Life Prints

The Cross-Cultural Memoir Series introduces original, significant memoirs from women whose compelling histories map the sources of our differences: generations, national boundaries, race, ethnicity, class, and sexual orientation. The series features stories of contemporary women's lives, providing a record of social transformation, growth in consciousness, and the passionate commitment of individuals who make far-reaching change possible.

The Cross-Cultural Memoir Series

LIFE PRINTS

A Memoir of Healing and Discovery

MARY GRIMLEY MASON

The Feminist Press
at The City University of New York

Published by The Feminist Press at The City University of New York
365 Fifth Avenue, New York, NY 10016
www.feministpress.org

First edition, 2000

Library of Congress Cataloging-in-Publication Data

Mason, Mary Grimley.
  Life prints : a memoir of discovery and healing / Mary Mason.
     p. cm. — (The cross-cultural memoir series)
  ISBN 1-55861-237-8 (hc : alk. paper)
   1. Mason, Mary Grimley. 2. Poliomyelitis—Patients—United
States—Biography. 3. Women—United States—Biography. 4. Feminism.
5. Women Scholars—United States—Biography. I. Title. II. Series.

RC180.1 .M37 2000
362.1'96835'0092—dc21
[B]
                                     99-056912

The author and publisher wish to acknowledge use of the following quoted material: Epigraph on p. 2 from "Sketch of the Past" by Virginia Woolf, published in *Moments of Being: Unpublished Autobiographical Writings,* copyright © 1976 by Quentin Bell and Angela Garnett. Reprinted by permission of Harcourt Brace, Inc. Epigraph on p. 108 from "The Mental Traveller" by William Blake. Epigraph on p. 146 from *Remembering the Bone House* by Nancy Mairs. Published by Beacon Press, 1995. Epigraph on p. 208 from poem 1203 by Emily Dickinson. Reprinted by permission of the publishers and the Trustees of Amherst College from *The Poems of Emily Dickinson,* Ralph W. Franklin, ed., Cambridge, Mass., The Belknap Press of Harvard University Press. Copyright © 1998 by the President and Fellows of Harvard College. Copyright © 1951, 1955, 1979 by the President and Fellows of Harvard College.

Photographs on pages 103–106 and 204–207 courtesy of Mary Grimley Mason.

The Feminist Press is grateful to Florence Howe, Joanne Markell, and Genevieve Vaughan for their generosity in supporting this publication.

Printed on acid-free paper by RR Donnelly & Sons
Manufactured in the United States of America

05 04 03 02 01 00 5 4 3 2 1

For Cathleen, Paul, and Sarah

CONTENTS

Photographs appear on pages 103–106 and 204–207

ACKNOWLEDGMENTS

This memoir could hardly exist without members of my family and relatives, some no longer here and others still a part of my life. Their love and loyalty through the years has been a sustaining force for me. Their stories no doubt vary from mine, but I only claim to speak for myself.

I would probably never have started this project if I had not been shaped and inspired by the Women's Movement and feminism, both of which I encountered through fellowships and friendships at the Bunting Institute and at the Wellesley College Center for Research on Women. The Mellon seminars were particularly important in that journey. I am grateful to Carolyn Heilbrun and Nancy Miller, whose work I greatly admire, for their generous recognition of my research on women's autobiography.

In the writing and development of this memoir I was helped and encouraged by many people. My support group of writers—Jerry Bernhard, Lisa Colt, Mary Cowham, Britta Fischer, Toni deBonneval, and Marilyn Zuckerman—made suggestions for shaping and editing that were invaluable. Other friends read the manuscript in various stages. They include Jane Cooper, Carol Hurd Green, Lawrence Kinsman, Karen Schneiderman, and former editors of mine—Evander Lomke and Paul Wright. I am also grateful to many other friends, too numerous to list, who gave me support and resolve when this project seemed interminable.

My special thanks go to Florence Howe at The Feminist Press, who encouraged me to complete the memoir and made crucial suggestions when she read the manuscript. I am very grateful to Jean Casella for being such an insightful editor and for asking the right substantive questions.

I worked on early stages of this work at Cummington Community of the Arts and at the Virginia Center for the Creative Arts. Portions of this book in an earlier form appeared in *With Wings: An Anthology of Literature by and about Women with Disabilities* and in *New Hampshire College Journal*.

WHO SPEAKS FOR THE CHILD?

I look at myself in a photo taken at Ocean City before I had polio, sitting on a swing in a bathing suit, and another, standing on the wet sand at the ocean's edge, spattered with sand globs, arms stretched out leaning on a long shovel. I am squinting happily, my white sun hat flapped back. I look ready to dig and scoop or perhaps to abandon it all and race into the water. In another picture I am on a tricycle, my brother, Tom, behind me. Both of us are dressed in Easter finery—a white tam for me and a dark blue, gold-buttoned coat. Tom has on a tan cap and suit with a wide white collar sticking out. I am pedaling. Looking at the photos, I feel a longing for that little girl who could pedal and run in the sand.

I am a disabled person, but until I was a child of four when I contracted polio in 1932, I was not disabled. I think some part of my mind always remained able-bodied and functioned as an observer, creating a double consciousness. At times this second self took over and I acted without awareness of my disability. I felt like a "normal" person. At other times, this other self withdrew in sadness and I felt different and alienated.

I was very young when I was stricken with polio. Soon after I recovered enough to be on crutches and braces, my parents decided to seek advice about how I should be treated in the family. We went to visit a man who was then the principal of George School, a Quaker preparatory school in Pennsylvania. He had contracted polio in one of the earlier epidemics of the disease and had gone on with his life although he also used crutches and braces. He told my parents that they should expect the same from me as they did from my sisters and brother. They took his advice and I was never treated as an invalid. I went to the same schools as my sisters and brother. So I grew up not thinking of myself as disabled.

On the other hand, of course, I soon began to perceive that the world saw me as different and, indeed, in many ways, so did my family. They carried me around a lot. I could not easily ride our pony although I was put up on his back (without my braces) and led around the pasture a little. I did not appear during the games in the family home movies where you had to run an obstacle race, the one in which you carried a suitcase and had to put on different pieces of clothing at each stop—shoes, dress, hat, scarf, gloves.

When I started school, I noticed that my peers treated me differently, too. I was given a front row seat in the first grade classroom and I did not run out to recess. My classmates were curious about my crutches and braces—I wore short half braces then—and they fought for the turn of handing me my crutches. I became a kind of celebrity. But I wanted to think of myself as just like everyone else. I began to build up a double consciousness. I was both the girl with polio and the girl like everyone else. I had started to mentally "pass" as able-bodied.

I started to consider myself a writer at sixteen and the problem of identity became acute. I would begin a story and halfway through discover that the protagonist was disabled even though I had not acknowledged it in the story or in my own mind. This double awareness became a dynamic in my life. For instance, in adolescence I often forgot my disability and enjoyed life with my friends in my all-girls school. At the same time, as I matured, I realized I could not be like my two older sisters who were dating boys and who seemed glamorous to me. I grew up determined to do everything a "normal" girl and woman could do, but sometimes I paid for not acknowledging my limitations.

In my memoir there are different voices—the young able-bodied child, the disabled child, and the girl and woman who struggled to integrate the two selves into one consciousness. All of these voices are separate parts of me but in my narrative as in my life the voices have finally come together. As I start my memories of my early childhood, I need to reach back for the child of one, two, three, and four—the child who could run, walk, skip, hop, jump, and dance, who wore shiny black Mary Janes and who scrambled onto the white garden bench to have her picture taken.

PART I

MEMORABILIA

In certain favorable moods, memories—
what one has forgotten—come to the top.

—Virginia Woolf, "Sketch of the Past"

SNAPSHOTS: BEFORE AND AFTER POLIO

Memories of the child before infantile paralysis are hard to isolate from other memories that people have told me. I was born in Camden, New Jersey, an industrial town on the other side of the Delaware River from Philadelphia. We lived in Moorestown, one of the many small southern New Jersey towns that served as commuting suburbs.

I remember our house on Stanwick Avenue. It was white stucco and in the back it had a blue door—a door with a latch that shut off the rest of the world and which later I identified with the hidden garden door in one of my favorite childhood books, *The Secret Garden*. Our blue door opened to the kitchen entrance and to the backyard, which seemed very big to me at the time. It was bordered by low hedges and beds of flowers. There was an arbor covered with roses. When you walked through the arbor you could actually sit down on white slatted seats facing each other, and I have the impression that if two people sat inside the arbor their knees would be touching. On the other side of the yard was the white bench where we had our pictures taken. Children's play equipment was at the back of the yard under tall trees: a sandbox that I dug in (my sisters had told me I would see "Chinamen" if I kept digging) and a slide and a swing, which consisted of two large wooden benches facing each other that you rocked back and forth by pushing your feet on the slatted floor and pumping. You could also come into the yard from the tiled porch connected to our sun porch. In the front yard there was a long narrow cement path to the street which was excellent for riding a tricycle. In the spring a family of Italian Americans would come and ask if they could pick the dandelions. When I asked my mother why they wanted to pick dandelions, she said that they used them for making wine and that they were poor people who needed help.

Years later, the summer I had orthopedic operations after my freshman year in college, I sat on the back porch in a wheelchair looking out over the yard, painting what I could see of my childhood playground. The vista, which as a child seemed so vast to me, had diminished considerably.

I had a friend whose name was Louise who lived across the side street from us, in a house that was bigger than ours and very dark inside. I remember that Louise's bedroom walls were covered with newspapers and magazine pictures instead of real wallpaper. I wondered if that meant they were poor like the Italians who picked dandelions. It was the Depression and her father was out of work. Her family were Quakers and most of the local Quakers were prosperous people. But they prided themselves on living simply and on taking care of those in their congregation or "meeting" who needed help. Louise went to Moorestown Friends School as my sisters and brother did and where I would go when I started school. Her mother—a soft-spoken woman who greeted me with "How's thee do?"— gave me cookies when I came to visit. On the other side of our house beyond a tall hedge was a very large house with big pillars on the front porch and a black and white marble floor in the entrance hall. I was aware that this house was a contrast to Louise's and that somehow our home did not belong to either category but fit somewhere in the middle—in other words, that we were neither rich nor poor. We got to enter our neighbor's marbled hallway every Halloween when we went trick-or-treating. The owner, a white-haired widow, would ask us to perform something for our treat—a song or a recitation. I hid behind my sisters and brother while they performed.

I remember too cutting the heads off of dozens of beautiful yellow daffodils in our yard. They were so pretty that I wanted to make a bouquet for someone—my mother, perhaps. Louise was with me, and we were very absorbed and serious in our task. I had taken the scissors from my grandmother's sewing basket. She was my father's mother and lived with us for most of the year and did all the sewing in the house. My mother was very angry and I got spanked. I don't think I would have been spanked if I had already gotten polio and was walking with crutches. But then I don't think I would have cut off daffodil heads. It was very difficult to be bad when you had crutches. You could never sneak quietly into someone's room because your crutches made too much noise. Someone would say, "Are you all right, dear? Can I get you something?" Sometimes my brother would tease my sisters and they would start screaming and running in and out of their rooms. Or they would have pillow fights and get so carried away that they would knock something over or burst a pillow and the feathers would scatter all over the room, which would get them into lots of trouble. I could not do these things and I regretted that I had to be so good. I wanted to be part of the pillow fight or splash and push someone in the wading pool that we had in the backyard in summer. I imagined places I would hide when the others played hide-and-seek, and just once I would like to have slipped out the door and run behind a tree when my mother called me—but I was always where she could find me. When I was a little older I became passionate about sweets, which I wasn't supposed to eat because I had gained too much weight. I remember trying to sneak into the pantry where the cookie tin was kept and trying to quickly grab a few. Tom could have done it easily, but I had to swing open the door and then noisily lean on the counter while I opened the tin.

"Hello, there, Mary!" The cook had heard me and came in from the kitchen to see what I wanted. She was a round French Canadian woman who worked for us for a number of years after we moved to Montreal, Canada. "Do you want a cookie?" she asked.

"Oh, no, thanks," I lied. "I was just looking for Sandy [our cocker spaniel]. I guess he's upstairs." I retreated feeling ashamed.

I look at the photograph albums in my mother's apartment in a garden retirement community in southern New Jersey. I search for more pictures of the child who was not on crutches. I find a little girl with short bobbed hair, not as blonde as the others. She is part of the group of children posing for summer snapshots in the garden on Stanwick Avenue. "Is this me?" I ask my mother, just to be sure it is not cousin Anne or some other visitor.

My mother looks. "Yes, I guess it is," she says, sounding a little unsure of my existence.

Looking at these photographs reminds me of how little my mother commented on past events. She did not tell family stories. We would ask her about her childhood, about her father and mother, about her brother, Bill, whom we never knew because he died in the 1915 flu epidemic, and even about our own childhood, but we usually got the barest facts or, after a searching pause, "Oh, I don't really remember." However, she became an enthusiastic photographer of her grandchildren and kept albums of all of them. She also made a scrapbook for me of my stay at the Georgia Warm Springs Foundation, where I was sent at six years old for treatment and rehabilitation. She called the scrapbook "Memories," but she did not put it together until after I was married, when my aunt Edith gave her all of the clippings she had collected of the event.

I turn to this scrapbook of memories, the record of my illness and my days at Warm Springs. These were my allotted minutes of fame, as Andy Warhol would say. Newspaper clippings and photos record how little Mary

Grimley sat next to President Roosevelt at a Thanksgiving dinner at the Foundation. I was a "poster child" before the role was invented but I did not enjoy my part.

My father, who was general manager of the international division of RCA, was in Japan in September of 1932 when I was stricken with polio. My mother, after leaving us with my grandmother, had set out by train to meet him on the west coast for a vacation. I became very ill a day or so after she left. I could not move my left leg and my neck was stiff so the doctor, guessing it might be poliomyelitis, sent me to the hospital and my grandmother telegraphed my mother to come home. My father was at sea on the *Empress of Japan* when he received a radio cable from my mother. He made a record thirty-four-hour flight across the continent after he landed in Vancouver, flying to Seattle, and then changing planes for Salt Lake City and flying from there to Newark airport. His journey was written up in all the papers (my mother pasted the pictures and articles in the scrapbook): "Baby Sick, Dad Makes Camden from Vancouver in 34 Hours," the headlines read. The picture shows him as he steps off the plane. "How is Mary?" he is quoted as saying to my Aunt Jane, who has come to meet him. I'm at the Children's Hospital of Philadelphia. My mother has already arrived there from Montana, where she had received the telegram from my grandmother. I am off the critical list but I am still very sick.

I remember a stretcher in a hospital corridor. I was going home, but I was not allowed to take any belongings with me. The medical world thought that polio might be very infectious so everything had to be fumigated or taken away. I was allowed to keep my stuffed animals—my family had sent me a lot of toys during my four-week stay in the hospital—and my small cuddling pillow until the last minute, but then they were removed to the end of the stretcher. I tried to reach them but I could not sit up by myself. Finally, they were taken away.

While I was in the hospital I had gradually lost the use of both legs but it was not until I got home that I really discovered that my limbs did not work anymore. My legs lay helplessly before me, and at first, I had to be lifted into different positions. I had to learn how to shift myself and use my arms to lift up my legs. Even after I had gained a lot of agility, I would have nightmares and wake up and be terrified to find that I could not move my legs, as if I were discovering it for the first time. My mother would come in and hold me on her lap in my grandmother's rocking chair. Rocking in her lap would calm me and take me back to memories of her cradling me as a baby and singing me a song about "Mr. Moon." The nightmares persisted for years and also became translated into general fears of the dark. I would dread the moment after my mother kissed me goodnight and left the room because then I would have to lie very still in the middle of the bed, far from the edges of the mattress so that something under the bed could not reach up a hand and grab my leg. Sometimes I would think about how I could escape from the bed and the room. I would practice lowering myself to the floor and crawling to the door, but I did not want anyone to know that I did that. I felt too ashamed even for my grandmother to find me. She was frequently upstairs in her room when I went to bed and that gave me some comfort. If she thought I was not getting to sleep she would bring me a cracker from the little tin box of supplies she kept in her bureau drawer so that she did not have to go to the kitchen when she was hungry. If I woke up in the middle of the night, I would call my mother and often ended up sleeping in bed with my parents until morning.

Many nights I dreamt of attempting to scream for help and finding that no voice came out, just a kind of guttural noise that eventually woke me up. Rarely, perhaps never, did I dream of trying to run away. The sensation of motion, so visible in the early photographs, was gone, except in fantasy—not dream fantasies at night but day fantasies, of dancing, floating as light as a feather, as graceful as a butterfly.

For several months after I returned from the hospital I was put in long plaster cast splints at night to keep my knees and feet straight, and then I was fitted into braces up to the knee and had to sleep in those instead. I was encouraged to crawl and stand, but although I learned to keep my balance, I could not walk more than a few steps before my knees collapsed. Despite physical therapy and massage in the next two years I did not improve in strengthening my legs and so I was given long leg braces and a corset for abdominal support. My father had insisted that I change doctors and the new doctor suggested that I be sent to the Georgia Warm Springs Foundation for more intensive treatment and care.

I look in my scrapbook at the many newspaper write-ups of my dinner with Roosevelt at the Warm Springs Foundation. "Patients to Eat with President at Thanksgiving," the headlines say, or "They'll Rub President's Elbows." The Foundation was a favorite spot of President Roosevelt's. After he contracted polio when he was governor of New York, he found the waters of the "health wells" in the little village of Warm Springs helped him regain his strength. In 1927, he founded the center, which is now called the Roosevelt Warm Springs Institute for Rehabilitation. Roosevelt owned a 1,700-acre farm near there on Pine Mountain and, as president, he kept a "little White House" at the Foundation. He celebrated each Thanksgiving with the patients. The year I was at Warm Springs, I was one of the lucky ones to draw a seat at the president's table; six boys and six girls were chosen. Along with sixteen other children, I lived in a house run by a housemother, Miss Harding, who kept in close touch with the parents. She wrote my mother every week, and a picture shows us gathered together with several attendants. Another photo shows my sixth birthday party where I am standing before my cake with my special pals, Roberta, Betty, and Druscilla. I am wearing long braces. One of my friends has an arm brace and the others have leg braces. We went to school in the mornings and in the afternoons each one of us had a physical therapist who supervised us in the pool. I was the youngest patient at the Foundation that year and I did not know anything about President Roosevelt so when we drew numbers from a hat, and I was told that I had drawn the lucky number and that I was going to sit at the president's table, I felt sure that it was something unpleasant that I had to do. Betty shouted, "Oh you lucky bum!" and I said that she could have my place, but Miss Harding said no, that I couldn't give it away because it was a great honor. I asked her if I had to eat with the president all the time he was there and I was relieved when she said, "No, only one meal."

One newspaper, the *Atlanta Constitution,* reported the coming event as follows: "Rays of happiness and pride are shining through the cloud of sorrow which has enveloped 6-year-old Mary Grimley, of Moorestown—for tomorrow the little victim of infantile paralysis is to sit beside the president of the United States at Warm Springs, Ga."

The write-up is at odds with the pictures that follow. I am sitting in a wheelchair, bow in hair, a very mad expression on my face, holding a string tied to a huge live turkey. My fellow patient, "Mary Elizabeth Runkle of San Diego, Texas, who will also sit at the president's table," is holding another string tied to the same turkey. She is smiling and happy and she makes my sour expression look even worse. I was the opposite of a March of Dimes "poster child." I refused to turn on the rays of happiness for the photographers and journalists even when they said, "How about a smile, Mary?" All of the fuss was annoying me. I would rather have been home with my sisters and brother and dog. I was already defiantly resisting the role of the disabled person. Later, in order to make peace with the world, I learned to smile and look happy no matter how stupid people were in their contacts with me. But I had not learned that yet.

Pictures and newsreels of the dinner table show that I am not much more cheerful. Seated at the president's left, I have a larger bow in my hair and I wore a blue dotted swiss smocked dress with rose buds embroidered on the smocking, but I am still looking sour. The banquet took place in the big dining hall, which was decorated with long white tablecloths, vivid autumn flowers, individual placecards, and chocolate turkeys. I was carried in to the head table where the president and Mrs. Roosevelt sat, surrounded by all of the Foundation patients who, like myself, had been chosen by lottery to sit with the president. I was given a cushion to sit on so that I could see my food and I remember that I felt rather tippy on the chair with my feet not touching the floor.

In an interview with Eleanor Roosevelt, the *Philadelphia Inquirer* quoted her as saying that the president cut my turkey for me on my plate but that I was so impressed with having dinner with him that I was unable to eat. Miss Harding sent a letter to my mother which quotes me as saying, "I didn't feel so very good sitting next to the president. The turkey was good and I ate all my dinner." In the news clipping the first lady went on to comment about me as the president's dinner partner: "The president worked harder at the meal than he has at any dinner party." I was very shy and when the president, who seemed to have a huge head and a big smile full of teeth, turned to me and asked me if I was all right, I could only nod my head. I saw my fellow patient, Peter Woodberry, talking a great deal to Mrs. Roosevelt (he was next to her) and I wondered what he was talking about. During the evening we sang songs accompanied by a man who played the banjo and we took turns by tables singing "Sweet Adeline." The president was asked to judge the best table of singers but he didn't count ours because he had been singing, too. I became very tired after the speeches, entertainers, and films about the Foundation and I had to go to the bathroom and didn't know who I could tell that to. Finally I was carried out of the dining room by one of the attendants. When I put my head on his shoulder, my eyes closed in sleep and the placecard, which the president had autographed for me, fell from my hand.

The next day all of the patients gave a performance for the president of a musical called "A Sailor's Sweetheart: The S.S. *Paral-Brace Lines*." We had been rehearsing it for weeks at school (we all went to classes every morning) and we were very excited. It was about Popeye and Olive Oyl and pirates and sailors. I was one of the sailors and sang in the chorus. We wore white sailor suits—a white middy blouse trimmed in blue over bell-bottom trousers. I was not nervous or shy in this performance and I sang hard and "looked right at the president with a big smile," according to Miss Harding. She added, in this letter to my mother, "In the play the president picked Mary out as being so cute."

My father came to visit me the Monday before Thanksgiving on his way to Mexico City. He didn't stay for the holiday but he spent two days with me following my routine, checking on my living arrangements, and pushing me around in my wheelchair. Except for exercise periods in the pool and fifteen-minute walking practice in the afternoon, I was in my wheelchair most of the time with my legs extended in braces. I could also do "free swimming" in the play pool, which was separated from the section of the pool where we had physiotherapy, and my father joined me there during his visit. One afternoon the president and Mrs. Roosevelt arrived while my father and I were swimming. They sat down in the sun to wait for the physical therapist who supervised me and watched while I swam around and ducked in and out of the big rubber rings that were there for play. My father wrote to my mother that the president watched me as I swam, and that he smiled and nodded, perhaps acknowledging that we had the same instructor. Later my father and I went to my walking class. Sets of wooden steps were assembled which I would go up and down, sometimes taking the steep ones backwards and learning different techniques for maneuvering difficult situations. I was very proud to have my father push my wheelchair, which was usually pushed by attendants. He was more important to me than President Roosevelt, but I was a little shy with him, too—afraid he would not think I was doing well enough in my swimming or walking. Even then I felt that somehow my father could not accept my disability, an idea that later absorbed me as he continued to search for cures. That night he had dinner with me. We enjoyed the meal but neither of us liked turnip greens, which they served quite frequently, so we made faces at each other when we saw that dish come around.

My scrapbook has two of my father's letters to my mother when he made that visit to me. They are dated Sunday and Monday, November 1934. More than sixty years later as I look at the beautiful handwriting in a script that is clear and flowing and full of flourishes (a writing style no longer taught in schools), his presence—so seldom evoked over the years—comes back to me. Most of the letters are about my adjustment to Warm Springs and whether or not I should come home for Christmas. He writes that "she hardly expects to come home for Christmas" and that "her spirit and determination are wonderful" but I know that I wanted to go home for the holidays very much. I found it very difficult to ask my father for anything or to complain in any way. He mentions in the letter that I "raised the issue," so I know that I did bring up the subject, but I could not have told him how I really felt.

My father was a self-made man. His father, E. Charles Grimley, a musician and owner of a musical instrument business, died when his oldest son

(Elmer Charles) was twelve, leaving his wife, Jenny Parker, with two girls and two boys and very little money. After graduation from Newburgh Academy in 1907, my father worked for a number of businesses for five years before he went to New York University and graduated cum laude in business and accounting. He got a commission in the navy in 1917 and was sent to the Victor Talking Machine Company in Camden, New Jersey, to oversee war contracts; he eventually joined the company and rose through the ranks until he became the president of the Canadian branch. In his college graduation picture he already appears very responsible, serious, and sincere. His formal high white collar and tie make him look handsome and distinguished. His heavy dark eyebrows and penetrating eyes, which seem to reflect on the future, make him look like a scholar. All his pictures show the same serious expression. Even in the family photo in the backyard of Stanwick Avenue, he has only a slight smile as he sits with my mother, his arms outstretched to include my two older sisters, Betty and Jane, one on each side of him. My mother, sitting next to Betty, holds me in her lap and my brother, Tom, sits on his tricycle beside her. My father's gesture of protection is like a pastor embracing his flock. My mother, sitting with her one-year-old on her lap, her three-year-old and her six- and seven-year-olds around her, is an icon of domesticity.

One of the happiest memories of my father's visit to Warm Springs was the evening we waited for the adult dinner hour and had a table of our own. My father was very handsome with dark wavy hair and brown eyes. I often liked to look at his blunt hands with their square-tipped fingers. There was a slight sprinkle of hair on them and his skin was never pale like those in the family who inherited my mother's fair complexion. He loved entertainment and all kinds of music—from classical to Broadway shows to jazz. That night Fats Waller, the jazz singer and composer, performed after dinner and we stayed to see him. Our table was close to the stage and my father wrote a note and sent a request for a song via the waiter. The song was "I'm Going to Sit Right Down and Write Myself a Letter and Make Believe It Came from You." Fats Waller sang it for us and I was completely spellbound. He seemed to spread all over the piano and his mouth opened so wide you could see all of his teeth including gold fillings. He nodded to us before he sang and I was thrilled that I was sitting there with my father who laughed and clapped enthusiastically. The pleasure my father and I shared that evening remains the counterpart of other more hostile feelings that I developed toward him over the years. Memories of him are always bittersweet.

One day many years after that Thanksgiving banquet at Warm Springs, my daughter Cathleen came home from junior high school one afternoon and said, "I saw you in a newsreel today, sitting next to President Roosevelt at Thanksgiving dinner." The social studies class had by coincidence shown the March of Time newsreel of the event. My other two children had the same experience in junior high. I had not thought of the newsreel since the Criterion theater in Moorestown had a special showing of it on a Saturday morning after I returned from the Foundation and my mother took me to see it with some friends and family. The event had long since faded from my memory but for years I had kept the image of FDR as a model of achievement and of the limitless possibilities in overcoming a disability. At times, I despaired that I had achieved so little compared to this great man. Then one day I had a revelation: Think of the networks of people and resources at his command! People to drive him, to arrange the details of his life: secretaries, aides, servants, a wife, and a mistress! Unlimited medical and physical facilities at his disposal! I felt better after this insight and I remembered the little girl with the bow in her hair with renewed tenderness.

After I returned from Warm Springs, I started biweekly physiotherapy in Ardmore, Pennsylvania, with Miss Dorothy Burns, who became a central part of my life. She helped me fake normalcy so that I could do just about everything that everyone else did despite my crutches. I accepted her unquestioningly because I knew she would help me convince my father that I was doing everything I could to improve my condition.

In one of my sessions with her, she asked me if I would like to spend a weekend at her country house in the Amish section of Pennsylvania. The idea sounded fine to me. I was about nine years old at the time and my family often spent weekends doing things I could not do, such as playing tennis or some other sport. I was aware of the difficulty my mother had of making plans for me on Saturdays and Sundays. Everyone else—my two sisters and brother—hurried off to their various social activities, which my age and my disability kept me from joining. Better to be somewhere else, I felt.

A few weeks after I had been to the country with Miss Burns, I was reminded of that weekend by some remarks of a fellow patient, Dorothy Klauder, who was a friend of the family's. She was a young married woman who had also contracted polio and had spent some time at Miss Burns's country house in the summer, working on her walking and her recovery. She was visiting us and I heard her talking to my mother in the next room about Miss Burns. "Dorothy Burns is certainly talented as a physical therapist, but she takes on some pretty depressing cases, like that weird boy, Bobby, whom she took with Mary to her country house."

Her remarks upset me. Those two days with Miss Burns and Bobby, the other patient, came back to me in a flood of conflicting images and feelings. My mother had driven me to Ardmore on Saturday morning, and that was the first I realized that Bobby was going, too. I had seen him from time to time, coming and going on weekly visits. He was a tall boy about fifteen or sixteen—his age was hard to judge because cerebral palsy had not only distorted his movements but had also affected his speech and had left him mentally childlike. I found him frightening and disturbing. Miss Burns put him in the back of her small station wagon, however. We drove off, chattering, and I soon forgot he was there.

The little house was all she claimed it to be. A whitewashed, stucco and stone Pennsylvania Dutch house with blue shutters in a lovely valley of wildflowers and trees. There was a fair-sized barn where Perry, the old caretaker, lived, a stone well, a root cellar, a grape arbor, and a gazebo covered with honeysuckle. Two or three dogs greeted us and Perry made a tilt at the baggage, but Miss Burns bustled through most of it herself, bounding and jogging as she carried armfuls of food and supplies. She was a plump woman with auburn hair and dark eyebrows, and she sang cheerfully as she unloaded us into her house.

We had a picnic lunch outside on the stone patio. Bobby seemed very content and didn't try to speak much. That was a relief because his speech was very unnerving, a kind of jabber with very few intelligible words. I did not know how to deal with it, and I was further relieved when he was taken inside for a rest. The remainder of the day went quickly. An hour of exercise, a trip to the local village for groceries and ice cream cones. Miss Burns fed Bobby his cone in the back of the car. She talked to him constantly, encouraging him like a small child. I avoided looking at him because he made a mess of eating, and I felt increasingly repulsed and tense about his presence. After supper Miss Burns and I played cards while Bobby sat near the radio and listened, rocking back and forth to the music and occasionally looking over at us and making a loud sound that seemed to be laughter. At about nine she got up to get Bobby ready for bed. He was going to sleep on the screened-in porch. Miss Burns and I had the two little rooms upstairs. She had difficulty getting him out to his bed and finally, when she had succeeded, she shut the door to the living room. Bobby was shouting loudly now, almost bellowing. I heard a heavy thrashing around, and I felt nervous. He was taller than she was and had a strong, though helpless, body. There was a loud thud onto the bed and a final roar from Bobby. Had he knocked her down? I wondered. Then gradually he subsided into a low crooning sound as if he was being lulled and soothed to sleep. I was glad that I was staying upstairs and that there would be a door or two closed between me and the porch. I went to bed later, after we had some cocoa and marshmallows before the fire, and except for the scurrying sound of mice, which kept me rigidly alert for a few minutes until I established the certainty that they were in the walls and not under the bed, I forgot the anxieties of the day and fell asleep to the sounds of the soft rustling leaves outside my window.

Late on Sunday morning I read the comics on a chaise lounge in the gazebo and looked idly across the field where Bobby was being instructed in walking by Miss Burns, who had all she could manage to help him put one foot before another—he lurched and swayed and shrieked as he made an effort, and she sang a marching song to try to establish a tempo through all the din. Shortly after, the two of them disappeared and the noise ceased so that I read on drowsily to the sound of some bees around the honeysuckle and the mixed songs of unfamiliar birds. I guess I had closed my eyes and momentarily fallen asleep in the warmth of noon. I opened them with a start and a jerk when I realized that Bobby's asymmetrical face was peering through the honeysuckle. He was saying something that approximated my name, and his voice rose shrilly as my eyes met his. His mouth fell open excitedly, and he crashed around the gazebo to the screen door.

I was terror-stricken, frozen to the chaise lounge. I could hear my heart beating, and feel the panic in my stomach rise to my throat. I was not even sure of what terrified me; there was something uncontrolled and violent about Bobby's movements that grew more chilling as I realized he showed pleasure in seeing me. I was sure that if I tried to scream now only a dry croak would come out of my mouth. I looked across the field to the house for Miss Burns. The screen door of the gazebo was being rattled, and with an increasingly wild babble, Bobby struggled to open it.

I heard a scream as he pushed open the door. It was I who had screamed. Immediately I heard Miss Burns running across the yard.

"Bobby, what are you up to? How did you get over here?"

He crashed though the door and she plunged after him, catching him as he fell. I noticed that his hand, so often clenched in useless strength, opened and dropped a crushed twig of honeysuckle just beside my chaise. He blurted my name almost audibly and looked at me. Now I saw only his eyes, not the crazy contortions of his face. They were shining brightly but seemed to have a bottomless depth. I felt a constricting sob in my throat, partly from released fear and partly from sorrow and shame. I picked up the honeysuckle. Miss Burns grabbed Bobby and propelled him toward the house, half pushing and half leading him as he continued to babble.

"Sorry if we disturbed you," she called cheerily.

We left soon after so that we would be home before dark. I deliberately looked in the back of the car as I got in. Bobby was sitting in his characteristic folded-up position, resting his chin on one crazily bent arm, gazing out the side window.

Weeks later Dorothy Klauder's gossip brought all of these emotions back to me—the fear, the revulsion, the shame. "She brought that boy out to the farm one day when I was there, but I told her it would be too disgusting to spend the weekend with him," she said to my mother. "I don't think she should have forced him on Mary for two days."

For a moment I relived everything I had felt in the gazebo, but then I recalled the sweet fragrance of honeysuckle. At the time I didn't understand my complex feelings about Bobby. I was unaware of the hierarchal context of disabilities—how some are more socially acceptable than others, even among the disabled, depending on physical or mental characteristics. I didn't identify with other disabled people. Yet I knew I did not belong to the world of the able-bodied either. The image of the honeysuckle "offering" stayed with me, unsettled and unresolved.

2

FAMILY ALBUMS

My mother was my caretaker as I grew up but when I visited her on her ninety-first birthday our roles had begun to reverse. I looked through an album of her life before and soon after her marriage. I wish there were more photos so I could know what my mother was like when she was young. The old faded pictures of the young woman dressed in 1920s flapper style in pre-Depression Philadelphia made a poignant contrast to the elderly—though still spry—lady whom I was visiting.

My mother, Clara Mildred Stauffer, was born in 1899 in Downingtown, Pennsylvania. Her father, William Stauffer, owned a dry goods store, and her mother, Clara Dauman, had been a school teacher before she married. My mother, who was known as Mildred, grew up in a family dominated by women although she had two brothers, one of whom died at twenty-nine. As the youngest, she was told what to think by her older sisters Edith and Mabel, who were eleven and ten years older respectively. Her sister Mary, only three years older, shared the end of the line with her. Mildred attended Wilson College for two years, following the Dauman tradition of educating the women in the family, but she decided not to finish college and went instead to Drexel Institute to get secretarial training. There she met Jane Grimley, who introduced Mildred to her brother, Elmer Charles. She never used her secretarial training in a job because soon after she met Elmer Charles, they married.

I find a picture in the album of my mother and my aunt Jane. I go through these photos eagerly, trying to find clues to my mother's past. She rarely spoke of her childhood or adolesence—or of any of her past life, as a matter of fact. I don't think she was trying to hide anything but she lived very much in the present and was not a reflective person. Suddenly I feel an urgency to reconstruct her life. Who was she at twenty-one when this picture was taken? I look closely. Aunt Jane is seated. Mildred is behind her with her arms draped affectionately around her friend's shoulders. Mildred—

blonde, blue-eyed—is looking at the camera with the smile of a contented "buddy"; Jane—curly, black, bobbed hair, a large mouth, dark eyes that crinkle at the corners—has a mischievous, daring look as if she was ready for action. The two were odd "best friends," so different in temperament as well as looks. Aunt Jane was extroverted, self-dramatizing, hyperbolic about life. She loved to dance, sing, and talk of "good times" at the Victor Talking Machine company where she worked as a secretary after her brother (my father) was assigned there as a naval officer to negotiate defense contracts during World War I. My mother was more reserved and was used to following others—or so she said in the rare moments when she talked about herself. However, in this picture of the two young women, Mildred's smile suggests an almost conspiratorial contentment: she married her best friend's brother and has her world just where she wants it.

My paternal and maternal aunts presented two very different influences on my life. Aunt Jane clearly represented the patriarchy: the world where women pleased men and were rewarded with admiration and—if they were lucky—with being taken care of. She married a tall, handsome, charming young man whose father, an erratic millionaire, abandoned his son in the Depression, leaving him unemployed. Subsequently, Uncle Henderson developed periods of depression, accompanied by a violent temper. After years of struggling to stay together, the couple broke up, although my aunt remained in touch with her husband and even close to him until his death. She developed a business, marketing a line of clothing for wealthy middle-aged women, and despite tough times, she always remained an optimist. Aunt Jane loved a party, and to this day, I can see her holding a drink in one hand and a cigarette in the other while showing my sisters how to do the Charleston. Although I had to look on as an outsider because I could not dance, I didn't feel excluded by Aunt Jane. In my sophomore year of college, when I had a series of orthopedic operations, she celebrated my leaving the hospital by taking me to see Ray Bolger, the great soft-shoe dancer, in a Broadway musical. We laughed until tears rolled down our cheeks in a kind of abandonment to pleasure that was never characteristic of my mother. I always looked forward to Aunt Jane's visits.

My maternal aunts, particularly my mother's two oldest sisters, were strong independent women who had careers and never married. I am not sure if they remained single by choice or by circumstance; Mabel began to lose her hearing when she was quite young, and Edith was lame from an illness in her twenties. An art student and a painter, Mabel appears in my mother's album with a group of house guests, fellow art students perhaps, circa 1918; the women are wearing white middy blouses and are standing with their arms entwined while the young men—one holding a guitar—seem an afterthought to the group, placed there solely as troubadours for the women friends. My aunt, standing somewhat apart, is wearing a jaunty hat and carrying a rake and basket, perhaps in parody of the pastoral life. We always thought of Aunt Mabel as bossy, but here she looks dramatic and captivating. She became a teacher and art director for the Atlantic City elementary schools, and held these positions even after becoming totally deaf in her middle years.

During our time in New Jersey, I always looked forward to our annual Easter trip to Atlantic City, where we would stay with Aunt Mabel in her apartment by the boardwalk. After looking at our Easter baskets in the morning, we would go to the boardwalk for the Easter parade, the boardwalk chair rides, and the saltwater taffy, which I would take home with shells from the beach. Easter was also one of the few occasions when I would see my grandmother Stauffer, who lived with my aunt during the winter months. Grandmother Stauffer was a small woman with gray hair that escaped into wispy curls from a tight bun. I remember her hair particularly because it contrasted with Nana Grimley's, which was pure white and twisted into a thick bun.

Aunt Mabel was a competent artist and liked to paint still lifes of flowers. Her best works were her watercolors of foggy scenes of Vinalhaven on the coast of Maine, where she and Edith vacationed several summers. I tried to get one of these paintings by hints and compliments but she always preferred to give us what she liked—or, we used to say, what she wanted to get rid of. I remember, however, a touching scene near the end of her life when she had gone into a Presbyterian nursing home in Pennsylvania.

I insisted that my mother, my sisters, and I go see Aunt Mabel, fearing we would not have many chances to visit together as sisters and nieces. In fact, it was the last time I saw my aunt. We met at my mother's and then drove together to the Presbyterian retirement home. Mabel was waiting for us at the front door and, still imperious, she waved us around the premises, showing us the garden, the recreation room, and the chapel. During dinner she introduced us to the other residents, who looked frail and retiring compared to my aunt's stocky figure and shrieking voice. (She could not hear the sound of her own voice because of her deafness.) I felt put on edge by her manner and perhaps a little apprehensive that I might be swept into the group as one of the disabled and infirm. But after dinner when she took us back to her room and sat us down in a row, I was soon brought to tears by her presentation—obviously carefully thought out—of her legacy to us.

"Mary," she screamed, "sit in the comfortable chair." She gestured me to the modest bedroom's only armchair, while the others were motioned toward the bed. Then my aunt brought out a basket of carefully wrapped treasures, one for each of us: a silver centenary spoon, a mug from Queen Elizabeth's coronation, a lusterware pitcher that had been a wedding gift to Nana Stauffer, or a needlepoint evening purse that she had beautifully crafted. Each item was explained in the wild piercing voice, giving us a small piece of Stauffer family history and particularly the history of the Stauffer women. We all fought back the tears to thank her.

My other spinster aunt, Edith Jane Stauffer, was my favorite Stauffer aunt, perhaps because she took a special interest in me for years, collecting Warm Springs and Roosevelt memorabilia (she was a fan of Eleanor Roosevelt and the only Democrat in an otherwise Republican family) and spending time with me in her regular visits to our house. She would arrive in her little blue Plymouth coupe and blow the horn until someone came out of the house to meet her and carry in her bag. Then she would sit in the big armchair in the living room and embrace each one of us with loud enthusiasm. My sisters and brother would try to escape these audiences because they claimed they got sprayed everytime she opened her mouth to greet them. I didn't mind because she was always ready to hear about everything I had done, including a newsletter that I once wrote announcing her arrival.

Aunt Edith was the oldest daughter in the family. In her photograph she stands looking majestic but rather forbidding. She had a handsome face with prominent features and a very firm jaw—a look that was justified when she became an elder in the Presbyterian Church. Aunt Mary once showed me letters of recommendation written by professors at Teachers College, where Edith was the first woman to graduate. They praised her work and predicted a fine career for her. However, like other women in her era, her career was limited. She became a dean of the Moravian College for Women in Bethlehem, Pennsylvania, where she was much appreciated but poorly paid. She retired without a pension.

When I was twelve, I spent six lonely months away from home with my physical therapist, Miss Burns, and I was grateful that Aunt Edith tried to console me. She came for me several weekends and took me from Ardmore, Pennsylvania, to her college in Bethlehem. I loved visiting her and walking through the gothic buildings on the campus. Her rooms included a study with shelves of books and an atmosphere of reflection that appealed to me. However, when I returned to my therapist's house on Sunday nights, I was always desperately homesick.

One weekend during Aunt Edith's spring vacation we went to the Stauffer home in Downingtown. The two unmarried sisters would eventually retire to this large Victorian house and produce multicolored zinnias in the garden (Mabel was the gardener) and "made from scratch" angel food cakes in the kitchen (that was Aunt Edith's domain). The house was red brick but trimmed with brown and tan gingerbread abutments and flourishes. It had wraparound porches with rocking chairs, stained glass windows over the front door and on the landing of the staircase, and, upstairs, long corridors with many rooms furnished with massive, dark mahogany beds and dressers. My only memory of Grandfather was in his sleigh bed in the master bedroom—only head and shoulders and white beard outside the covers. He gave me a silver dollar and patted my hand. Downstairs, the front parlor had stiff Victorian settees for afternoon callers. The adjoining parlor was more comfortable, with a large desk, and a couch with cushions and pillows that you could get lost in. The Downingtown atmosphere had a lasting effect on me. It directed me to Victorian literature and to a fondness for daguerreotypes and needlework.

During that spring weekend visit with my two aunts, I discovered the source of Aunt Edith's limp. She was a heavy woman and walked slowly with a slight lurch to one side. Sometimes she used a cane and her shoes were always sturdy orthopedic oxfords that seemed to bind her swelling ankles. Because the house was empty and dark, I did not object when my aunt said that I could sleep with her in her big mahogany double bed. I would have been frightened to be alone in one of the other rooms that had once belonged to my dead relatives. However, I was a little embarrassed about seeing my aunt get undressed as I lay on my side of the bed. I kept my head turned a little but after she pulled on her nightgown, my aunt sat down and pulled up the gown to take off her stockings. I saw deep scars on one thigh—almost as if a piece of flesh had been cut out. "Those are my scars," she said. "My leg became infected from bedsores when I was ill many years ago."

"Does it hurt?" I asked sympathetically but remembering that people often asked *me* that question and I would get annoyed. It always seemed so obvious to me that I didn't have anything that *hurt*.

"No, it doesn't hurt me now," she answered, "but it has affected my walking."

I wanted to ask her more about her illness and her recovery and how much it had affected her life. I wondered whether her disability had kept her from marrying and whether she was drawn to me because of my polio. But my aunt was climbing into bed and turning off the light so I knew that the subject was closed. The Stauffers did not talk about their personal problems very much. I had heard vague references to a nervous breakdown earlier in Aunt Edith's life but, of course, I would never ask her about that.

During the weekend Aunt Edith showed me the family Bible where she had recorded all of the births and deaths in the family. She also gave me a flower paperweight from her desk and showed me her sterling silver flatware, which she had begun to collect. It was a rosebud pattern and she said she wanted me to have it eventually. When I went to graduate school I felt that I was following my Aunt Edith's tradition of scholarship—I was the only one in my family to get a graduate degree—and she certainly encouraged me and followed my career with interest, although we talked more about politics than literature when we saw each other. I wanted her to be a role model for me so I was surprised and hurt when, after she went into a nursing home in her late eighties, she gave her leather-bound set of George Eliot to my sister Jane, and her silver to my niece Carol, Jane's eldest daughter. I expected to receive from her some sign that I was heir to her professional career, and I also expected some recognition of our shared experience with disability. Sometimes I wonder whether she thought I would not marry because of my disability. I even wonder if she was disappointed when I did marry because I would not carry on the Stauffer tradition of the strong single woman. In any case, I am sorry that she did not see herself as my mentor.

The last time I saw Aunt Edith was a few years before her death in her mid-nineties. Her Presbyterian nursing home was very different from my Aunt Mabel's; Aunt Edith's home was for parishioners who could not afford to pay monthly fees. My mother and I made the trip into the Pennsylvania countryside on one of my visits to New Jersey. We arrived at a big nondescript building on a bare hillside. Right away I noticed the contrast with Aunt Mabel's nursing home, which was a large Tudor house surrounded with well-kept flower gardens. We found Aunt Edith in a small room that she shared with another patient. She had not been allowed to bring many possessions with her, so the room was hospital-like in its bareness. We had brought her a plant and some candy and we helped her into the wheelchair she had to use because of severe arthritis. She was radiant and smiling and overjoyed to see us. Her commanding voice boomed as we went down the concrete halls to the reception room. She spoke to all the attendants we passed, and knew each one by name.

"Janice, I want you to meet my sister and my niece," she proclaimed. "My niece lives in Boston. She is a graduate student at Harvard University." The attendant smiled and stopped to shake hands with us.

We walked through the dreary halls to a visiting room with vinyl couches. My aunt seemed almost ecstatic. She told us about the daily religious services and the sacred music concerts on Sundays. Bach was her favorite composer and she had often spoken of my attending the Bach festivals in Bethlehem when she was still at Moravian College. Sitting at the entrance doors as we left, she waved and called to us and told us to drive carefully. She no longer looked like the big woman I remembered. She had lost a lot of weight and seemed literally to be turning flesh into spirit. Eventually, she died of an infection. There was almost nothing of hers left in her room to turn over to the family, but when I told my mother that I was sad not to have anything of Edith's to remember her by, she gave me a small antique Victorian pin made of twisted strands of family ancestors' hair set in a filigreed gold frame. I treasure the memento but still feel puzzled that she could not acknowledge that she had been my role model.

As I turn to other photo albums that record my own childhood, I am struck with how young my mother seems in her pictures, but then I realize that she had her four children while she was still in her twenties. She looks very slim, but she must have been strong because I remember her carrying me into her bedroom at night when I woke up with nightmares. She comforted my night terrors, but during the day she was absorbed in running my father's household. We had a cook and a gardener and a young woman would come a few afternoons a week to baby-sit. Mother ran the house efficiently and organized the lives of my grandmother and four children without drama. She also directed my rigorous routine of treatments, and kept a record, painstakingly typed, of everything that was done for my care. I found this record recently in a file marked "Polio—History of Mary's Case." In it I read about the changes doctors prescribed for me during the four years after I contracted polio: short braces and night splints, one long leg brace and one short, two long walking braces with joints, and always with crutches. I initially wore an abdominal corset to keep my back straight, but it was gradually cut down and finally removed. During the two years after I returned from Warm Springs, the record shows that my parents tried some nontraditional approaches to my condition. I had twenty weeks of what are described as "short wave treatments"—no explanation of what these were—and then osteopathic treatments three times a week for three months. Meanwhile, my physical therapy with Miss Burns continued twice a week, I returned briefly to Warm Springs to see the doctors there, and I started with a new doctor in Philadelphia whose specialty was polio. Reading over this report I wonder how my mother managed to do it all. She was the one who took me to these constant appointments, although my father researched and decided upon them, determined to leave nothing overlooked that might lead to my recovery.

My dependence on my mother and on the endless treatments and consultations I endured made me occasionally wild with frustration and anger. I remember one particularly hot and humid summer day when we had to drive into South Philadelphia, to Sauer's—the bracemakers—to try on some new braces. I dreaded these trips because we usually waited for hours to be seen and there was nothing to do but look at the other sad-looking people who were waiting to be fitted. Sauer's was in an ugly part of the city on a street lined with dingy office fronts. It was so hot that day that the sidewalk seemed to exude steam. The office was not very crowded but we still had to wait a half hour. I sat on a chair with a torn leather seat and stared out of the large dirty window, reading backwards the letters that spelled out "H. Sauer and Sons." Mr. Sauer, the son, was a tall, balding man with rolled-up shirt sleeves. He ushered us into a cubicle with a long leather-topped table, which he helped me onto. The braces were lying on the table, stiff with new leather straps and gleaming with aluminum metal.

"Now," he said, "we can see how these fit. I'm sure you are going to like them."

I was certainly not so sure and said nothing as Mother helped me off with the old braces and on with the new. When I stood up, I felt as if a hundred little fingers were pinching me up and down my legs, into my crotch and around my shoes. Mr. Sauer had me walk across the room with my crutches. He inspected the tops of the braces where they were pinching into my skin, and looked at the angle of the shoes.

"I think we have a good fit," he said.

My mother looked at me and I shook my head, tears of frustration welling up in my eyes.

"They're no good," I said. It took another half hour to try to show Mr. Sauer where the braces pinched and pressed me. He agreed reluctantly to make some changes, remarking that I was probably just not used to them. We waited while he took them back into the shop to bend and mold them and to cut down some of the leather.

When we left the office, I was wearing the new braces under protest, but my mother felt I should try them immediately and see if I could get used to them. As we drove through the hot city and over the Benjamin Franklin Bridge, I sat in the back seat of the car feeling that my legs were encased in some monstrous instruments of torture. I began to cry and pounded on the back of the front seat in fury. "I won't wear them, I won't wear them," I shouted.

Mother tried to drive and calm me, but I would not be consoled. Finally she told me to take them off, which I did, and when we got home, she carried me inside.

Eventually I did get used to the new braces, but as I got older, I learned how to describe very specifically what needed changing and when to insist on more exact fittings. Sometimes I found a skilled and patient orthotic practitioner, and at other times I had to become combative and call in a doctor to back me up. However, the prospect of a brace fitting still fills me with dread, left over, no doubt, from the helplessness I felt as a child.

We moved from Stanwick Road to Prospect Avenue in Moorestown the year I returned from Warm Springs, and although we only had a year there before my father got transferred to Montreal as the president of the RCA Victor Company, I remember the house as a wonderful new world of wonders. The move was a change in status as well as in space. Stanwick Avenue was on the edge of town, that is to say, *just* in the middle class. Now we lived in the center of town but not in the "club estates" where the really wealthy residents were currently building their houses.

Our Prospect Avenue house seemed like a castle to me. It was a sprawling hybrid of colonial and Victorian design, with many porches and odd rounded balconies and dormer windows and here and there some fancy leaded windowpanes. It was a dark color when we bought it but we painted it white. It sat on six or seven acres of land including a wooded grove on one side and a sloping lawn that went down a hill dotted with apple and peach trees. We rented out the farm at the bottom of the hill and were supplied with corn, tomatoes, lettuce, and other vegetables from the farmer. The flower beds and trees were well pruned but there was also an uncultivated feeling, too. I would sit on the wide porch and look into the trees and imagine myself disappearing from sight or I would imagine climbing the apple tree where my brother had built a tree house. He would take a friend and a supply of food and stay up there for hours. I longed to go there, too, but it was too high to boost me up into the branches.

Inside the house I could go anywhere and there was plenty of space to explore. The living room and dining room looked out onto one of the big porches with its view down the hillside. My mother and father's room was set apart and had its own bathroom and balcony. My room was small but at the top of the stairs, which I liked, because I was put to bed earlier than the others and I was comforted to hear voices downstairs. My sisters still shared a room because my grandmother was with us. There was also a sewing room off of the upstairs hallway, often the workplace of my grandmother, and the place our Easter baskets were put. It was that year I received only maple sugar candy in my basket instead of the chocolate eggs that were in all of the other baskets. My father decided that I had to watch my weight so he told my mother to buy only maple candy for me. She saw my pained surprise as I went through the contents of my basket, and I could tell by her expression that she was not happy about it. I was heartbroken and could barely pretend that I didn't mind. My sisters and brother looked at me sympathetically but didn't dare give me any of their candy and disobey my father's orders. He had been converted to a health food diet long before its commercial popularity, and we had a number of strange foods, such as "Dr. Jackson's Roman Meal," a kind of multigrain hot cereal which had that consistency of glue and which all of us refused to eat. But I felt miserably singled out because of my Easter basket.

I did not translate my misery into hostility toward my father until early adolescence. At this point, I just accepted my disappointment as part of the frustration of my disability. My anger, which occasionally erupted, was at the world in general. In retrospect, I know my father always intended to do what was right for me and what he hoped would better my condition, but he was often insensitive to the feeliings of his children. In any case, my mother—or perhaps my grandmother—must have told my father how I felt because I was never given a "special" Easter basket again.

Mother continued to be the energetic facilitator in my life for many years. She moved and installed me in many places—college and summer programs and graduate schools and my first job in Providence, Rhode Island. Even after I could drive a car and transport myself, Mother loved to help me get settled: arranging the furniture, buying curtains, and setting up the kitchen. She was very much a woman of her time—trained and socialized to use her practical gifts and her creativity for running a home and for being a caregiver. I think she was very happy in these roles. She loved everything connected with housekeeping and domesticity: beautiful and useful household things, gardens, lawns, babies, small children and grown children. Later in life on her many trips abroad with her jaunty widowed (seldom divorced in those days) friends, she would collect treasures for her three "girls": lusterware teapots with sugar and creamers, fine English china teacups, handpainted trays, or fine linens from Italy. In her summer house in Maine, which she bought in 1953, she collected stacks of summer china and glassware and matching towels and bathroom accessories. At the same time, she was frugal and a conserver. All household possessions were kept in tiptop shape—from the polish on mahogany tables to the repair of lamps and screens and appliances. Nothing was wasted or allowed to deteriorate. Cleanliness really was next to godliness and her grandchildren discovered her passion for keeping their clothes clean when in the morning they would run down the long stairway in the Maine cottage and try to dodge "Nana" on washing day to avoid her demanding that they surrender slightly soiled socks or tee shirts to the washing machine.

Now, when I visit her, she is no longer able to be the manager. We are disabled together. She still tries to take control. "You can't make that bed," she says. "Let me do it." Or, "I'll get the breakfast. Just stay there." I object and try to finish the bed before she notices. Then I realize I shouldn't. I should try to accept the help graciously, gratefully. Someone still wants to take care of me.

3

MONTREAL, CANADA

We moved to Canada in August 1936, when I was eight. On the wall of my study I keep the photograph from our Christmas card in 1938. Standing in our snow-covered yard, we are all dressed in ski outfits, except for me. I am wearing my hated winter outfit, a dark blue wool coat with a red knitted toque, knitted sash, and mittens. My coat is bulky and prevents me from moving my arms freely. I am sitting on the toboggan, holding our dog, Sandy, hiding my face in his fur. The rest of the family, except for my mother, are actually on skis. Everyone grumbled about posing; my sisters, who are fifteen and sixteen, feel the whole thing is silly. Yet in the photo they are already adopting the "blonde Grimley girl twins" pose and the look of 1940s glamour girls, with hairdos long and curled at the end. My mother stands between them and looks like one of their contemporaries. Tom, my thirteen-year-old brother, is crouched on his skis in front of my father, ready to take off. He was a natural skier and ski jumper. In the photo, he and my father are a little separate from the rest of us, an important reminder of how the men are kept apart from the girls in our family.

My brother and I drifted apart as he entered his teens. His room was on the third floor. I thought it would be scary to go to bed alone up there, but my father was still afraid that Tom might be influenced by too many women. This separation may have hastened our growing apart after being somewhat close as children, but I think Tom was just moving into another world of adolescence, making him closer to my sisters. In our last house, on Lexington Avenue, we were more crowded together and my brother's room was next to the young people's study on the third floor. My sisters were usually there in the evenings doing their schoolwork or playing records or trying out new dance steps like the "shag" or the "dipsey doodle." Hearing them laugh and dance above my room, I felt pangs of jealousy at being the outsider. Tom adored my sisters and became like a mascot to them, piling into cars with their friends at the summer cottage, sailing with them on the lake, or playing tennis and swimming. Any closeness he and I shared was lost by this point, and we became strangers to one another.

Loneliness was part of my life in the midst of our busy family, but it was relieved by the presence of Nana, my beloved Grandmother Grimley. She became the most important person in my life—besides my mother and father—for my first thirteen years. It was for her that I made the most serious bargain I ever made with God and experienced my first spiritual crisis. She was dying of cancer in our Lexington Avenue house in Montreal at the age of seventy-six. Nana had been my constant companion and friend throughout my childhood. When all the rest of the family would take off for a ski weekend in the Laurentians—banging around with long ski poles, my father growing more and more irritable until my sisters and brother exchanged the well-known look of fear and cowardice that develops under an irascible leader—I would remain on the upstairs landing looking down at them, sitting next to my grandmother's bedroom. She would be in her rocking chair, sewing, her pincushion-round figure comfortably filling the chair. She always seemed caught in a spell of serenity. When you entered her room, you crossed into a charmed circle around her where no human tensions could penetrate. She was always there unless she went to visit her daughters, Jane or Emma. She would look up, not say very much, but enough. Sometimes the twinkle would appear. That was one of her nicest gestures, a slightly ironic but benign comment on the world from the eyes. She was great at communicating this when my father exploded. The twinkle and a marvelous grimace of the lower jaw, saying, "Look at him. Beware the green dragon!" Only for a second. Then she'd resume an imperturbable poker face that said, "Who me? I didn't say a thing!" She was the only one who called my father by his christened name of Elmer.

In 1942, Nana had become ill and had been taken to the hospital against her wishes. The doctors found that she had inoperable stomach cancer and so she was returned home. The house was permeated with white uniformed nurses, low voices, the odor of the fatally ill. I knew she was not going to get better. Every day I would go in and sit beside the bed, holding for a moment her yellowing hand. Sometimes she had a Bible on the covers beside her. Later she was barely conscious or awake, but I still sat there and held the ungrasping hand. Grief was not really part of my life, but I knew that I could not lose Nana. God must know that. What did he want from me?

My communications with God were usually carried on from my bed at night, never at our church, the United Church of Canada, down at the foot of the hill. I only play-acted my prayers and conversations with God in church. It was too difficult to talk when you had to be mindful of how you looked praying. A few streets up from our house stood the large Catholic cathedral of Saint Joseph's—an alien and grotesque place of worship to our family, who shared a general Protestant prejudice against Catholics for their alleged superstitions. But its very pomposity, sitting at the top of Westmount Mountain, at the crest of three or four hundred steps, was to me a compelling sign that it might be a good place to contact God, and so it was to Saint Joseph's that I turned in my terror about Nana. I had been there a few times before when we showed visitors the city and had already tried to make a deal whereby my crutches would join the stacks of crutches and canes left there by the faithful after they had been cured. I had not yet passed judgment on the practices of any religious group so I tried a number of bargains, from giving up candy to reading a whole chapter of the Bible each night, yet nothing worked out. But now, I reasoned, I would be asking for someone else.

The first question was how to get there. It was not easy to convince someone that I needed to go to Saint Joseph's, and it was too far for me to walk. Walking uphill was difficult for me and anyway, my mother always felt she needed to account for my whereabouts and such an outrageous request would be inexplicable to her. My problem was miraculously—I hoped—solved by a visiting cousin from New Jersey to whom we had to "show the sights." Mother was going to drive by the cathedral and take Jan on to the wax museum, which specialized in religious martyrs. (Mother did not seem to associate the museum with the saints and martyrs she so disliked in Catholicism.) I chose my moment just as we paused in front of the massive set of steps, dotted with kneeling pilgrims.

"Let's go inside the cathedral and look at all the crutches and canes," I ventured.

Mother looked particularly incredulous and slightly offended. "Jan wouldn't want to see that, would you, Jan?"

My cousin was seventeen, attractive, pleasant, slightly indifferent. I looked at her apprehensively, but was relieved when she said, "Oh, let's go in."

My first step was achieved. Now I had to get in front of the altar without too much obvious purpose and make my plea. While Mother and Jan were looking at the white and pink and blue statuary with disapproving appraisal, I stumped down to the front of the pews, my heart pounding with shame as I knew everyone would think I was praying for my own cure. I was given a religious medal on the way by a woman in black, her face circled in a dark kerchief. She spoke in French and looked curiously, perhaps compassionately, at me. I smiled a ghastly false smile, took the medal, and reached the steps of the altar. My message was brief. "Let Nana live and forget about my ever being cured and able to walk."

I hadn't really decided on my bargain beforehand, and only tried out a number of minor and major sacrifices. When the moment came, the words just blurted out—in my mind, that is. I don't think I had ever consciously thought about whether my "cure" was physically possible. Residual polio, my medical condition—I was weary of my father's insistence on trying to find a cure, but I always held a scrap of hope in the miraculous. And here I was giving it up! I was astonished at myself and caught my breath in surprise.

"Mary, let's go, dear." My mother and Jan had approached, and we went on our way.

The next few days were hard. Every day before school I would check with the day nurse, who had just relieved the night shift.

"Is my grandmother any better?" I'd ask.

"No, dear," she said on Wednesday morning—I had made my bargain on Saturday. "Our patient is not too well today." Then she raised her eyes— she was a prim, starched lady. "It's all in the hands of God," she said.

Wow, I thought to myself. Does she know? Then I realized her expression had been a commonplace, like a comment on the weather.

The next afternoon I went swimming at the Montreal Athletic Association, where Mother would take me after school. I had a special weekly lesson with the instructor and hated the damp, hot indoor pool. I could never get dry and could not leap out like other swimmers and run through the showers. It was January, cold and wet in Montreal, with snow, slush, a seasonal thaw. I was particularly hot from the struggle of loading on winter clothes and when I went outside, the cold bitter air turned the heat to a chill sweat. Mother's face looked crumpled when she came to pick me up. Something was wrong, I knew.

"Nana has taken a turn for the worse, dear," she said. We drove home without speaking. Mother did not discuss these things very much.

When I went in, I realized Nana was dead. The "turn for the worse" had been death. My father was home, although it was only four o'clock. My father came out of Nana's room with the doctor and the nurse. He didn't speak to me and his eyes were blurry.

I took off my heavy clothes in silence with mother's help. "When will there be a funeral?" I asked.

"Tomorrow." Mother patted my arm. "You'll stay home from school."

I went upstairs to my room, passing my grandmother's room at the top of the stairs. Just the nurse was at the door now. All the others were downstairs. It was the "in the hands of God" nurse. I wanted to avoid her if possible, but I took a considerable time to get up the stairs and couldn't slip by unnoticed. She stood in the doorway, her arms crossed and her hands grasping her elbows neatly. She smiled at me as I approached.

"She's in the arms of Jesus," she said, with honey in her voice.

I crashed around the corner, achieving my room. I didn't even try to sort out my conflicting emotions, simply closed the door and sat on my bed—heart thumping, hands clammy, my breath short, my still damp hair clinging with a chill on my head.

"So I can get better!" I said it out loud, and it was a sob. Then I pulled the pillow to me to smother the dull ache I felt in my heart.

Nana's death and my bargain with God marked a maturing in my life to the reality of my disability. My grandmother did not live, so I should have been cured. I had offered up my cure for her life, but my bargain did not work out. I could no longer count on miracles and I had to redefine my faith in a God who did not directly respond to me. Moreover, I understood that I would probably have to walk with braces and crutches for the rest of my life.

My father, however, had not given up on finding a cure for me or at least changing my condition substantially, so now I turned to his approach of relentlessly seeking to fight my disability by any means possible. We had not found a satisfactory physical therapist in Montreal so he suggested that I spend some time in Ardmore, Pennsylvania, with Miss Burns, concentrating on my walking and possibly moving from crutches to canes. I could also have a checkup with my Philadelphia doctor. I agreed, but I had no idea how miserably homesick I would be.

I was eleven years old when I arrived at the large near-empty Victorian house in Ardmore where Miss Burns lived with her two elderly parents and an aged deaf uncle. I was determined to work hard and go home with great physical accomplishments, but I had not anticipated the isolation of my life there and how it would affect me. Despite a number of entertainments for me on the weekends—the circus and movies and an occasional visit to Miss Burns's house in the country—I was virtually alone all day except for a woman who tutored me three hours several mornings a week. I had a study furnished with a desk, a chair, a chaise lounge, bookshelves, and a table. My companion was my radio. I listened to soap operas (*The Guiding Light* and *Mary Noble, Backstage Wife*) and longed to be home in my busy household where someone was always around. I had physiotherapy daily in the pool that was attached to the house and I occasionally saw other patients coming and going, but I had no contact with anyone my own age. I can remember the smell of chlorine that came up to my study from the pool and the white almost translucent look of Miss Burns's skin after she had been giving treatments in the water all day. She wore glasses even in the pool and a black bathing suit, which was covered over once a month when she got her menstrual period (and did not want to get wet) with a huge tan rubber suit like a pair of overalls. She inspired us, her patients, to do impossible things—to raise a leg that was almost lifeless or take steps you didn't think you could make. She willed us to achieve and I worked hard despite my loneliness.

Occasionally I would join Miss Burns's mother and her retired father for their afternoon soap operas in the parlor, a gloomy room full of over-stuffed chairs covered with small lace antimacassars. The uncle was too deaf to hear anything but he would join us before dinner, which we ate together. I was given lunch upstairs by myself. Sometimes my tutor, a young woman with light red hair, took pity on me and had me to her house on Saturday where I had lunch with the welcome noise of other children and dogs and a canary. I would go with her children to a double feature matinee in the afternoon and eat popcorn and candy (both frowned upon by Miss Burns).

My letters home were cries for help. But when my father stopped by to see me during a business trip, I could not tell him how I felt just as I could not speak to him about my loneliness as a small child at Warm Springs. Something about his dark eyes and stern look made me unable to state my case of homesickness. As always, I felt that I must not fail him and that I must try harder to do the impossible. He left and apparently told my mother that I was doing well. However, three weeks later, when I was left alone in my bedroom until quite late at night—Miss Burns was out for the evening and our two rooms were the only ones on the top floor—I went nearly out of my mind with pent-up homesickness that took the form of an acute attack of terror.

I had gone up to my room on my own, climbing the third floor steps from the dark second floor corridor. Everything was silent because the elderly people had retired at their usual early hour. By the time I got to my room, I could hear a hundred creaks and cracks throughout the house and imagined footsteps coming up the stairs from the first floor. I turned on my radio and got ready for bed. I was reluctant to take off my braces, feeling I should be ready for flight. Eventually I took them off. I could not even think of going to sleep or of turning off my light. I tried to read but could not. I kept turning my radio down so I could listen to the house and to any signs of danger. I began to feel a cold sweat and I was sure I heard the footsteps of someone stealthily coming up the stairs to get me. I prayed that Miss Burns would come home, but I knew she had said that she would be late. By the time the grandfather clock on the first floor struck eleven o'clock, I was shivering and sobbing and gasping. I must have let myself down from the side of the bed to the floor. I dragged myself on all fours down the steps, bumping and bruising my legs as I went. I became conscious of myself pounding on the closed doors of one of the second floor bedrooms. It was the door of the deaf uncle but I got no response from him. Mr. and Mrs. Burns, startled from sleep by my pounding, appeared in long white nightshirts at their door. Mr. Burns must have carried me up the stairs to my room. He was not a big man but he was strong with the sturdy hands of a carpenter. I don't remember falling to sleep but I did.

The next day I remained in a state of shock. Miss Burns did not say anything about the episode at breakfast but she looked very serious. Her mother asked me, "Are you all right this morning?" Her daughter gave her a silencing look. She said, "We'll talk about it later." It was not until I was in the pool that she brought up the subject. "My parents were frightened by your behavior last night," she said, without looking up at me as she started my routine of leg exercises. "I don't know what happened to you."

I was going to say something about my terror, but she stopped me. "I don't think it is going to work out keeping you here any longer. I wrote to your mother this morning and asked her to come and take you home." I was stunned by her coldness and detachment. I had expected her to say she was sorry that I had been so frightened. Instead I felt as if I had committed a criminal act. I was relieved when my mother came for me a week later, but for several years I had nightmares about that night flight.

When I returned home from Ardmore, I felt that my mission had been a failure and I resolved to give up my father's obsessive drive for making me better. I wanted to get on with life and not dwell on my disability. I began to turn more to my sisters for companionship. They had always been figures of awe to me—glamorous and popular and very self-sufficient. We were five and six years apart in age so I was out of their world anyway, but they were tolerant of my tribute and usually I was welcome in their bedroom to watch them dress for parties. They often dressed alike, but not for dates so there was much discussion about who would wear what each date night. It was the era of elaborate evening gowns with hoop skirts, low-cut bodices, rhinestones, black velvet chokers, and spiked heels. Hair was worn straight and long, evolving later into the Veronica Lake peek-a-boo look over. I watched in fascination as wet dripping hair and bodies were transformed into glamorous "dates." The male counterparts seemed practically irrelevant.

In the summer, in our rented summer cottages at the Hermitage Club on Lake Memphremagog, sitting on the long sprawling porches or in front of the big fireplace, I got to see the string of eligible young men who would appear on the weekends. I was almost unnoticed as I watched but I took it all in—the plots and schemes and heartbreaks and triumphs. I would report it all to my friend, Mary Skelton, who also had an older sister and brother, although they were not into the social set of the Club as yet. Mary and I would spend long afternoons eating and swimming and comparing notes. We swam until our hair was waterlogged and our skin as wrinkled as prunes. Sometimes we would be harassed by Jeffrey, her twin brother, but we were generally free of much contact with the opposite sex and were just as glad to experience them vicariously.

Sometimes I was given a special place of honor by my sisters. They would insist that I be taken along in someone's red convertible for ice cream or included in trips to the movies in the local town. At times, my presence came in handy if one of my sisters wanted to distance herself from her weekend guest who had turned out disastrously. I am sure that my sisters were unaware that they caused a deepening of my double consciousness as a disabled and an able-bodied person as I approached adolescence. On the one hand, I identified with them as I grew into womanhood. On the other hand, I realized I could never fully be like them, popular with boys in an exciting social life.

One occasion that I regularly shared with my sisters was the annual costume party for adults and children held at the clubhouse at the end of the summer. One year my mother got me dressed up as the picture "Springtime," one of those English garden portraits of a little girl in a long Empire-style yellow dress, wearing a sunbonnet and holding a big basket of summer flowers. I was posed in a huge gilt frame made for me by a local carpenter. My mother made the dress and perhaps even the bonnet. The preparations were elaborate. I won a prize and I felt like a fool. I was sure I had been given the prize because I was disabled and everyone felt sorry for me. I was no happier than I had been holding the Thanksgiving turkey at Warm Springs, and I remained a reluctant "poster child"—but now I smiled and played the part. My sisters came as rhumba dancers—Xavier Cugat was popular then—and they won a prize, too.

Fortunately, in my all-girls school in Montreal I felt very much at home and I was not an outsider among my friends. At thirteen and fourteen we had not yet entered the world of romantic relationships partly because we went to a girls' school and partly because in the culture of the 1940s dating did not begin until at least high school. In any case, our experience with the opposite sex was limited to fantasy and what we could observe (and exaggerate) about our older sisters' love lives. Together with my friend Barbara, who was then a gangly and awkward teenager, I acted out fantasies by drawing fashion models or putting together outfits on fashion dolls—precursors of Barbie dolls. The women in our drawings had tiny waists, huge breasts, and long pageboy hairdos and we thought them the epitome of beauty. We were offended when Barbara's mother, a pretty Englishwoman who had been a nurse in Jamaica, would laugh tolerantly and ask us if we thought our models could keep their balance with such top-heavy chests.

I was spared from confronting how my crutches and braces would affect my social life. My friends seemed almost oblivious to my disability. However, when I was fourteen, Ann Thompson, one of my best friends, had the first coed party that I remember. It was a pretty grim affair, held in her basement playroom. The motley group of boys she had gathered (I wonder now where they came from) huddled on one side of the room while the girls surged impatiently toward them from the other side of the room. But the two forces would not meet. Ann tried to bring us together with food and drink and records, but nothing lured the boys away from each other. I felt uncomfortable with my false smile, and the other girls did not feel much better. That same year my friend Barbara, who was turning into a beautiful young woman, began to talk about a boyfriend—a summer acquaintance of her family—and brag about long telephone conversations with him. Barbara's parents were very strict so she could only see the boy at her house, but others, like Liz Thatcher, boasted of meeting a boy at a drugstore for a soda. The rest of us felt cut off from these fortunate few, but we consoled ourselves with gossip.

One of the things that my sisters and I shared was the Trafalgar School for Girls. My brother was sent to the local public school and then given an extra year at Deerfield Academy in preparation for college in the United States. At Trafalgar we wore uniforms—short black tunics that had to measure four inches above the knees when you knelt, a white blouse, black stockings, shoes, and bloomers. Our ladylike principal, Miss Cummings, always wore black or other dark colors and, despite a sweet and gentle voice, could make you rigid with fear if you had to appear in her office because you had received a black mark. An accumulation of black marks could get you suspended or even expelled from the school. When Miss Cummings retired, she was followed by Miss Foster, whose homeliness stays with me vividly. She had red kinky hair drawn back in a bun—her hair would have made a handsome Pre-Raphaelite portrait if allowed to fall loosely around her face—and she had remarkable buck teeth, keeping her mouth ajar, punctuated by the mole on her upper lip.

Neatness, good posture, civility, obedience, and good study habits were the Trafalgar School heritage. The intellectual achievements were modest: some fundamental skills in math and writing, a spark here and there from a Latin teacher and literature teacher, a little drawing and a little music. I do remember that Miss Bedford-Jones provided me with my second and only other chance to perform onstage (the first was my debut at Warm Springs as a sailor). In our eighth grade Shakespeare performance, sitting in a regal chair onstage in black robes, I played the Duke in the court scene of *The Merchant of Venice:* "How shalt thou hope for mercy, rendering none?" was, I recall, one of my most forceful lines. (I had about twenty-five lines in all.)

I was disappointed at the thought of leaving my friends at Trafalgar when my father decided to move back to New Jersey in semiretirement after he had suffered a heart attack the previous year. He had been confined to bed for a month or two—there was very little heart surgery performed at the time—and I was aware of how unusual it was to have him at home but I didn't know how serious his condition could be.

I had told the school I would not be returning in the fall, but I was surprised when Miss Harvie, my ninth grade homeroom teacher and also my teacher of ancient history, called me and said she would like to say good-bye and invited me to her tennis club for tea. I was rather flattered even though I found her a dull teacher. She was a slim woman in her late thirties with short-cut graying hair, a tight expression and a ramrod straight back developed from her own student days at Trafalgar before she went to McGill University and to Oxford. On her way home to Canada in 1939 she was shipwrecked and rescued from the SS *Athenia,* the first ship to be torpedoed by a German submarine in World War II. As her students, we knew none of this but only that she was a rather severe teacher and taught us a dry subject.

I was dropped off at the club in the afternoon and found Miss Harvie waiting for me. She was wearing a white frilly blouse and a full bright blue skirt instead of her usual gray or tan sweaters over straight gray or tan skirts. She greeted me with a wide smile that startled me because it was so uncharacteristic. Her face was usually immobile. I got used to her new look quickly; she seemed very attractive, like a totally different person. After English tea with crumpets and cakes, Miss Harvie pulled out some photographs and shyly pointed out her fiancé, a dark-haired young man who she said was Polish and whom she had met the previous summer, bicycling in Europe. I was astonished to think of Miss Harvie with a fiancé and was, of course, dying to dumbfound my school friends with the news although she asked me to keep it a secret since the engagement had not been announced. As she talked of her romance, I realized that indeed it was a secret, perhaps even from her own family, and that she had chosen to tell me because she could not contain her joy and wished to share it with someone. She showed me many more pictures of the two of them on their bicycles, standing in front of churches and monuments and mountains. She offered her news shyly but her face was radiant and she looked quite pretty. This would be a revelation to my friends. We naturally talked a lot about who was pretty and who was not but our teachers rarely qualified. Miss Harvie was definitely not considered pretty and not even remotely likely to have a boyfriend; in fact, in our minds she was totally outside the realm of romance or sexuality.

After I left Miss Harvie, who promised to write me when she got married, I puzzled over the reasons that she chose to share her happiness with me. My departure did make me a safer confidant because I would soon be gone and theoretically less likely to spread the news. But I wondered too if being a disabled person made me seem more sensitive. I never knew the answer but I did learn that Miss Harvie did not announce her engagement and did not leave Trafalgar to join a young lover in Poland—he probably died in the war. Rather she stayed on at the school, teaching ancient history and Latin and becoming part of the establishment. She became the vice principal and then the principal, and finally she retired in 1975. In the spring of 1993, I received my Trafalgar newsletter, "The Victory," featuring a memorial article on her. She died on February 12, 1993. A cover photograph of her as principal showed that she still had gray hair, an unbending neck, and a steady gaze. Her expression around the mouth, however, was softer than I had remembered it, somewhat mellowed. In the account of her funeral service, a tribute by one of her students was quoted. The eulogy ended in Latin: *Ave atque vale cara amica. Requiescas in pace.* (Hail and farewell, dear friend. Rest in peace.)

Miss Harvie was, at the time I knew her, a model I wanted to avoid at all costs—a spinster school teacher who had little chance of romance in her life. However, after our visit, I wished fervently for the success of her romance because I wanted to believe that a lonely Cinderella could be transformed and find her prince. I felt that I, too, might be a Cinderella.

Death marked my childhood years twice in Montreal. My grandmother's death was followed one year later by my father's. He had a heart attack on our sailboat in August of 1943 at Lake Memphremagog. My mother and my cousin were sailing with him and saw him fall into the water and sink out of their reach. It took five days to find his body.

Two nights after my father drowned and they were still looking for his body in the lake, I dreamed that they had recovered the body and revived him. He returned to the summer cottage through the front door, dripping with water and wearing a red and blue striped towel around his shoulders—the way my mother had come in two afternoons earlier after the boat accident. But this time—in my dream—it is my father who enters. He is with my sister's fiancé, who is still in his swimming shorts and who, I believe, has dived down to the bottom of the lake and brought up his body. Their entrance shocks me. I am sitting in the wicker rocking chair, trying to grieve for my father's death and then he walks in and the rug becomes wet with the water dripping off his hair and body. Immediately in my dream I feel tension in the air, the same tension that I felt three afternoons before when I went out on the porch and met my father's disapproving look: "Mary, why aren't you doing your exercises?"

"I'll do them later," I replied defensively. Talking with my father made me nervous that summer when I was fourteen. He needled me constantly about exercising, about trying to walk with canes instead of crutches. I was impatient and just wanted to get where I wanted to go quickly. But my impatience didn't satisfy my father. In a letter to my mother, he wrote, "Mary's thinking should be switched from the present groove to physical improvement." He was investigating a nerve-crushing treatment at the time that allegedly regenerated nerves in some patients, including one with polio. However, a series of letters from doctors concluded that the treatment would not benefit my case. That did not deter my father from pressing me to work harder to make some improvements on my own. We became engaged in a battle of wills. I wanted to be left alone. He would insist that I sunbathe down on the dock and brown the back of my legs, even pulling up my bathing suit to expose my buttocks, which humiliated me terribly when other people were on the dock. I'd pull my suit down and watch out of the corner of my eye to see if he was reaching over to pull it back up. If so, I'd let myself roll into the water and swim out to the raft—perhaps even go under the raft and come up in one of the open spaces between the row of barrels that was the understructure of the float. It was dark and cool under there and only the lapping of the water would disturb the silent oblivion I sought.

My father was angry with me that afternoon on the porch and shouted that I'd never get well if I didn't try. I didn't reply, but dark obliterating rage, mixed with fear, blinded me. He had a nasty temper and could speak cuttingly. I sometimes felt that he was going to hit me. Once at the breakfast table, we quarreled. As usual he was ordering me to do something that I sullenly resisted—and when he raised his hand, I was sure he was going to hit me. I almost wished that he would so that I could respond violently, shouting or hitting back. My mother intervened and my grandmother looked pained so I was sent up to my room where I sat shivering in anger, blinding tears rolling down my face. Suddenly I started to hit the front of my bureau drawers with my clenched fist. I continued hitting it until my hand was limp with pain.

Once I heard my father slap my mother in the bedroom next to mine and my mother cried and then my father cried, too, and said he was sorry. But he never told me that he was sorry for anything he'd said, and that afternoon on the porch, three days before he drowned, I vowed that I would rather die than tell him I was sorry. I resolved to resist his tyranny forever. And so I stood in front of him, fearful, but immobile. Perhaps because of his heart attack months before, he wished to avoid extreme anger. In any case, he stopped shouting, and I went inside, trembling but stolid. In the dream, when my father comes in dripping from the lake, I do not feel a rush of love and joy. However, I am relieved because I feel guilty that I have not grieved for his death. When I awake the next morning and find that my father's body has not yet been found, I can hardly believe it. I was completely convinced of his presence in my dream. I feel the heavy suspended pain return, but at the same time, I have to admit, I feel a release from tension. I am suddenly free to live without the impossible goal of being cured.

In the days following my father's death I lived with my dreams, recreating his presence over and over again. Sometimes I would lie awake and daydream about him, rifling through the images of him in my life and trying to remember images of tenderness, searching for moments of his humor and practical jokes, the side of him that was often reserved for friends or for my grandmother, whom he loved to tease. I remembered the time he stood in the hall coat closet with a shawl over his head knowing his mother was going to open the door to get her shawl. She screamed when she saw the silent ominous figure standing behind the coats and scolded, "Elmer, stop that! You scared me to death." He was very fond of my grandmother and wept at her deathbed. We had cried together.

I could not recall many occasions alone with my father, except the time he came to Warm Springs and the time he visited me in Ardmore, Pennsylvania. Once when I was eight and taken to New York City to see one of the many doctors my father insisted on consulting, I was alone with just my parents. We stayed in a hotel and had dinner brought to our room by a white-coated waiter who served the meal elegantly. My mother and father whispered together during dinner and I gathered that they were trying to find a way to spend the evening at Radio City Music Hall but they could not find a baby-sitter for me. Finally, after much suspense, I was told that I was going to go to the show. It was my first experience in a theater. In fact, we rarely went to the theater or even the movies as a family so this occasion became even more precious to me because it connected me to the world of entertainment that my father loved. He had collected all of the recordings of popular Broadway shows and would sing along with them and reminisce about his brother, who had a brief career in show business before he died in the same flu epidemic that took my mother's brother. I was fascinated that night by the Rockettes' dazzling precision and high-kicking leg art. Perhaps this was the beginning of my fascination with dancing of all kinds, an art totally impossible for me.

I do not have many other memories of being alone with my father. In Montreal, when my grandmother was still alive, we would play Chinese checkers with him after dinner if I had finished my homework. After Nana died, my father and I would play double solitaire together. He insisted that the goal of the game was for both of us to uncover all of our cards, not for one of us to win. I became so accustomed to this rule that when I played with my brother, I had to remember how to be competitive and slap the cards on fast. Now I see that my father's version of solitaire—principled and rational—comes right out of his "Philosophy of Life," notes for a book that he left among his papers. In the notes, he reveals himself as a believer in the golden mean, firmly rejecting greed and excessive wealth and defining accomplishment as the cultivation of a "human organism acting as a whole." Had he lived a long life, we might have discussed such matters, overcoming the emotional conflicts that separated us then.

Growing up, I both revered and feared my father, and his death caught me in a tangle of emotions. During those tense days when everything was focused on recovering my father's body, the house was muffled but active. People brought food to us although we still had our summer cook so meals were regularly served even when my mother was not there. My future brother-in-law stayed with us and helped to coordinate the recovery efforts. I felt useless and numb and was glad to have some packing to do as we got ready to leave the lake. Finally after five days, my father's body was found by the local police. It had been washed ashore halfway down the lake.

The funeral was in our church in Westmount. It was very formal and the church was full of workers and associates from my father's company as well as friends and relatives. The casket was closed and the minister, Dr.

Lloyd Smith, gave a long eulogy. I felt separated from everyone. I didn't think about the quarrel my father and I had before he died; I couldn't think about anything. My mind shut down, focusing on little details around me, such as the creaking shoes of a pallbearer and my mother's black veil caught just under her nose. There were many officials from my father's company—his assistant vice president, Harry Marpole, and other officers I didn't know. Outside, important-looking men arranged parking going to and from the church in long black cars. In the church, sextons, dressed in formal striped pants and cutaway black coats, told people where to sit and walked with their heads slightly bent down. At the funeral reception at our house the housemaid served trays of sandwiches and cakes, moving silently back and forth among the guests. My sisters and brother helped distribute coffee and tea. They talked quietly to some of our aunts and cousins who were staying with us and with friends. I endured people patting me on the head sadly or embracing me, but I concentrated only on how I could escape upstairs to my room. It was difficult to go up the staircase in the middle of the front hall without people noticing. I couldn't slip up silently. My crutches made too much noise. I finally managed to disappear with only two or three people asking me if I was all right as I went up the stairs. I sat on my bed and thought about my grandmother and how much I missed her. I felt guilty that I could not feel the same pain about my father and then I began to cry about that. My real grief and sorrow for his loss was repressed and not resolved until years later when I was able to come to terms with my anger and better understand his influence.

We had planned to move back to Moorestown in the fall but the return was hastened after my mother accompanied my father's body to New Jersey to be buried. The war was still on and my sisters' boyfriends were all in the service overseas or about to be sent there. My sister, Betty, married in November in a quiet wedding in our Prospect Avenue house. Her husband was commissioned as a doctor in the Royal Canadian Navy. Jane, my other sister, was married in January in Montreal when her fiancé was on leave from the Royal Canadian Air Force. I returned to Moorestown as a tenth grader in the Friends school and my brother, Tom, went to Dartmouth College and then was transferred to Harvard in the Naval ROTC. I could not have imagined then that his funeral would follow my father's by only five years.

4

COMING OF AGE

After my father's death in 1943, we moved back to New Jersey where I attended Moorestown Friends School and graduated in 1946. I had a relatively easy time going through my teenage years because MFS was a small low-key school and there was not the usual kind of social pressure to have a boyfriend or be a pin-up girl. In fact, we didn't have typical high school heroes—the kind you would find at the town public high school. We didn't play football. Like most Quaker schools, we only played soccer and basketball. Furthermore, it was wartime and the gravities of the war effort muted our social expectations.

Despite the noncompetitive atmosphere at MFS, I became self-conscious of my image in tenth grade. I was overweight and I began to look despairingly at myself in the mirror. Up until then, I had not been preoccupied with my body. My sisters were the glamour girls and I did not relate to them except in romantic fantasies when I would be transformed into a beautiful, slim heroine without crutches and braces. Suddenly I felt the humiliation of having my clothes specially made and I hated the plaid yellow and tan jacket that I wore with a tan skirt that was tight around the waist. I went on a diet—under a doctor's direction—that was all bananas. I was to eat six bananas a day with skim milk. I still hate the smell of bananas but I lost twenty-five pounds and discovered a new image. I was still "the handicapped girl" in the class but no longer "the chubby handicapped girl." My mother and I actually could buy clothes for me at department stores. We had a whole new way to relate to one another and I felt as if she treated me more as she did my sisters.

I remember a particular dress Mother bought me for a dinner party that had been arranged for a group of my classmates in a hotel. We had gone to two department stores in Philadelphia and we were having lunch at Whitman's—a favorite in-town restaurant. We had not found any dress that I liked.

"Let's try that specialty shop near Rittenhouse Square," mother said, referring to a very expensive boutique where my sisters had done some shopping. I was impressed but a bit nervous about going into any place so fashionable. What would the saleswomen think of me? I wondered. Mother seemed confident about taking me there so we left Whitman's and drove to the shop.

The saleswoman knew Mother and did not blink when she said I was looking for a dress. She brought out several selections and I immediately saw one that I liked. It was a soft cotton—Wedgwood blue with a slightly darker print in it. It had a full gathered skirt that emphasized a small waist-line and capped shirred sleeves framing a sweetheart neckline. I picked it out and went into the elegant dressing room to try it on. For a moment as I stood looking in the mirror, I did not recognize myself. The skirt was quite long so it hid my braces and I hardly noticed my crutches.

"Now that's perfect," the saleslady insisted. "Isn't she lovely," she said to my mother.

Her flattery brought me back to my senses. I was still on crutches and I wouldn't forget that, but I did have a new sense of myself and I was elated at the approval that my mother showed. She hardly looked at the price although it was very expensive.

"We'll take it," she said decisively, a rare gesture for her. She was usually cautious about spending.

The dress was wrapped in a large box and we drove home to New Jersey, talking about our day in town. It was probably the first time that I thought of myself as becoming a young woman, aware of my sexuality. Of course, my mother did not discuss such matters. The words were not part of her vocabulary, but the fact that she had taken me to purchase the dress, as she might have done for my sisters, told me that she looked at me differently.

The Second World War, which ended in my junior year, cast a shadow over all of our lives. The heroes of the school were the graduates who came back in uniform with medals even though many Quakers were pacifists and refused to serve in the military. Some pacifists had been sent to jail; others did alternate service in mental institutions or prisons. But we did not hear about such people at MFS.

There were a few teachers who did convey the Quaker philosophy. Some were memorable teachers as well. Miss Jackson, my tenth grade English teacher, was inspiring. She encouraged me to write. She had the poet Sarah Cleghorn visit our class one day. Cleghorn was a small gentle woman who seemed ancient. (She was actually sixty-eight at the time.) I did not know that Robert Frost had called the elderly woman "a saint, a poet, and a reformer," but she became special to me primarily because she read one of my stories and encouraged me to become a writer.

In the late 1940s, there were no black children at MFS even though it was a Quaker school. They all went to the public school. But racism did come to my high school class when Nancy Stokes, who graduated with me, married a young black man when she went to college in Chicago. She returned home with her baby to visit her family and found herself beseiged wih people coming to call on her to see the new, racially mixed child. One of my mother's friends said she stopped by the house to ask for a drink of water just so she could get a chance to see the baby. "Why, it's a cute little thing," Mrs. Rogers said, "but all that nappy black hair! I wonder where the couple will live?" Some of Nancy's relatives tried to persuade her to give up the marriage and the child. The town's frenzy of gossip and voyeurism ended when her brother got up in Quaker meeting and told the congregation that they were a flock of hypocrites. The people were shocked but the visits stopped. Nancy's marriage did not last and she eventually moved to Hawaii with her child, but her father wrote a beautiful article for the *Atlantic Monthly* on the joys and privilege of being a grandfather to a child of mixed race. It was not until I read the article that I realized how much the fabric of my southern New Jersey town was racist and how much of it I had unconsciously absorbed. I also realized that my own experience of "otherness" as a disabled person made me respond almost viscerally to other marginalized people and connect with them.

Later when I was in college and had come home for the holidays, I became more and more intolerant of the town's racism and specifically of my mother's unawareness of it. One day when I drove into the town's segregated black section to deliver a Christmas gift to someone who worked for my mother, I noticed to my astonishment that there were no sidewalks on any of the streets. There was a paved road and then dirt and sometimes grass and then the houses. I pointed this out to my mother. "Did you notice that there are no sidewalks in the black section of town?"

"Oh really? Yes, I guess you are right. I never thought of that," my mother replied noncommittally. "Maybe the colored folk don't want them," she said.

"What do you mean, they don't *want* sidewalks?" I was immediately outraged but realized afterwards that I obviously never noticed the unpaved streets before and so had been at one time just as unconscious of racism as my mother.

By twelfth grade, I was part of the ruling elite. Not only was I an editor of the yearbook but I was in the debating club and the choral society, and I was one of the class speakers at graduation. However, the yellowed notes of Mr. Deyo in history class and Miss Harding's plodding exegesis of Hardy's *Return of the Native* convinced me that better things must be coming in college. Everything would change, I thought. I would make exciting new friends. I would have inspiring professors. I would become something—what I was not sure, probably a writer. I couldn't wait to get on with my life. I decided to go to Wheaton College in Massachusetts because it was close to Boston and small enough that I could walk around campus.

Despite my excitement, Wheaton was a disappointment to me and by the end of my second year, I couldn't wait to leave. Nevertheless, I remember the people there vividly. When I look over one of the yearbooks that I kept, the pages evoke a strong sense of a community of women, a community which at that time I did not appreciate fully. I was too intent on passing as a "normal" college coed.

The campus was modeled after a New England village with the white chapel predominant and brick buildings built around the green. Mary Lyons Hall, named after the founder, was proof that the college had been one of the first seminaries, started, like Mount Holyoke (also founded by Mary Lyons), to further the education of women. I arrived at the college enthusiastically, but I forgot how difficult it had been for me to leave home as a child. I never experienced the regimentation of summer camp so I did not realize that I would feel trapped by rules and regulations. There were a lot of parietal rules in women's colleges in the 1940s: lights out for freshmen at ten o'clock, signing in and out when you went off campus, compulsory early morning chapel several days a week and a forced freshman fellowship—bonfires and sing-alongs and special hats. I longed to flee. Also the old night fears and nightmares returned during the first weeks.

In these postwar years the campus was still suffering from wartime inconveniences. Cars were scarce and transportation by bus or by train to Boston or anywhere was difficult. By the end of the week most of the women felt trapped and claustrophobic and took off—rather desperately —for blind dates at Brown University or MIT or other male institutions. Saturday morning classes were obligatory—attendance was very strictly required—so my music appreciation class was usually filled with young women with shiny clean hair, high heels, shetland sweaters and polo coats in contrast to the weekday look of messy hair, loafers, and long crumpled shirts over bluejeans. As the class drew to its close the professor—a commuter from Boston University—became more and more ironic. He noticed the closing up of notebooks, the tidying of pocketbooks, and the faraway look in the students' eyes as they prepared to rush out the door to catch the bus to different destinations. "I'm sure you young ladies won't mind if the class runs over a little today," he would threaten and then laugh as he saw the looks of horror. In those days we were polite and deferential to professors—particularly if they were male—so no one would leave until he dismissed the class. He never carried out his threat but always enjoyed his joke.

The return after the weekend was grim. The sleek hairdos were flattened and the bright looks of expectation became dark circled eyes. I heard accounts of the weekends in the "smoker," which was a dreary basement room where smoking was allowed. It was furnished with a shabby couch, a table, and some chairs and, of course, it was always filled with clouds of smoke and ashtrays full of cigarette butts. I smoked, like most people there, to be part of the social group and to hear the tales of disastrous blind dates and drunken fraternity parties. There was usually an attempt to make the weekend sound like fun but underlying enthusiastic descriptions of how cute Bob was or what a great car Dick had there was a current of despair. How could you meet someone you really liked? When would that special person come along?

The weekend student body divided roughly into three groups: first, the majority, who went away on these weekends; second, the more fortunate, who had already found their special person and spent weekends more happily; third, a small group of outsiders, who scoffed at all of the above and who either studied all weekend or hinted at less conventional adventures (I never knew what these were). I was somewhere in the last group, not identifying myself with the grinds or the bohemians. I went into Boston to the theater or concerts as often as I could, taking the taxis and buses that were necessary to make the trip. I found some friends who wanted to join me but even my closest friends would give up a play or film if a blind date was available. Most of them did not have steady dates those first two years. I didn't blame them but I began to feel that I wanted to be somewhere where there was more of an intellectual life and where the primary focus was not the next date. I knew I would never go on a blind date—perhaps that I was not really "datable"—but I did not rule out the idea that I could have a relationship with men. Just what that relationship would be I was not able to determine, but the life at Wheaton did not offer me any options.

I did not easily think of myself as an intellectual probably because in my family it was not a category offered as a model. But in my second year at Wheaton I found Mrs. Boas, who became my first mentor and encouraged me to think of myself as "brilliant"—an extravagant compliment that had to last me through many academic years ahead. She and Mr. Earle, a tall transcendental-looking Emerson scholar, picked me out as superior and encouraged me to transfer to a more stimulating academic campus.

Mrs. Boas remains in my memory vividly. A small bent woman with short gray hair and thick glasses that could not hide a piercing gaze at the world, she was my first encounter with a feminist, albeit a Shavian feminist. From her course on modern drama she preached the Shavian doctrine of salvation from the conformity of the middle and upper classes through the specially chosen: the poet, the lonely genius, the iconoclast, the woman of strength and will power. Mrs. Boas's husband, who had died just before I arrived at Wheaton, had been a popular Shakespeare scholar and teacher. The two of them had been the center of much intellectual fervor on campus. She was herself a Shelley scholar, and over the years of our friendship she gave me a number of Shelley books and mementos. Years later I was astonished to find in the Boston Athenaeum a book of hers on Elizabeth Barrett Browning. It was an incredibly sentimental account of the "perfect couple" and I wondered if she had thought of her own marriage in the same way. Even before I read Mrs. Boas's account of the Brownings, she had conveyed, along with her revolutionary messages, a romantic notion of the perfect marriage, a meeting of minds, bodies, and souls.

Despite her romantic excesses, Mrs. Boas was a feminist keenly aware of the particular needs of her students. For years afterward, whether she took me to the Harvard faculty club for lunch to discuss my work or came to my Cambridge apartment to scold me for not having a dishwasher when I was trying to raise children and teach and study at the same time, Mrs. Boas always focused on my particular circumstances as well as my intellectual aspirations.

While I was at Wheaton Mrs. Boas let me use her house and her library as a retreat from dormitory life. She usually greeted me at her front door with some provocative declaration: "Einstein has just taken infinity from me," she said one day and followed it with one of her bursts of cackling laughter. Her voice was anything but "soft and gentle" and although she was from the Midwest she had picked up an English accent from her many years traveling back and forth to England with her husband. I found in her a whole new model of femininity. Despite her eccentric appearance and her independence, she was very conscious of herself as a woman who had won her way with men. She was a little vain about her custom-made silk dresses purchased on visits to Hong Kong and was very sentimental about young lovers.

At the end of my freshman year, I had a series of orthopedic operations to stabilize my ankles and knees and I was in casts for eight weeks. The doctors failed to tell me what happens to your limbs when they are immobile for that length of time. When they took off the casts, I could hardly stand and I was in extreme pain when I attempted to walk. My mother—dauntless as ever—found a motor scooter that had already been adapted for use by another disabled person. I was able to return to college almost on schedule but now on wheels. I had a sidecar for balance and for books and occasionally for a passenger, but few trusted me enough to take a ride. I never completely mastered the machine. Rather I would start it up and let it drive me. It made a loud zooming noise that gave everyone in front of me plenty of notice to scatter and to leave the paths clear for the onslaught. Nonetheless it became a well-known mascot on campus.

Despite the help with mobility, my return to Wheaton in my sophomore year was difficult. I developed an ulcer in high school, probably due to the excesses of my dieting, and the stress of the orthopedic operations and the readjustment of the first weeks back on campus brought back the ulcer and landed me in the infirmary. I fell into the hands of a handsome but bored young college physician who told me laconically that I should return home and give up this impossible idea of coping with campus life. I am grateful to this wretched man because he gave me just the shot of adrenaline from anger that I needed to persist through the fall semester and get back in control of my life. Once I had done that I began once again to feel suffocated by the smallness of the campus setting, the inanity of the weekend life, and the lack of intellectual stimulation. However, I don't think I would have really believed that I could transfer to another college if I had not met a psychiatrist at a cocktail party during the Christmas holidays. After talking to me about Wheaton (which I described as "just right for me because I can get around the campus"), he said bluntly, "Why don't you get out of there and go someplace you want to be. You can always hitchhike around." Suddenly I realized I could change my life if I wanted to and so, with further encouragement from Mrs. Boas and Mr. Earle, I transferred the next fall to Radcliffe College. That summer I drove my first hand-controlled car and felt the shock of freedom. A whole new sense of power opened up to me. I was able to move under my own volition. It was a large car—there were no compacts then—and I could hardly see over the dashboard, so I drove most of the time by intuition. I was told by many people in Cambridge that when they first caught a glimpse of my gray Oldsmobile, they thought they were seeing a driverless automobile.

5

TRANSITIONS

One of the first trips I made alone in my new car that summer was to Tanglewood, the music school and festival in Lenox, Massachusetts. I wanted to do something exciting before I started Radcliffe, particularly because I had spent the prior summer in casts in the hospital. My family knew the manager of the Boston Symphony—he had grown up in Moorestown—and he suggested that I come and sing in the festival chorus at Tanglewood. During that summer I met a dancer, my roommate Naomi, and it seemed as if the image of the dancer that sometimes appeared in my dreams had become a reality. We would experience a strange and touching encounter at the time of my brother's death.

Tanglewood introduced me to a world that was different from my familiar Wasp world. A heady combination of art and ambition surrounded me and unchecked emotional self-expression stunned me. I was particularly fascinated by many of the women students and musicians, who seemed to me provocatively sensual. They wore their sexuality openly and they expressed their feelings unreservedly. Jeanne Schmidt, for instance, a University of Chicago student who had overwhelmed me with her self-confidence and sexy husky voice, acted out her crush on the young star of the summer, Leonard Bernstein. When we sang Mahler's Second Symphony, which he conducted, she collapsed into semi-hysterical weeping. No self-respecting college student that I knew would let herself fall apart like that; we had scorned the groupies around Frank Sinatra. Of course, Bernstein took her tribute in stride and later he even had a brief conversation with her, which put her into an ecstasy for days.

I was very much an observer that summer, treated with some indifference, not because I was disabled necessarily but because I was only there for the pleasure, rather than to advance a career in music. Most everyone was too busy forwarding his or her own personal agenda to pay much attention to me. In the midst of this anonymity I had a unique communication with my roommate, Naomi. She was not my assigned roommate. When I arrived in Lenox, I found that the girl I was to room with was another member of the chorus who, like myself, had been disabled by polio. She met me incredulously at the door of the room and without saying a word fled to the main office where she asked for a room change. I think she spent a good deal of the summer trying to avoid me, for I hardly ever saw her again. The experience was painful but the gesture understandable. It took me years to overcome a distinct squeamishness with other disabled people. In the 1950s we were a generation with very little political consciousness and I had did not identify with disabled people as a political group with rights and issues. Naomi was my next assignment. She said simply, "The girl is crazy. What difference does it make?" I was grateful for her lack of commiseration or analysis. She didn't talk a great deal anyway, I was to discover.

I had never met anyone who looked like Naomi. She had a long-nosed Eastern profile. Her eyes were just slightly tilted, small but very black, and she had a wide full mouth. Her close-cut black hair revealed a long, graceful neck. To my eyes she was beautiful and her face made me recall profiles I had seen in museums on scrolls or sculptures. She told me that her father was a rabbinical scholar in Chicago and that her life had been made painful by the contrast of a brilliant, articulate, red-haired sister, who had not only finished her undergraduate college career but who had married a scientist and was studying to be a social scientist herself. These accomplishments were considered by her family to be the complete recipe for success, according to Naomi. Her family tolerated her dancing as a way of keeping her occupied, she told me.

We were dramatically different from each other, Naomi and I, but each of us was intensely private so that we got along easily. She was hopelessly pursuing a young conductor with curly black hair and cynical eyes, and unlike many of the other eager summer residents, she seemed in perpetual melancholy. We had not done a great deal of talking—not from lack of inclination, but because she was almost inarticulate in expressing herself. When she wanted to make contact in a group, she would drop off from everyone else and start to dance. Sometimes she did this in odd places, such as the lobby of a theater. No one paid much attention to her, preferring not to acknowledge her at these moments. Thus ignored, she would address herself to me as if I were her audience. I found it embarrassing but touching and compelling.

There were times when I would not see Naomi for a couple of days. I did not know where she went. I found out that it was not with her conductor but with a number of other brief alliances. She would come back even more depressed. Sometimes she would talk a little about her troubled life. It seemed unhappy. She had tried to take her own life several times. She had changed psychiatrists three times. Her mother disliked her. Her father filled the house with visiting scholars and rabbis who created a world from which she felt excluded. Despite this, Naomi was at other times light-hearted and would join us in evening gatherings at the local restaurant. We were a fluid group but it usually included Jeanne, a brother and sister from New York, a singer named Lenore from Long Island, and a bassoon player, Howard, from the Bronx, whose dark eyebrows knit in one sullen, dark line of scorn and who particularly liked to sharpen his insults on Naomi. He laughed at her when she broke into a dance and accepted her exhibition-ism as a personal proposition to him. Occasionally he would bait me too, asking about my life or background. Whenever I told him something about my family, that my father had been the president of a company, for instance, he would gasp in mock awe and say, "Oh, I guess I should be impressed."

I am not sure whether Naomi ever went off with Howard on her nights out because I never saw her leave or return. She just slipped away unno-ticed. Jeanne, who knew Naomi's family in Chicago, told me that her dis-appearances were not unusual. I could see that the Tanglewood romantic alliances were far more sophisticated than the equivalent relationships among my college acquaintances. The sexual revolution of the 1960s was still long off, and girls at college who had affairs were considered far-out and daring.

I don't remember anyone talking about anything that happened in the "outside" world that summer. There was no other subject but music, musi-cians, or intracommunity gossip. It was as if we were cut off from the rest of society. So the evening when my brother-in-law arrived suddenly from the cottage in New London, Connecticut, to tell me that my brother Tom was dead, the news came to me as if it were a message from another planet. I was in my room alone getting ready to go to an evening concert when Hugh found me. I knew something terrible had happened when he appeared at the door. He came over and hugged me.

"What's the matter?" I asked. "Is Mother all right?"

"It's Tom. He shot himself last night." He paused. "He killed himself, Mary."

"Oh my God!" I felt myself crumpling inside. "With my father's revolver?"

"How did you know?" Hugh looked at me in surprise.

I sat down. I couldn't answer. My heart was racing and my head was throbbing. Hugh helped me pack up my things. I was in a daze and when Naomi came in, Hugh explained to her what had happened. She put her arms around me. As I was leaving, I said, "I knew it was going to happen." She looked at me in surprise and horror.

Later in the car on our way back to Connecticut, where my mother, my sister Jane, and her family had taken a cottage for the summer, I wondered why I had said that. I certainly had not known it was going to happen and yet I had immediately recalled an April morning about a year ago when I was home for spring vacation and Tom had almost shot the milkman.

I was awakened one morning at 4 A.M. by the sound of Tom shouting out of the window of his room.

"Stop! or I'll shoot!" I heard.

Terrified, I sat bolt upright in bed. I heard my mother running into Tom's room.

"What's the matter, Tom? What are you doing?" Then after a pause, "That was the milkman. You almost shot the milkman!" Their conversation then broke down into murmurs. After a few minutes, my mother stuck her head into my room.

"Tom had a nightmare. He heard the milkman at the back door and thought it was a burglar. Everything is all right. Go back to sleep."

Tom said nothing about the incident in the morning. I thought he would at least make a joke about it. He hurried off to work, taking his coffee with him. I asked my mother where he had gotten the gun and she told me it was my father's revolver, bought after a robbery one summer in our house in Montreal. I expected more of a reaction from her. It seemed to me like very alarming and dangerous behavior, but she dismissed the incident as a nightmare. Mother usually explained things in some physical or practical way. We did not speak of it again.

I felt during those years that I no longer knew my brother very well, particularly since we moved from Montreal. He came home from college for my father's funeral and only returned home again to do the honors of giving away my sisters at their weddings. I do not really know what impact my father's death had on him. A handsome but serious young man, he was three years older than I but younger than my sisters by three and four years. After the war, when he was discharged from the navy, he came home but seemed to be lost and without direction about what career he wanted. My father's insistence on his finding definite career goals had not succeeded and, of course, the war had interrupted Tom's college years. He chose to go to Dartmouth College after being sent to Deerfield Academy, a prep school in Massachusetts, but he was transferred to Harvard in the naval officers' training corps to study naval engineering, which he hated. My mother put him in touch with my father's business associates and friends when he returned, and after about six months of consultations and interviews, he started working in a training program for junior trust officers in a Philadelphia bank. He seemed to settle comfortably into a gray flannel suit, a maroon convertible, membership in a tennis club, and an attractive girl-friend.

Now as Hugh drove through the night, I recalled that terrifying April morning and for a moment his death seemed inevitable. Hugh and I spoke about Tom's life, about the fact that he had been living at home that summer with a young psychiatrist and his wife, who were renting mother's house, and that no one knew that he was troubled and suicidal. I recalled a note that I had recently received from Tom. He returned some money that I had lent him. In the note he apologized for taking so long to repay me. It was a small sum and I had actually forgotten about it. The note read, "Sorry. This won't happen again." Now those words seemed ominous and I shud-dered as I told Hugh about them. I wept and I wanted to scream in protest.

We arrived into a broken and dazed family. We clung together in incredulous sadness trying to make some sense of what had happened. Tom had not confided in anyone. Later that summer a minister in Moorestown told my mother that Tom had come to him telling him he was confused and did not know why. The note he left my mother said simply that he did not feel he could go on with his life. In the last photograph we have of him, he is holding a young nephew in each arm beside his shiny convert-ible on one of his weekend trips to Connecticut. He is wearing chino pants and a white tee shirt and looking steadily into the camera. His embrace of my nephews looks warm and protective.

The funeral was in New Jersey and we drove there in several cars, stay-ing with our friends, the D'Oliers. The service was as small and private as my father's had been elaborate and public although both had closed caskets. We went to the chapel next to the funeral parlor and sat huddled together. My aunt Jane was with us. My other aunts were on their vacation and could not get back from Vinalhaven in time. Our local minister's eulogy was very short but I still could not concentrate on what he said. I felt suffocated in the dark unctuous chapel and I wanted to shout out, "Why did you do it? Why doesn't someone tell me?" A number of friends came up and silently embraced my mother. They murmured a few words and I heard her respond several times, "It was like a sickness, you know. He was ill." I wanted to go up to the closed casket but no one else did so I felt too awkward and wor-ried that I would upset my mother if I left the family group. I felt as if Tom's whole existence was being wiped out. There was no reception after the funeral; we simply went back to the D'Oliers and had a light supper.

Aunt Jane—my father's sister—stayed with us that night. She was the only one who talked about Tom. My sisters and I sat in the living room with her after the young children had been put to bed in cribs borrowed from friends. My mother was still in the dining room with my brothers-in-law and the D'Oliers. Aunt Jane shook her head, "If only someone had known he needed help," she said. My sisters and I nodded. "You know nervous depression runs in your mother's family. Your mother's sister Edith had a nervous breakdown and then there was your Uncle Sam." (He had taken his own life.) She didn't finish because my mother came into the room with the others and the conversation shifted to what rooms each of us would share. I stayed with my mother that night and I slept with her in the big double bed, holding her as she cried. "I'll always be here," I said, but I couldn't cry.

It was not until years later, when I was separated after more than twenty years of marriage and grieving for the good years lost that I finally also grieved for my father and for Tom. It was as if I felt all my losses as one. I would drive to work with tears streaming down my face, completely unable to stop them, or I would have to leave in the middle of a class I was teaching so that I could wash my face and recompose myself.

By the time we left Moorestown, the family had reestablished a reserved composure—not that we ever really expressed our grief. Our family found it hard to acknowledge deep feelings, and later in life I found the ritual and even the sociability of a Catholic wake a pleasant relief from our repressed ceremonies. We were left to deal with the tragedy as best as we could in our family, and we turned to practical matters. It took a few days to attend to details. I was designated to write some thank-you notes to people who had sent letters and flowers. I wrote a note to my brother's former girlfriend. He had broken up with her quite a while before but they had remained friends. My letter was appallingly sentimental. I could not seem to say anything genuine.

I had left the Tanglewood grounds feeling as if I would never see anyone there again, but my family's stoicism convinced me to return after the week of the funeral. It would have been difficult to stay in the small summer cottage, which was full to capacity. Hugh drove me back to Lenox. We arrived back at dusk, the time I had left the week before. The dormitories were vacated for supper and early evening rehearsals or concerts. Hugh took in my bag and we exchanged a few words, an embrace, a promise to write, to look after my mother, to see each other in another few weeks. I sat on the bed after he left and stared into space. Someone came into the room. It was Jeanne. I hardly noticed her but she swept in to embrace me and then swept out again. Naomi came in soon after. When she entered the room, she looked at me rather closely. "Are you all right?" she asked. I nodded. "Can I get you some dinner?" I shook my head and thanked her.

As I remained seated on the bed, Naomi slowly began to dance, bending and curving in the movements I had grown somewhat used to watching. I followed her in a daze. The moment seemed full of chaos and madness. I thought I must be losing my mind. Here I had returned from a numbing tragedy and she was dancing as if nothing had happened. As I half stared, I began to notice a pattern in her dumb show, and her dancing took on a form and beauty I had not noticed before. Her eyes were almost closed and she seemed unaware of my presence, but she was telling a story of grief and despair and of her own experience with annihilation. Her body was frail and graceful but she danced with increasing acceleration, circling around in smaller and smaller space as if confined by invisible walls that closed in on her. I took her silent communication without comment, but I knew she was making an offering of sympathy to me. Her dance paralleled my grief. It also expressed a shared confinement of spirit—trapped, fluttering like a butterfly in a net. We were both trapped in our own kind of inarticulateness—she so often without words, and I still inarticulate about myself as a woman. I had been introduced that summer to a new kind of world—a more emotional and sensual world than my own. My eyes were now open to the frank sexuality surrounding me, but I was still just an observer and did not know where I would fit into this world. After the summer I spoke to Naomi a few times on the phone, but I never saw her again although I often recalled that dance.

In the remaining weeks at Tanglewood, I tried to lose myself in the music. We sang Brahms's Requiem and Mahler's Second Symphony and I felt I was singing the requiem for my brother, giving him the ceremony and mourning he had been denied. The deaths of my father and—five years later—of my brother often seemed connected to me. Perhaps it was because they were the two male members of my family: my father, who was such a patriarchal figure, and my brother, who was almost a casualty of that inflexible system. Perhaps Tom felt that he could not adequately take his place in my father's world. I wondered if he felt overwhelmed by the pressure of my father's purposefulness. I would never know, but whatever form of depression he suffered from was not identified. He could not or did not ask for help. And we all blamed ourselves for not recognizing his pain.

After I left Tanglewood that summer, I once more had the dream of my father's death—the dripping figure coming through the cottage door. And once I dreamt of my brother. I met him in the garden by the blue gate where the milkman had been startled that morning—and I talked to him, but in my dream I could not hear what he said. Was he telling me why he had withdrawn so mysteriously from life? After that dream, I found myself praying every so often for my father and my brother. At night, before I went to sleep, I would say like a child, "May their souls rest in peace." I had heard that said at my grandmother's funeral.

One night I had a new kind of dream. I dreamt that I was a dancer, like Naomi, and that I could float across a stage making my feet carry my body like a feather, barely disturbing the silence with a rustle. In my dream I experienced this so intensely that when I awoke I was in shock at the reality of my clumsiness. I know the dream expressed my desire to be transformed into another kind of being—one that was free to walk and dance, but I also believe that it expressed another kind of release—a separation from the oppressive role my father played in my life. I would now be able to reclaim the positive part of his influence in my life.

My introduction to Cambridge and my junior year of college was overcast by this family tragedy, but nonetheless I was happy as a student at Radcliffe and Harvard. Driving a car gave me great independence and I loved being in Cambridge, going to classes in Harvard Yard, studying in Widener Library, and meeting friends in Harvard Square, quieter then than it is today but still a social and cultural center for the university students. I went to poetry readings and films and other events and felt comfortable on my own. More often than not, I would meet someone I knew or start an acquaintance with someone I didn't know.

I was able to park in the Yard for my classes probably because very few people needed that privilege. I rarely saw a disabled person—occasionally a veteran returning as a student—so I was almost one of a kind, yet I experienced an anonymity that was no doubt due to Harvard's studied diffidence toward anything or anyone who was different. I enjoyed that anonymity and often forgot about my disability—or at least about it as a dominating factor in my consciousness. In my last year I did meet another disabled student, Ilona, a Holocaust survivor who came to Radcliffe and was publishing a novel about her Holocaust experience. We met when I offered her a ride—she lost a leg during her brutal experience in Auschwitz and walked with a cane—and we became friends, but we talked about our interests in writing more than our stories of disability. She was perfecting her English prose style and I discussed some of her drafts with her. I think Ilona, as I, wanted to be identified as an individual and a writer, not as a disabled person. In any case, we did not talk about our disabilities when I first knew her. In later years we shared information and experiences from the perspective of longevity, frustration, and humor. Ilona became a major literary figure at Harvard in Archibald MacLeish's fiction writing classes. When I was a senior, I too approached MacLeish about joining his class, but when I told him I was writing an honors thesis, he said that the combination would be too difficult. He wanted a total commitment to being a writer and, unlike Ilona, I was ambivalent about that.

Cambridge in the late 1940s was very literary. The Harvard I knew still turned toward Europe and especially England. We went to hear Dylan Thomas and T. S. Eliot as much as e. e. cummings and Robert Lowell. The Brattle Theatre, which was started by a group of World War II veterans, produced season after season of Shakespearean repertory, sometimes importing an English actor, such as William Devlin, to perform the role of King Lear or Macbeth. The Poet's Theater did Yeats and other Irish playwrights, although the founders and creators of that theater were young American poets like Robert Bly, who dated my roommate.

I was never in the elite literary groups but I did think of myself as a writer and I took two fiction writing classes, one of them with Albert Guérard. In order to get into the class, we had to submit a writing sample based on an autobiographical passage by André Gide, Guérard's favorite writer. We actually sat in the classroom and wrote and then waited as Guérard read them and picked out the class members. I felt very special as the number of applicants was reduced from about thirty to fifteen. I do not remember that the members of the class were very supportive of one another, despite their being the chosen few. I began to recognize a common theme in the literary or scholarly world at Harvard: if you were a woman and attractive, you would be accepted and judged on the basis of the connection you had with a male student, graduate student, or professor. Adrienne Rich (who was in another writing class that I took) wrote in "When We Dead Awaken" that after she had written to please (or to not displease) her father for twenty years, she went to Harvard and wrote for other men, "writers teachers—the Man, who was not a terror or a dream but a literary master and a master in other ways less easy to acknowledge." Like Rich—who wrote this sometime later—my feminist consciousness was not raised enough at the time to know how sexist the atmosphere really was. The word *patriarchy* was not even part of our vocabulary. Of course, we had the the deans at Radcliffe to give us some alternative mentoring, but even Radcliffe's president at the time was a man, President Wilbur Kitchener Jordan.

As I look through the pictures in my Radcliffe yearbook, I spot Roger, the head cheerleader at Harvard, who was my first date at college. Raised in the Midwest, Roger was full of college spirit, leading the all-male cheerleading team at football games and participating in everything he could—the Hasty Pudding, sports teams, and clubs. He first saw me at Emerson Hall in Harry Levin's Shakespeare class and claims he didn't see the crutches until I stood up. He was taken aback and then decided—"what the heck"—to approach me anyway.

I am grateful to Roger. It made a difference to be chosen and it was the first time I had really been asked on a date, not just included or paired at an arranged party. I think I was embarrassed and didn't know how to handle the idea of a date. I know Roger dealt with my disability better than I did. He pretty much ignored it as something that would not limit our relationship. We went out several times, including the Yale-Harvard game when I rode to New Haven in a van with the cheerleaders and watched the game from their bench. The cheerleading team was fun to be with, and I felt very special but at the same time awkward sitting with them. I knew I wasn't showing enough college spirit when Roger was leading the cheers. I should have been jumping up and down with excitement, which I couldn't do, or at least shouting and screaming wildly, which I didn't do. Was I thinking of myself as like my sisters who went out with the football stars, not the cheerleaders? Or was I really identified with the intellectuals and the writers and embarrassed at Roger's Midwestern school spirit?

All in all, our New Haven weekend was not a great success. After the game we attended several dark and smoky fraternity parties and did some pretty clumsy "necking" (the current term). However, I got a few calls from Roger, one of them late in the evening from the Hasty Pudding Club. Merry and drunk, he wanted me to come pick him up. I said I was too busy. In retrospect, I seemed like a prig. In any case, before long Roger found another Midwestern girl and they got engaged. I didn't feel sad when I saw the photos of the two of them together; Roger was not my Prince Charming.

Most of my other dates—there were not many—came from meeting someone in a class or in Widener Library. (Radcliffe women could not yet use the Lamont undergraduate library.) I had some strange encounters. John Diebold, a tall blond Harvard Business School student, stopped me in Widener and asked me to join him for coffee. He came for me at Barnard Hall in a gorgeous black convertible, which did not go unnoticed by the other residents—a brief moment of triumph for me. John soon found out about my Thanksgiving dinner with Franklin Roosevelt and admitted a passionate interest in the former president. After eating out, we went back to his suite at the business school and he showed me his FDR collection, which included all of the president's recorded speeches. As he revealed his treasures, his roommate came in but quickly apologized and left. He seemed to be following some code of action that went along with dates. He needn't have bothered to leave because John spent the whole evening playing one FDR speech after another. I felt part of his collection. We went out a few more times and then he disappeared.

While I enjoyed the novelty of dating, I had a much more significant friendship with John Fulton. With him, I could relax; I didn't have to figure out any romantic part in our relationship. He was safe because he was committed to his high school sweetheart, a young Austrian girl whose family, like John's, were also refugees. He was planning to marry her after our graduation, when she would just be starting as a student at Radcliffe. John was a friend of Lenore's, a singer whom I met at Tanglewood. He was a physicist, born in Hungary, whose family left to escape anti-Semitism in the 1940s. We became good friends and companions during my two years at Harvard, and he advanced my cultural education in the arts, particularly music. We went to concerts, poetry readings, and plays, and we drove to the ocean for picnics. Both of us studied a great deal and were committed to doing well academically so we both graduated Phi Beta Kappa and with honors.

John and I became very attached to one another during our two years in Cambridge, and as our graduations approached—his parents and fiancée were coming to his, my mother and a family friend were coming to mine—we realized we were saying good-bye to a part of our lives. As we sat in the car at the end of our last evening together, I could feel his growing emotion. His eyes, which were dark and very large, were almost tearful and his mouth trembled. I don't know why we didn't at least hug each other but we didn't. We were both restrained—he because he was committed to someone and I because I found it difficult to express my emotions. We actually just shook hands. We stayed friends for a long time afterwards. He married while he was still a graduate student at Harvard and had two daughters. I visited them as a family when he was a fellow at the Institute for Advanced Study at Princeton. Later he became professor of physics at Johns Hopkins University. They visited me in our summer cottage in Maine where my mother made a heroic effort to be hospitable. She found it almost impossible to relate to people who were a centimeter outside of her own Wasp world and she was constantly challenged by my bringing home Jewish friends. By the time I had finished college, she had adapted, although she never managed to be at ease when she met a person of color.

I last saw John when he and his wife called on us in Cambridge after I married and had two children. After that, we lost touch, but I always treasured the friendship we had and the way he enriched my college life.

When I began to think of what I would do after graduation, it seemed natural to apply to Oxford, the place everyone wanted to be. I had briefly considered the advertising world. We had family friends at Young and Rubicom and at J. Walter Thompson, both big agencies in New York City, and I could have gotten a job through them. In fact, one of the vice presidents of Young and Rubicom, a summer neighbor in Maine, gave me a little course on copywriting and predicted that I would do well in the field. It never occurred to me that my disability would prevent me from advancing in any professional world. I was naive and only realized much later how I might experience discrimination in the corporate world—or the academic world, for that matter. I had been protected and never experienced discrimination as long as I was a paying student at Harvard. In any case, I drifted toward graduate work instead, although I did not have any compelling goal except a desire to see new places. When I did not get a fellowship at Oxford, the dean at Radcliffe urged me to go to the University of Chicago, which was the center of New Criticism, an innovative school of literary theory. On her recommendation, I applied for and received a scholarship from a fund for children of World War I veterans. Thus my father's life touched my own again.

6

CHICAGO AND AFTER

I was politically and socially naive at twenty-two when I went to the University of Chicago in 1950 to get a master's degree in English literature. The university was situated on the south side of the city along the Midway, a parkway separating it from the black ghetto that pushed against its borders like a surging tide. Jobs and housing were scarce and it was a period just before the explosion of major race riots in many parts of the country.

One night when I left the library where I had been studying late, my car wouldn't start. I was living at International House on the Midway, not far from the university. At first I was not concerned and looked around to see if I could find someone to help me, but the street was deserted. I tried to start the engine several times, hoping I would not have to go back into the building to use the phone because the library was just closing when I left. I began to panic a little. I knew it was too far for me to walk with crutches back to International House. Besides it was not safe to walk alone at night on the Midway. As I glanced at my rear view mirror I noticed a car moving up the street behind me. It slowed down when it passed me and then parked in front of my car. A tall black man in a handsome camel's hair coat sauntered up to my car window.

"Do you need some help?"

The man was handsome but dressed too flashily for someone at the university. He leaned on the open window and I noticed that he had big gold cufflinks and wore a gold and diamond ring. All the clichés from my racist hometown crowded into my head.

"My car won't start." I spoke as casually as I could. He told me to open the hood. He fiddled around inside for a minute and then gestured for me to start the engine. Nothing happened.

"Are you a student?" he asked. I nodded noncommittally and decided to get out of the car and look for myself. I noticed he showed some surprise that I was using crutches.

"Do you live near here?" he persisted. Was he offering me a ride? Should I take it? I wondered.

"Not far. Just at International House." I hoped to imply that many students from the house would be soon dropping by. I went back to the car and turned on the ignition and unaccountably the engine started. With great relief I prepared to say good-bye and leave hurriedly. He handed me a card through the window.

"Here is my name and number. Y'all give it to your lady friends if they get bored." I drove off as calmly as I could wondering what he meant. Was he a pimp suggesting that I solicit my friends? I returned quickly to the house. When I told my friend Lee about the episode, she gasped. "Wow, you were lucky your car started." I nodded but I wondered if I was also lucky to have crutches. Would I have been in danger of being abducted? Or raped? Or was I just exaggerating the danger? I felt confused. I was more vulnerable because of my disability. I could not run away from someone. At the same time, perhaps I was less vulnerable because I was not a desirable woman!

I was still shy and insecure about my sexuality when I moved to Chicago. As a result, I was obsessively self-protective about my relationships with the opposite sex. Alan Finkelstein, a bushy-mustached geologist smelling constantly of garlic, was the first person to lecture me on my bad self-image. "What the hell's the matter with you, Mary? You're a well-stacked woman." We had met at a poetry reading and he took me for bagels and lox at a Jewish delicatessen. I liked Alan for telling me that but I did not go out with him, although we saw one another from time to time. He was too much of a culture shock for me then. I had certainly been liberated from my narrow Wasp world through my friendships at Tanglewood and at Radcliffe, but Alan's exuberant, unassimilated type was still strange to me. It is difficult now to understand the provincialism of the 1950s and of my family, but I was expanding my world little by little. As someone who had often felt like the "other," I was gradually able to identify with people outside of my own tribe.

I spent most of my time that year with graduate students in the English department, and it was during my evening library hours that I met Lenny Dean, my first romance. My fantasy of a Prince Charming was replaced by a real person although he did not carry me off to live happily ever after. Lenny was my passion for that year and several years after. He worked in the English section of the library where we all had our carrels. I noticed him right away and found him very attractive. He had an extremely sensual mouth and eyes, a tooth slightly broken off in front and eyebrows much darker than his hair. He was twenty-six and had been in the navy as an ordinary seaman which qualified him in my eyes as an older man who had lived around a lot. I was fascinated by him but didn't expect him to pay any attention to me although he was always very friendly and helpful in the library. Naturally I thought he was just being nice to a disabled person. Alan's lecture had not done me much good.

Gradually I became aware of the fact that Lenny always came over to my carrel to talk as soon as I came in the library. Finally one night he stopped by just before closing time. "Would you like to go out for a coffee or beer after I close up the library?" he asked.

I was thrilled and a little nervous. "That would be nice. I'll wait for you," I said as nonchalantly as I could.

We went to the bar that was a frequent hang-out for the English graduate students. I drove my car that night but soon, as we started to spend a lot of time together, Lenny did the driving. I saw parts of Chicago I had not discovered before: jazz at the Blue Note with Louis Armstrong, the Italian section of town with outdoor festivals and good restaurants, and picnics by the lake. Sometimes we were joined by other graduate student friends.

When I first went out with Lenny, I talked constantly. He suggested on our third date that I had developed that habit to protect myself. Then he kissed me and laughed and said he could have as easily kissed a telephone pole. It took me a while to learn how to let my emotions go, but Lenny was a patient teacher. He broke through my defenses. I would have probably drifted into an affair with Lenny, but he never asked me to his room on the other side of the Midway, claiming it was too depressing. I was a little disappointed. Even though it was the 1950s and only older women and wild young women had affairs, I now felt more sophisticated as a graduate student. Besides, I knew that he had been having an affair with someone before we started to go out. She was a fellow graduate student in the English department and she also lived in International House. I found out about their relationship by accident one evening when I visited her in her room.

Cathy was a slim dark-haired Southern girl perfectly turned out with a touch of the professional woman but with a sly mixture of femininity that only Southern womanhood can master. She had dark sparkling eyes and casually curled hair just recently shortened as if to acknowledge her maturity and set herself apart from women like me in the younger set. Her mouth was full and had an odd immobility that went with her Southern drawl except when she broke into a smile or laughter; even then she held her mouth half shut so that her slightly crooked front teeth would not show. She had come to graduate school after ten years of teaching school and caring for an elderly father. Cathy was a pioneer in breaking the mold; this was before the Women's Movement and the influx of nontraditional women students at all levels of the university. She held her own among the predominantly male intellectuals by a combination of sharp wit and intelligence and outrageous feminine wiles.

In her room that evening, I found her standing before her mirror putting on makeup and joking about the "coming of wrinkles." While we were talking, we both heard a soft scrape against the window, the sound of pebbles being thrown by someone outside, three floors below.

"That will be Lenny," she laughed. "He sometimes stops by late like this and we go out and have a drink." That was the first time I heard of Lenny. I said good night and went upstairs to my room. In the next few weeks I would often come upon Cathy walking across the Midway early in the morning when I went out to an 8:30 A.M. class. She would hail me cheerfully, looking self-conscious but jaunty.

Meanwhile Cathy introduced me to Lenny at the library and he turned out to be the same man I had been watching. I soon figured out that she was coming from his apartment when I saw her early in the morning. When Lenny began to seek me out a month or so later, I wondered whether he was still with Cathy. She had not been coming to the library as regularly as she once had. I asked him about her on one of our first dates.

"Oh, that's all over," he said. "It was a dreary affair. We both were trying to find a way out." I was impressed by his nonchalance but still was not completely convinced until I noticed that Cathy had taken up with Jim, a bespectacled graduate student with thinning blond hair who seemed as if he might resist all human entanglements. But Cathy could be persistent. She kept leaving little notes on Jim's carrel and I began to see them together at the university restaurants. She and I waved to one another at International House but she rarely joined me at a table and seemed to be taking her meals elsewhere.

One Saturday evening Lenny mentioned that Cathy wanted us all to go out for drinks together—he and I and Cathy and Jim.

"Do you want to go with them?" Lenny asked.

"Do you?" I responded warily.

He shrugged noncommittally. "It's okay with me, but we don't have to go."

"Oh, sure, why not," I said bravely. I felt a tinge of jealousy. Be sophisticated, I thought.

We drove downtown to the Italian section. Cathy talked incessantly from the backseat, trying to get a response from Jim, who sat beside her, immobile. He insisted upon wearing a brown fedora when he went out, and Cathy made this the target of her attack.

"Jim, you can't really go into a restaurant like that now. Can he, Lenny?"

"I like my hat," Jim said.

"But it's silly," Cathy giggled. She snatched it off his head and put it on her own. He visibly winced.

"Jim, you're too solemn," she continued relentlessly. "Lenny, don't you think he's too solemn?" She tapped him on the shoulder as he drove.

"Just let me get out at the nearest bus stop," Jim said, seething.

"For God's sake, Cathy," Lenny said, "quit it. Where are we going to eat? We're headed toward the Amalfi."

"Oh, here's your old hat," Cathy said, putting it on Jim's lap. "Lenny, let's go to the Amalfi. That was our favorite place."

We reached the restaurant and the atmosphere got better as we concentrated on antipasto, lasagna, and Chianti. Cathy made frequent references to food that she and Lenny had tried and she punctuated the conversation with "do you remember?" Lenny acted as if nothing unusual were going on. Jim interspersed sardonic asides, and I was completely silent, feeling as if my tongue were stuck to the top of my mouth. I heard a kind of ringing in my ears that was interrupted by Cathy jumping up to look at the selections on the jukebox.

"Lenny, here's our song, Sarah Vaughan's "Ain't Misbehavin'," she said. "Quick, give me some change. I'll play it."

"For old times' sake," Lenny said acidly. "Sure, here's a quarter."

Cathy put the money in and as the music began to play, she began to dance slowly back to the table.

"Come on, Lenny. We have to dance to this." She lightly took his arm and pulled him up. Her eyes were bright and her breath came short; everything about her was energized, taut, electric.

I turned to stone with a frozen smile on my face. I could hardly lift my hand to clutch my wineglass. Jim puffed a cigar. Lenny shrugged. I remained immobile while they danced. Jim stayed silent or if he spoke, I didn't hear him. When they came back, Cathy let go of Lenny's hand reluctantly.

"Oh, that was grand!" She sat down. "Jim, you old stick-in-the-mud, will you dance with me?"

"I never learned," Jim retorted. "I came to graduate school so I wouldn't have to dance at the country club."

"Well, I never!" Cathy laughed. "Let's drink to all of us!"

"I'm going home," I heard myself saying.

"Oh, you're tired?" Cathy looked at me for the first time that evening and her tone was all concern.

"I'm going, too," said Jim. "I don't stay up after midnight. It's not good for my liver."

Lenny looked at me. "You want to go back?" He looked concerned.

"Yes, I do." I got up and so did everyone. We drove home with little conversation. Cathy badgered Jim in the backseat. He got off at his corner before we got to International House. Cathy jumped out of the car ahead of us and called, "Goodnight, you all!" as she ran up the steps.

I started to open the door as Lenny put his arm around me. "You mad?" he said.

"Yes, I'm mad."

"Why?"

"Why not?" I asked. "Why don't you decide whether or not you and Cathy are still on and let me know when you've come to a decision." I tried to sound as caustic as I could.

"I'm sorry. It was nothing. She's a little desperate. Jim's completely asocial, maybe not quite human."

"Well, that's their problem. I don't like being put in the middle. Let's take a break for a while." Lenny looked hurt. I went in. The next evening at the hour he usually called from the library, I didn't answer my buzzer when it rang to announce a phone call. I was miserable, but I went down to the lobby and talked with some friends. I had neglected most of them since I started seeing Lenny. When I went up to my room, there was a note on my door about a second call from Lenny. The next night I had supper with some graduate students from England and we sat around talking until about ten-thirty, about a half hour after the time Lenny usually called. I went upstairs and found no note on my door. I felt a numb pain and I was angry. Good, I thought. He's throwing pebbles at her window. Just as I was about to go in my door, Cathy came down the hall.

"Mary, can I come in?" She flashed a bright cheerful smile. I felt like stabbing her.

"Sure," I said indifferently. My friend Lee, my only confidant, was going out and raised her eyebrows.

Cathy followed me in, chattering. I didn't offer her a chair (there was only one), but she sat on the edge of the bed and crossed her legs neatly. I turned on some lights and sat down in the chair. I stared at Cathy. She looked tired, drawn. Her face appeared older when it was not animated.

She had no little nervous habits as I did such as smoking or twisting her hair, so she folded her delicate hands primly in her lap.

"There's nothing between Lenny and me anymore," she said. "I like Jim; he's more my age but he's knotted up like a gnarled tree emotionally."

I found nothing to say.

"I just wanted you to know that," she continued, "I acted like a fool at the restaurant. It was all my fault."

"It doesn't matter," I said. "Besides, it wasn't all your fault. Lenny likes having us both on a string."

"No one can commit themselves around here," Cathy said bitterly. "It's like a community of ghosts—ships that pass in the night. I'm sick of them all." She sat as still and composed as ever but tears were in her eyes, blurring her mascara, streaking her powder. She took out a handkerchief and carefully wiped her eyes.

I put out my hand instinctively, but she jumped up, looked in my mirror, dabbed a little more with her handkerchief. "Well, I'll soon look a fright this way." She started toward the door. "I just wanted to let you know Lenny's too young for me. Our affair is completely over." She laughed almost gaily. "Not many real men around here," she joked. "Half of them are fairies, the other half are hopelessly neurotic."

She turned at the door. "You look so young and untouched," she smiled, not maliciously but sadly.

"I wish I had your poise and experience," I said.

Cathy laughed a little bitterly. "No hurry," she said. "There's plenty of time. You know," she continued quite seriously, "we probably both need to cry more." Then she laughed again. "Maybe some of us are made for broken hearts. Good night now," she called in her Southern drawl as she left.

I sat just where she left me for about ten minutes, staring at the door, before I finally felt the tears stream down my face.

Lenny called again the next night and I answered the call and we went back to our routine of late night dates and weekend plans. We spent most of our time either alone or with other students from the department.

Although my social and emotional life was very intense, I was disappointed in my academic world and the graduate program in English. The courses were given by faculty who were interested in New Criticism but most of the brilliant originators of that literary theory had moved on to other universities. The professors I had were either dull or excessively arrogant. My facility for writing and expressing ideas became stunted and dried up; I felt that I had lost my voice. I also discovered that graduate school in the 1950s—and particularly the English department—was a little world of its own, an autocratic state that demanded full obeisance to the hierarchies and eccentricities of its entirely male faculty, who had arbitrary control over graduate students' lives. The department had become notorious for not getting its students through their degrees, failing them almost automatically on their first try at Ph.D. comprehensives and encouraging them consequently to become eternal ABD's (All But Dissertation), living on meager scholarships and bits of teaching. One such student was George, from New Mexico. Years after his arrival at the university, he was still using benefits from the G.I. bill and he was a fixture on campus, always about to take his final comprehensive exams but constantly postponing them. Surprisingly, George was seen not as someone who failed to finish his graduate work, but rather as someone who had escaped the narrowness of academia. I remember an evening with George that seemed to illustrate his status among graduate students.

Lenny and I had been invited to a party at George's basement apartment. There was the usual mixture of couples—one or two married pairs and the rest oddly matched English graduate students. The women were dressed in wool tweed skirts and cashmere sweaters, the men in casual pants and sweaters. George wore a suede jacket and cowboy boots. Suddenly an exotic-looking girl came out of the bedroom. She was Wanda, George's girlfriend, obviously not a graduate student but described as someone in theater. She wore a slinky salmon pink dress and had long perfectly shaped fingers with tapered oval nails colored to match her dress. She exuded sex and when she approached, silence fell on the group. The men tried not to ogle her too obviously and the women laughed nervously. George enjoyed the moment, presenting her as a prize with a blasé air of proprietorship. After the introductions, the conversation returned to its normal level of interdepartmental gossip, literary jokes, and academic showing off. George talked a lot about D. H. Lawrence, his dissertation subject, and about his visits to Taos to meet with Lawrence's friend Mabel Dodge Luhan and others. Although I was fairly confident in intellectual conversations, I was certainly silenced that evening, first by what seemed to me to be George's literary sophistication and second—perhaps even more so—by the exuding sexuality of Wanda that literally dominated the room. Such overt and awesome sensuality challenged my very being. I could tell that the other women felt the same way. There was no way we could compete with someone like Wanda, who didn't have to do a thing all evening except just be a presence. She hardly spoke except to demand drinks and cigarettes from George and she made no attempt to be a hostess. George cooked a delicious chili and he served it with the help of one or two of the efficient wives. Later a group of people played chess and others continued to talk. We drank a lot of red wine until finally everyone got the feeling George wanted to be rid of us. Wanda kept disappearing into the bedroom—and so we all self-consciously left. All of our intellectual pretensions were no match for Wanda's magnificent indifference. Even Lenny, who joked about George's "woman" on the way home, had a slight tinge of envy in his voice.

Although my graduate program was a disappointment to me, I still found the university an exciting place to be in the 1950s. Robert Hutchins, president and then chancellor of the university, created a unique model of college education. Recruiting bright students after their sophomore year of high school, he admitted them to a program based on general education. Using the idea of his colleague Mortimer Adler, he developed a curriculm of "Great Books"—a canon of selected works representing the great intellectual traditions of Western culture. The students took survey courses and comprehensive examinations and were given a B.A. at eighteen or nineteen. They were then encouraged to specialize in graduate programs. There had been as yet no feminist critique of the patriarchal nature of the Great Books canon nor any test of the diversity of the system. There was, however, a broad interdisciplinary literacy in the college faculty, who were still enthusiastic about the Hutchins system. My friend Louis Crompton was a graduate student in English but also a mathematics instructor in the college. He took me to his departmental events—cookouts and picnics—and I found the young male faculty (no women) were not only informed about many fields, including my own, but were also unassuming people full of energy and humor. It was a contrast to the stuffy Harvard faculty that I had known.

At International House I met students from all over the world, but I found the more casual acquaintances that I made at the university also constantly opened new doors for me. I was introduced to the work of the Russian filmmaker Sergei Eisenstein by a couple whom I met at lunch in the cafeteria. Elena offered to carry my tray over to a table where her husband Victor sat. He was legally blind so he was waiting for his tray, too. A tall, slightly stooped man with a shock of hair that fell over his dark glasses, he began talking immediately after we were introduced. He was fascinating to listen to, plunging headlong into one subject after another. Elena was Russian and Victor was American and they were working on an interpretive biography of Eisenstein, whom they had met in Russia. They were involved in his life and work with religious fervor. They asked me to their apartment several evenings later where we drank beer and I listened to their discussion and analysis of Eisenstein's work from *Potemkin* to *Alexander*

Nevsky to *Ivan the Terrible.* They insisted that his films were encoded with symbolic messages, suggesting a mystical reading of his life, and they supported their interpretations with narratives of their encounters with "the master." From remarks they made, I gathered they belonged to the radical left, particularly Victor, although we didn't discuss politics or Henry Wallace, the former vice president of Franklin Delano Roosevelt. Wallace had started the Progressive Party, popular on the campus with many liberal democrats. Elena, a dark-haired intense person with a volatile set of expressions and moods, seemed to add a spiritual dimension to the two of them. During our acquaintance we attended a series of Eisenstein films sponsored by the university. They returned to New York at the end of the year to do further research on their book, leaving me with a broader cultural and political consciousness.

More important, that year I really felt that I had become independent. I had begun to feel liberated at Radcliffe, partly because I could drive a car and be mobile and partly because I was exhilarated by the challenges of a big university. Now that I was farther away from home, I felt even more in control of my life and I expected the future to hold many possibilities, including a teaching job that would enable me to support myself. Actually it was a few years before I was completely independent financially, but I was doing more than many of my friends, who were choosing the security of marriage after a year or two of working.

I drove home to New Jersey in June for a break before I returned in the summer to take my comprehensives, which would finish up my master's degree. Lenny and two other friends went along so that we were able to travel nonstop by taking turns driving. My mother had heard me speak of Lenny and she welcomed him, I thought, a little too enthusiastically. I felt she was relieved that I could produce a boyfriend and was eager to make him part of the family. I felt nervous and embarrassed by her enthusiasm. Lenny and I had not come to any understanding about permanence. In fact, he had accepted a teaching job in Beirut, Lebanon, for a year. His graduate work had become stale, and he could not get on with his thesis. Nothing was said about what would happen when he came home. However, he seemed to thoroughly enjoy himself in Moorestown and kidded me about coming from "class." He liked to claim his family was working class but his story was weak. His father taught in a community college in Indiana and Lenny had middle class written all over him. He went abroad before I returned to Chicago and sent passionate, devoted letters. Mine were more cautious because I already felt that I should protect myself from an emotional crash if we should break up. After a year of correspondence—I had taken a job at a girls' school—I found Lenny's letters getting more and more like travelogues. I began to visualize all the beautiful women he was becoming involved with and I pined away secretly. Characteristically, when I realized he was gone, I cut him off sharply; I wrote a stiff little farewell letter and told him not to write to me again. Then I tore up his letters and his picture, cutting every trace of him out of my life. Several years later, a mutual friend from the university, Lloyd Dodd, looked me up when I was living in Cambridge and we went out for a drink and reminisced about Chicago. Lloyd had remained at the university working on a doctorate in fine arts. He had unsuccessfully pursued a young woman—a fellow graduate student—for a year or two and was also down on romance.

"What happened to Cathy?" I asked, rather surprised that it was one of the first questions on my list.

"She took a job supervising education students at the college," Lloyd replied. "Jim went off to Iowa to teach. I don't know who Cathy's attached herself to now."

"And Lenny?" I asked.

"Don't you know the latest on him?" Lloyd looked surprised.

"No, I lost touch. Did he finish his degree?"

"He's finishing. And he's about to get married. Didn't you know?"

"No, I said I'd lost touch." I spoke irritably. It was still hard for me to talk about him.

"She's a first-year graduate student." Lloyd scanned me a minute. "Looks a bit like you," he chuckled. "Blonde, blue-eyed, bourgeois" (one of his favorite epithets).

"My first rejection," I said.

"Yeah, that's me, too. Well, it's good for you, they say. Think of poor Cathy. She's really over the hill, now, you know."

"I just thought of her," I said and I did not explain my reference. I saw her again in my room that night, turning at the door—"maybe some of us are made for broken hearts!" Her laughter trailed off in my memory.

"Let's drink to broken hearts!" I raised my glass.

"Yes, let's," Lloyd agreed. And we drank.

You were supposed to be able to teach college courses with a master's degree in 1951, but Napier Wilt, the chairman of the English department, called the graduate students together and told us we would probably have to work in factories. After a summer of unsuccessful applications and interviews, I took a job in a girls' boarding school in Providence, Rhode Island, after my predecessor left in October with a nervous breakdown.

Except at Wheaton College, I had never been in a community of as many women as we were on the faculty and student body of Mary C. Wheeler, and I learned a lot about women's lives in those two years of teaching. The head of the school, H. Rowland Morgan, was a prematurely white-haired, crew-cut man, newly appointed to bring fiscal order. He presided over the women and the two lone male teachers with an ineffective good nature. Many of the women faculty had been teaching there for a number of years and represented a generation of bright women whose only outlet for a respectable career—other than marriage—was teaching in a fashionable school at very low wages, which assured them a life of spinsterhood and minimal social status, unless they had their own money. Some of the women prevailed with great dignity over their restricted options.

My immediate superior, Miss Baechle, was one of these women. She impressed me from the start with her snapping blue eyes and white upswept hairdo, which gave her a classical regality that she intensified by wearing a blue draped dress, pinned at the waist with an incongruous Victorian brooch, a golden love knot. She was not tall in stature and she walked with arthritic difficulty in orthopedic black shoes, but neither that limitation nor her ill-fitting bridgework—noticeable when she spoke at length—spoiled the dramatic effect she could create when she spoke, sweeping her arms in Shakespearean majesty. Her apartment was off campus—a luxury that most could not afford—and she asked me formally to "a little supper" soon after I arrived. She had a studio above an old carriage house and it was, I thought, right out of a Pre-Raphaelite world—peacock blue and brick-colored drapes, Indian prints, Chinese and Japanese vases and lamps, lilacs on a dark mahogany table, and rows of beautifully bound leather books on her shelves. Her cooking was gourmet. I had my first acquaintance with an artichoke, which I manipulated cautiously, watching Miss Baechle's slightly freckled plump fingers pluck the leaves and dip them rapidly into sauces. She spoke of her travels, her life abroad, her years as a student. Our friendship was formal but respectful and I learned much about teaching English literature before her unexpected death the second and last year of my stay at the school.

Another memorable figure was the head of the art department—Miss Louise Davis, who also had a place off campus and had won a kind of singular position, not only from her economic independence, which was marginal, but also from her artistic eccentricity. It was accepted that she did not have to appear in the neat drab attire of other women. In fact, she wore large paint-smeared smocks, wool skirts punctured with cigarette burns, and multicolored spattered shoes. Her hair was tied with different color ribbons or scarves and stuck out in uncontrolled clumps. She was accustomed to having at least two young assistants, art students from the Rhode Island School of Design, whom she could order around. She was known for fits of violent temper, alternating with off-color stories. The demands she put on her staff for preparing the school's magnificent spring and winter pageants were completely unreasonable; one year she had them painting plaid designs by hand on one hundred yards of cloth to be used as Scottish kilts. Since I was the drama coach, among other things, I fell under her domain, and it was with difficulty that she restrained her authority over me, giving me a slightly higher status than her assistants. She often communicated to me through the morning assembly, a time when faculty were obliged to gather in front of the student body and join them in prayer and hymn as well as in daily announcements. Miss Davis would arrive late to these gatherings, if she came at all. She would elbow her way to my side and sing her message to me—"Meet me at eleven o'clock in the lounge"—to an off-tune version of the hymn "God of Our Fathers" or whatever it happened to be that morning. Often she would be finishing her breakfast, which was a hard-boiled egg carried in her pocketbook, taken dry and producing an electrifying spray when she sang. The students believed that Miss Davis had remained single by choice but they concluded that as an art student she had had her share of romance. She sometimes intervened to help the older students arrange clandestine meetings with local boyfriends. It was also said that Miss Davis drank a lot when she went home in the evenings, but on the whole, she kept her after-school life to herself.

Most of the women on the faculty did not fare as well as Miss Baechle or Miss Davis, either in the independence of their lives or in their assessment by the students. For instance, Miss Buxton, the Latin teacher, was not a popular woman. Despite her handsome bearing, a product of her proud Nantucket heritage, she was a bitter woman and presided over her table at the evening meal with silence, broken only by an occasional sarcastic comment on the tardiness of a latecomer or by a pointed remark about how some faculty members could afford to eat out all of the time. (She was referring to my frequent absences from dinner.) Students tried to avoid sitting at her table and looked anguished when there were no other places in the dining room. She took a kind of triumph in seeing their despair as they sank to the empty seats beside her. They would much prefer to rush to the table of Miss Rochefort, the mild-faced language teacher with frizzled hair and wide dazed eyes, who once surprised us all at a faculty party by becoming quite tipsy on Harveys Bristol Cream. She started to dance to someone's phonograph record and on her third whirl around the room, she flung off her shoes and her belt. We all watched in frozen wonder, waiting to see what she would take off next. The bespectacled music teacher finally turned off the record and Miss Rochefort fell into hysterical giggles, ending in hiccups and in a sad departure with one of the older teachers.

My position in the school was closer to the students in age and perspective. I was the youngest faculty member, and I sensed from many of the older women a certain distrust and outrage that I could be so young and so eager to take on a job that I would probably not keep beyond a year or two. I would move on. They would stay. I was getting experience and would probably return to graduate school. They would have to content themselves with the rewards they had managed to collect over the years of dedicated teaching.

As soon as I began to teach I knew that this was something I could do well. It came naturally to me, and my students were touching and seemed fond of me. Many of them were poor little rich girls abandoned by parents who dumped them at boarding school during the year and left them to spend their holidays in luxurious homes, empty except for servants. The girls were incurably romantic and liked to imagine me as a kind of Elizabeth Barrett Browning (they had read *The Barretts of Wimpole Street),* an invalid who would one day be carried off by a devoted Robert Browning to live happily ever after.

Student-faculty contact hours were overwhelming, however. I saw students from morning until night because my room and private bath were on the students' floor and I was often on duty to enforce "lights out." I was also required to chaperone them in taxis to the railroad station when they were taking a weekend. We were not responsible for what they did once they got on the train!

Finally, at the beginning of the second year, I moved to my own apartment nearby and took, as a result, a further cut in my minuscule salary. But I was relieved and excited to have the first place of my own. It was in the basement of a tall Victorian house inhabited by an elderly lady and her daytime servant. At night when I arrived home, there was hardly the sound of a mouse above me. I was nervous at night, pulling my curtains tightly across the windows that looked out on the ground above me. I kept the radio on a lot. I had become used to living among many people in International House and in the boarding school dormitory. Even so, I was glad to get my freedom. The dreary after-dinner coffee hour at the school and the smoker for the faculty depressed me at the end of a long working day.

I enjoyed cooking meals and having a few people over. Among them were a thirtyish, just-divorced secretary at the school and a couple of young elementary school teachers who lived on the school farm in the country about ten miles outside of Providence where the younger children boarded. There was also Mrs. McGrath, housemother and manager of the farm, who seemed to me a motherly figure, a pleasant relief from the more eccentric unmarried women of the upper school. She was in her late fifties and had been widowed young, raising on her own two magnificently handsome sons who had gone to Harvard, graduated, and moved to other parts of the country. I saw their photographs and Mrs. McGrath could have been one of them thirty years before. Although she had a handsomely feminine face and abundant honey-blonde hair, which she pulled back in a plain bun, she walked with the stride of a man. She could shoot and fish and haul wood and she rarely appeared at the upper school because she didn't want to get out of her corduroy trousers and plaid shirt. She guffawed when she laughed, squinting her bright blue eyes and banging her solid fist on the arm of her chair. When she needed to retreat from the duties of the farm, she went to a little beach cottage that she had bought for her children's summer vacations. There she could relax in her oldest clothes and sit with her legs outstretched and her heavy boots propped against the wood stove. She took Corinne, the secretary, and me with her occasionally in the late fall and early spring and we sat around the stove and drank beer and talked and joked. Corinne told her stories of sexual escapades as an army wife with casual bluntness and humor, and I realized that my life had been sheltered. Mrs. McGrath would slap her thigh and roar with laughter. "You're something else, Corinne!" she would shout. We discovered that she was a heavy drinker and Corinne and I quietly agreed that she would not be the one to drive home late Sunday afternoon.

One Saturday night after we had cooked a steak and sat around the stove with wine far into the evening with Corinne's stories of bizarre escapades among army couples, Corinne announced that she was tired and went to bed in the next room. I was correcting student compositions for Monday and didn't notice that Mrs. McGrath had disappeared. A surprised shout startled me as Corinne came running into the room half-laughing but not with her usual lightheartedness.

"My God, she's trying to get into my bed," she said, grabbing her jacket and putting it on.

"Did she know you were in it?" I asked.

"Yes, she knew. But she's quite drunk. Help me try to shove her into the bed. I'll sleep out here."

We had quite a time getting Mrs. McGrath's feet on the bed. She was lying across it and kept flailing out and grabbing Corinne. She finally sprawled out on the bed and we covered her over with blankets. I felt guilty seeing her lying there, her hair falling out of its pins, shirt pulled out, and arms flung out in abandon. Corinne giggled. "Why, the old reprobate. She attacked me," she said.

The next morning when both of us appeared for coffee, Mrs. McGrath was up cooking eggs and bacon. Coming out of the bathroom, I heard her talking to Corinne. "God, I'm sorry, Corinne," I heard her say.

"Forget it," was the reply, followed by Corinne's cheerful giggle.

I think I barely knew the word *lesbian* at that time, although my room-mate at college had introduced me to Radclyffe Hall's *The Well of Loneliness*—the famous English lesbian novel—and one or two students in my dormitory were known to be having affairs with other women. Corinne did not discuss the incident any further, but she took it very lightly. I could not draw any conclusions about Mrs. McGrath's sexuality—whether she was attracted to Corinne or just drunk.

We left rather early that day and all three of us felt strained. Despite our misgivings, Mrs. McGrath drove back fast and hard. She didn't do any drinking that day, however. She resumed her hearty laughter and conversation and nothing more was said about the weekend.

I spent the rest of the afternoon working, preparing my classes, fixing a light supper, reading, and listening to music. At about ten o'clock I heard a knock at the outside door of my apartment. At night I locked the outside door as well as the inside one, knowing that the janitor had his own key to get into the furnace room if he needed to. I was not expecting anyone so the knock made me a little jumpy. I considered not going out at all and just ignoring the knock, which was louder now and quite insistent. But I knew that if I didn't answer it, I could never sleep, wondering if someone was trying to pry open one of the basement windows. (I still suffered from nighttime fears left over from childhood and my feelings of physical vul-nerability.) Corinne would have called if she were coming over. I knew few people in Providence; most of my former college friends lived in Boston or Cambridge. The next knock was accompanied by my name. I recognized Mrs. McGrath's voice.

"Mary, are you home?" I was relieved, and then not so relieved when I remembered the events of the night before. It was her weekend off and she would not have to be back at the farm until Monday morning. I went to the door and opened it with false cheerfulness. "Well, hi!" I said. "Hello!"

She was standing at the door with a six-pack of beer in her hands. "I brought some good cheer," she said. Her eyes were twinkling brightly and her face was a little flushed. She has already started on her own good cheer,

I thought to myself. I stood quite paralyzed for a moment. I did not want to get into Corinne's situation last night. I didn't think I could handle it as well as Corinne did. I was not thirtyish and worldly wise. She peered at me a little.

"Oh, listen, I'm sorry. You're probably tired and have work to do. I'm an old fool. I was just delaying my return to the farm."

I felt ashamed and silly. Her big comfortable-looking frame seemed welcome in my lonely doorway.

"No, do come in. I'd like to take a break."

We talked for two hours. I fixed sandwiches and we drank beer. She told me about bringing up her sons alone, about how she married quite young. She was from a good Boston family and was given the customary education at that time for a young woman: horsemanship, hunting, some cello lessons and some language study, a trip to Europe, a good finishing school. Her husband was one of her brother's friends. He was the first to fly his own plane and was also a "bit of a sport," as she said. He died unexpectedly on the tennis court. Money was scarce but she had some connections, and with painful dependence on relatives, she got the boys through high school and college. Now they were on their own and she was on her own. No one was too interested in a middle-aged woman with little money whose handsome sons had grown up and gone. Particularly when she was socially inept, she added. She preferred hunting and fishing to garden clubs and volunteer Junior League work.

"I taught the boys all they knew about fishing and duck hunting," she said. "Used to go to all their sports events in school and college—that is, until they got kind of embarrassed when I'd show up at Harvard. I was pretty clumsy to tote around there. But we'd always have a whale of a good time when they came down to the cottage. Still do when they come to visit."

"Everyone was relieved when I took the job at Wheeler," she continued. "The boys were glad I'd finally found a place to roost, I guess. They still have some wild oats to sow, themselves."

"They'll marry someday," I said. "And you'll be a grandmother."

"Oh God, can you see it?" she roared. "Me, a grandmother!"

"Yes I can. I can see you hauling grandsons and granddaughters off fishing." I could, too. I could see her striding along the beach beyond the cottage, carrying the fishing tackle and pointing out the different kinds of shells and sea crabs.

We talked on and on until we were both tired. I told her about my loneliness in my apartment, but also about my sense of freedom and independence. I talked about my plans to return to graduate school.

"Yes, you must do that." She got very excited and waved her hand. "Don't get stuck here. Go on and get yourself a place in the world." She rose to go. "I'll leave you the rest of the beer," she said. "I can't drink it on the premises, you know."

"Come back and have it here then," I said, "whenever you want to get away."

"That's a nifty idea." She gave her characteristic guffaw and gave me a clumsy bear hug at the door.

"Good night, ladies," she half-sang as she went out, humming loudly as she got into her car.

I went to sleep quickly that night. Mrs. McGrath left me with a sense of well-being and warmth. I admired her as someone who had survived and prevailed in a hard world. She often returned on Sunday nights while I was there, bringing her six-pack and some good conversation.

After my first year of teaching I was glad to get away from Providence. I went back to Cambridge, where I had spent many weekends with friends that year, and took a summer course in fiction writing at Harvard with the Irish short story writer, Frank O'Connor. I was still confused about whether I wanted to be a writer or an academic so I thought a summer of writing fiction might help me decide the direction of my life. I shared an apartment with a friend from the Rhode Island School of Design and I hung around with the summer crowd of young and not so young folk who had come to taste the Harvard and Cambridge atmosphere.

O'Connor was charming and true to his reputation of storyteller, drinker, and womanizer. He was tall and angular with a shock of white hair, a little Joycean mustache, and a wicked smile. When we turned in our stories, he read them out loud pacing slowly back and forth in front of the class or draping himself over the podium. The horror that I felt when I first recognized that it was *my* story that he was going to read dissolved as I listened to the music of his soft Irish brogue, which made my prose unexpectedly beautiful.

Lillian was our class's self-proclaimed social secretary. A raven-haired self-confident graduate student, divorced and thirty-something, she organized a lavish evening at her Brookline apartment with a catered dinner and open bar. O'Connor arrived an hour late, obviously having stopped for a drink along the way. He was directed to the couch, a central position in the room, and the rest of us clustered around him. Lillian brought him his whiskey and soda and the maid passed around hors d'oeuvres and later served the cold turkey and ham and potato salad.

"Lily, you'll have me completely spoiled," O'Connor chuckled. "I'll never be able to return to the rigors of Ireland, ye know."

Someone asked him to tell us about Yeats and what it was like working as his secretary during the Abbey Theatre days in Dublin.

"Ah, Willie Yeats. Now there was a most peculiar man, a most extraordinary man. You could never tell what he would do next."

He went on to tell us stories of the Abbey Theatre—of Yeats's despair at the parochialism of the Irish Catholic audiences, who booed and threw programs in puritanical rage at J. M. Synge's line about Irish girls in their "shivies" (underclothes) in *The Playboy of the Western World*. Yeats insisted, he said, on going onstage and lecturing the audience on their abysmal ignorance.

After more stories and more whiskeys, O'Connor was reciting Yeats's "The Lake Isle of Innisfree" and his elegy "Under Ben Bulben," accompanied with sweeping gestures on the lines, "Cast a cold eye / On life, on death, / Horseman, pass by!" When I left the party after midnight, he was singing revolutionary songs from his days in the Irish Republican Army.

The highlight of my summer with O'Connor was his visit to my apartment on Ware Street. I was stunned when he said after class that he would return one of my papers, which he had not finished reading, in person if I would tell him how to get to my home. I knew that he had spent time with many of the class members individually but I was still impressed. I was a little apprehensive that I would not be up to the honor.

"That would be really nice," I said as casually as I could. "You can join me for a drink at about six."

I immediately telephoned Pam, my roommate. "You have to be in tonight," I said. "O'Connor's coming for a drink."

"Hey, all right!" she exclaimed. "I'll pick up some cheese and crackers. You get the liquor."

O'Connor arrived promptly at six o'clock. He obviously had not stopped for a drink on the way and he came right in and folded himself comfortably on the couch as if he lived there. After we served the drinks, he charmed us for an hour and a half with Irish stories and some tales of his American experiences on a lecture tour the year before. Before he left, he pulled out my paper and handed it to me.

"It's a grand story, Mary, a grand story." He had written good comments on the manuscript and had given me an A. I was thrilled.

O'Connor's influence on my writing that summer was very important. I gained more confidence because he liked my work. But his influence on my life as a writer was questionable. Pam's family friend, an editor at the

Atlantic Monthly, entertained O'Connor for dinner and told Pam that the Irishman had described me as "the perfect wife for a writer." I laughed when she told me but the remark penetrated my psyche disastrously, preparing me to become the wife of a writer and not the writer herself. In retrospect, it was a tremendous put-down, but at the time I didn't get it. I didn't see what a contradictory definition of selfhood I was developing. I accepted the woman's secondary role as supporter to a man; at the same time, I thought of myself as a writer. This contradiction was shaping my identity all too much. But in that heady summer atmosphere of writing, writers, and dreams, I blindly accepted O'Connor's remark as a compliment.

At the end of the summer O'Connor ran off with a student from another course he was teaching. She was half his age and had been introduced to him by Professor John Kelleher in the Celtic department at Harvard. Kelleher sponsored O'Connor's coming to the university and was furious at the writer, who had a wife and several children in Ireland. I heard that Kelleher had vowed never to speak to him again. I was not too shocked at the story although I did wonder how O'Connor found the time to carry out the conquest. As a student, I had been conditioned to accept male literary icons' promiscuity as part of their legends and certainly as their prerogative.

My summer experience also highlighted the other ongoing conflict in my life: my denial of my disability and my simultaneously constant awareness of it. Although I could not actually pass as able-bodied with crutches and braces, at times I was so convinced of my normalcy that it rubbed off onto other people. Occasionally, someone would break through this role playing with a remark such as "You are amazing the way you get around!" and I would be jolted back to reality. Or I would be asked to a party and have to decide whether or not I wanted to face a whole new set of strangers who would try desperately not to notice my disability. One such party was given by Joel, someone I had met at Tanglewood four summers before. I ran into him in Harvard Yard and he came up to me full of enthusiasm.

"Hey, Mary, good to see you," he said, and we talked a few minutes about why he was there and what I was doing. He was having a party that weekend and I would really have to come, he said. I jotted down the address, and after agonizing a while about whether or not to go and trying to persuade Pam to break her date and go with me, I decided to give it a try. I found a place to park and climbed up to the second floor apartment where the door was open, the music was blaring, and Joel was nowhere in sight. I eased in the door, smiling steadily but not getting much recognition.

Every time I met someone's glance I noted that theirs slid off of mine as quickly as possible. I inched around the room looking for Joel or a food and drink table so I would have something to do. Finally I bumped into my host. He was very welcoming and quickly brought me a strong gin and tonic, which grounded me permanently in one spot because I could not easily carry a full glass and walk at the same time. The best strategy that I found was to at least get to a wall to lean against. A chair was not the answer because if you sat in one, you were then totally incommunicado. Everyone towered above you or walked around you unless you had found a couch and someone else on it to talk to. I did find the wall and since I had only my drink to focus on, I drank it quickly in between a few bits of conversation with passersby. I had never been into drinking much, and I discovered that evening that I was definitely not a gin and tonic person; the room started to go around behind me instead of staying in front of me where it belonged. I decided I had better get outside to breathe while I could, so I put my glass on the nearest ledge and slowly and patiently moved toward the next room while keeping close to the wall. By this time I made no attempt to be friendly or make eye contact. I was intent on my mission: to get out of there. As my head kept getting larger and smaller I made my way to the exit, and I didn't stop to find Joel. I cautiously descended the stairs—my landing on each step resounded in my ears like thunder—and got to my car. As I started the engine, Joel dashed down the front steps and bounced over to my car window.

"You have to go so soon?" he said. "You just got here."

"I have to stop by another party," I lied, "but thanks a lot for asking me. Great to see you."

He concurred. We shook hands and I drove off rather precipitously, vowing as I always did after each such event that I would never go to a party again.

7

LOVE AND MARRIAGE

In 1953, after teaching a second year at the Mary C. Wheeler School, I returned to Harvard to work on a Ph.D. Although I liked teaching, I knew I did not want to stay in secondary school education and I could not imagine how I could make my living as a writer. Graduate school seemed to be the logical solution. Like many other would-be writers, I had illusions that I could combine the academic and the creative disciplines. Harvard took me back and I looked forward to returning to the Cambridge scene.

The summer before my return to graduate school I met Herb, my future husband, through my Chicago friend, Lloyd. Herb and Lloyd had met in New York and took a cottage together on Orrs Island in Maine where Herb's half sister and cousins had summer cottages. They both planned to write that summer. I spent most of the summer at Boothbay Harbor where my mother had rented a cottage for the last few years so that the family could reunite and I could continue my swimming and exercises. Nearby, Mother found a swimming club run by a couple who were in the health training and recreation business. It featured a saltwater pool blasted from coastal rock, tennis courts, and picnic grounds. My days at the club swimming and working with Walter Buzzell, a stocky well-preserved body builder, were my final attempts to fulfill my father's legacy of unremitting assault on my disability. Although I did not improve my condition dramatically, I kept in excellent shape. However, after several weeks of my healthy routine and sharing the beautiful setting with my sisters and their small children, I longed to escape to the crowded cafes of Cambridge and to others who shared my interests.

The daily routine in my mother's house was organized around the schedule of two- and three-year-olds, but Mother fixed up a small shed as a studio where I was to go every day to produce and create. It was "Aunt Mary's studio . . . She mustn't be disturbed." Whenever I left my retreat and appeared at the house, someone always asked if I had accomplished a lot.

All the neighbors on the point asked me if I liked my studio and if I was getting a lot done. I resolutely went there every morning, thinking that maybe I would be able to write that story or read that book but I accomplished nothing, wrote nothing, and was hardly able to read. I was consumed by a dark energy that was bottled up and screaming to be let out. So when Lloyd got in touch with me and asked me if I would come to Orrs Island, I was glad to escape and immediately accepted his invitation.

I found Herb and Lloyd in a tiny, rustic three-room cabin set amid fruit trees, wisteria, and uncut grass. Herb looked very young. (He was three years younger than I.) He was fairly tall—about six feet—broad shouldered, and blondish, with a Brahmin square jaw and a cleft in his chin. He walked at a leisurely pace, with a rambling gait. He often tilted his head slightly forward when he spoke to you, as if he might make a bow from the waist. Lloyd looked the same as he had in Chicago, but he presented a contrasting figure to Herb. Short, slight, and wiry, with black hair cropped short and a rather pointed chin, he darted when he moved and gestured intensely when he talked, moving his eyes rapidly from one person to another. They were an odd couple, but I immediately felt at home with them and welcomed the chance to be with my own contemporaries.

When I arrived at the cottage they were both unshaven because water was scarce in the cottage, and they said they were going to Herb's half sister Eleanor's house to clean up. She had invited us for drinks as well that evening, and they were served on the porch of her comfortable summer cottage, a leftover from better days when she and her husband were part of a smart 1920s set with inherited money and high expectations. Her husband, Jack, still dressed the part in a dark blue blazer accented with a yellow silk ascot. He waved his drink at us in a friendly but laconic fashion when we came onto the porch. Having gone through his inheritance the way he went through alcohol, Jack had settled into chronic unemployment and alcoholism. Eleanor, a handsome dark-haired woman, evidently took after the first wife. (Herb was the son of his father's second marriage, which followed a scandalous divorce that rocked the Boston family.) However, she had her father's square cleft chin so she and Herb showed some resemblance. She had managed to keep her family going with a number of cottage industries—one of them a hat shop—in Concord, Massachusetts, where they lived, patronized by her wealthy contemporaries.

"Hello, Uncle Herby!" We were greeted by Herb's two nieces, who were about his age but liked to tease him about being their uncle. "Come join the party!" They were both attractive dark-haired young women still dressed in shorts from sailing all afternoon. Eleanor, like her husband, was more formal and had on a green and gold printed caftan and gold sandals.

We all sat looking out to the sea, which could be glimpsed through the trees. Lolly and Peedie, the nieces, propped their feet up on the porch railing after they had brought out some nuts and cheese. Eleanor occasionally got up to pass the refreshments but she was relaxed. They all seemed amused at the odd couple and slightly skeptical about them as budding writers, but they spoke mostly about island gossip and events, such as the clambake that was to be held on Bailey's Island on Sunday night. They didn't question me much, accepting Lloyd's introduction—"my friend from Chicago who is going back to graduate school at Harvard"—with little comment or interest, partly from indifference and partly from politeness. And, of course, they were too genteel to ask me about my disability. I was relieved not to have to explain myself.

Later the three of us ate clam chowder and crabmeat at the local fish wharf and went back to the cottage with beer. Lloyd was intense about his latest French reading—Gide and Camus. Herb was reading Robert Lowell. They both recalled a dramatic visit from Herb's mother, who had descended on the cottage the previous weekend, filling it physically and psychologically.

"It was as if a storm had broken through the door when she arrived." Lloyd held out his arms as if to embrace the whole room. After I met Mildred Mason I could easily see how she would have filled the space—so deliberately and jealously guarded by Herb as his own. She was not exceptionally tall but she weighed over two hundred pounds and she seemed to expand as she talked to you—like a figure out of a play by Ionesco, the one Herb and I saw in Paris five years later, where a corpse keeps growing and takes over an apartment, eventually exploding out of the window like a meteor.

The next morning we all drove to a rocky point and walked out to a ledge where we sat looking at Ragged Island, where Edna St. Vincent Millay had lived and was said to have filled her motorboat at the general store with booze, which she took to the island for solitary binges. Lloyd went scuttling among the rocks along the shore, never able to sit still for more than five minutes, and Herb and I talked. We immediately connected. He spoke intensely as a young aspiring writer struggling to be born in Robert Lowell's "tranquilized fifties." I identified with the artist's voice and with his need to be heard though I am sure neither of us thought about a romantic relationship. I was Lloyd's friend first but I soon felt I was also Herb's friend.

I went back to Orrs Island several times that summer—once to a spaghetti dinner that Lloyd and Herb gave to repay all the meals and services Eleanor and others had provided. The house was jammed full of people glowing with sun and beer in contrast to the two hosts who remained pale and cloistered-looking because they did not spend their days on boats or beaches. When everyone had gone we found Uncle Jack passed out by the front door. Evidently Eleanor and the others had not missed him so Herb and Lloyd had to drag him up the road to his cottage. Another weekend we drove to Middlebury, Vermont, to visit Patricia, an artist friend of Herb's, who was a summer curator of the town museum. There were five of us pressed into my car—a brother and sister from New York who were friends of Lloyd's and the three of us. We drove up Friday night and arrived late, not sure where we were going to stay. Patricia said she could probably put us up, but her studio apartment above the museum had only a pullout couch and a single bed. Joan Gilbert and I got those accommodations. Lloyd and Bill Gilbert found a canopy bed in the museum that they agreed to share, while Herb and Patricia, evidently more than just casual friends, took over a colonial bedstead on another floor. The only alarm clock was in the apartment, so Joan and I were assigned the important duty of waking everyone before the museum opened for official business so that visitors would not be startled to find Lloyd and Bill or Herb and Patricia asleep under the handmade quilts.

As fall approached, both Herb and I realized we had to look for a room to rent in Cambridge—Herb was going back to finish Harvard—and it seemed only natural that we should look together. We each spent a day or so in Cambridge looking on our own and reporting on any good finds. We ended up both taking rooms in the house of Paul Frost, an elderly and eccentric landscape architect. I am sure we had no idea at the time how important that decision was going to be in both of our lives.

My friend Janet, a harpsichordist, also took a room in Frost's house and we moved in on the same day. Her fiancé, Fred, helped her bring in her harpsichord and my brother-in-law transported my things for me. Our rooms were furnished so it didn't take long to get settled. After they left, Janet and I decided to stake out the communal kitchen. We found it in a horrible mess, showing years of neglect. A group of actors from the Brattle Theatre had come and gone for about ten years and they did very little housekeeping. We made a start on a cleanup but realized we would have to get more powerful equipment. As we emerged into the front hall where our rooms were located, we ran into Paul Frost coming down the stairs. I did not immediately recognize him. When I first met him he had been dressed in a tee shirt and old khaki pants held up by a piece of rope. When he showed me the room, he had knocked tentatively on the door. "I don't think anyone is living here anymore," he had said. Then he opened the door to a room that was empty except for a bed, a bureau, and desk—all very handsome pieces of furniture that had seen better days. "Now you see, I was right," he said. "There is no one here so you can have the room anytime."

But now the man coming down the stairs was dressed in a handsome blue cape and a beret. He looked like someone out of a Toulouse-Lautrec poster. His white hair was well groomed and he carried a leather volume in his hand. When he saw us he stopped short and bowed.

"Well, young ladies," he said, "How do you do? Have I had the pleasure?"

"We're Janet and Mary, Mr. Frost. We rented the two downstairs rooms. Don't you remember?"

He made a dramatic gesture. "Why, of course I do. Welcome to Ash Street Place. I hope you will take a camellia from my greenhouse. I am going there now to pick one out to wear to the Shakespeare Society of Boston's meeting. We are reading *The Winter's Tale* tonight."

The greenhouse was off the dining room, and although it was wildly overgrown, there were a number of camellia plants blooming. Frost snipped off three flowers, gave us each one, and put the last one in the clasp at the neck of his cape.

"And now I must leave you. I mustn't be late," he said and swept out the front door.

According to neighbors, Frost had lived with his aunt and mother for many years in this charming colonial house set at the end of a cul-de-sac and surrounded by a lush garden that was now, like its owner, in decay. While the women were alive, the house and garden had been kept immaculately, they claimed, and Frost, who said he was a cousin of the poet Robert Frost, had been a successful landscape architect. They said he was imperious about his taste in landscaping and would occasionally decide to improve one of the neighbors' property. The owner would wake up one morning and find a flowering tree planted in his yard or a set of rhododendron bushes under his living room windows. Apparently the additions were so well chosen that no one complained. They also claimed that Frost had been one of Freud's first American patients and that the analyst had advised the American to follow his sexual preferences where they led him. Frost followed his advice and there was a series of alliances with young men who came and went. Janet and I discovered that one of his lovers liked to streak through the upstairs hallway. He would come down from the third floor where Frost lived among his aviary birds and run past the bathroom door when one of us emerged. Janet was the first to encounter him.

"Christ!" I heard her shout one morning as she ran down the stairs with her towel. "There's some creep lurking nude in the hallway upstairs."

When we reported it to Frost, he looked puzzled at first. "Oh, Jerry," he said with an enlightened look. "That's my good friend Jerry. He lives on a little island in Boston harbor with wonderful wildflowers all over."

Jerry, it turned out, was an occasional actor; he got the part of Bartolph in Shakespeare's *Henry IV* at the Brattle Theatre because of his red nose and florid face. He also spent time in the local prison in Boston harbor. Frost faithfully visited him there. Otherwise, he stayed in Ash Street Place. We finally met Jerry and he agreed to be more modest when he came to the bathroom, so peace was restored. Herb's room was on the second floor just above mine. The other two boarders were Allan, an anthropology graduate student from Brooklyn, and Henry, who was getting a doctorate in psychology and who became our financial manager when we discovered that Frost was not capable of collecting the rent and paying the bills.

We discovered the need to form a cooperative a few days after all of us moved in. Janet and Henry and I had just finished making breakfast and were drinking our coffee outside the front door, sitting on the bench on the small patio. The apricot-painted double doors were open as they often were and we saw Frost coming down the stairs waving his hand as if he were addressing an audience. As he reached the bottom of the stairs, we heard his words: "Touch not a hair on this gray head / But leave the electric on instead."

He waved some papers at us. Henry looked at them and found a notice from the electric company announcing that service would be cut off that day. The rest of the papers were back bills. We had a hasty conference and collected some advance rent and Henry became our agent. He rushed our payment to Boston Edison and the lights stayed on that day.

Soon we all became engrossed in our own lives and work. We did not think much about how our community appeared to the outside world. Even in Cambridge our lifestyle was considered bohemian in 1953. I became aware of how we were perceived by some people when I was visited by an insurance agent investigating a claim I had made for a crate of books shipped from Chicago and lost two years previously. The agent telephoned first and asked for an appointment, presumably to see if I was hiding the books I claimed were lost. He arrived, a round dumpling of a young man in a business suit, with a wide face and wide eyes. He looked around rather apprehensively when I told him to come into my room so I could answer his questions and fill out a form. When we finished, he glanced suspiciously into the hall through the open door.

"Do you mind if I have a look around the house?" he asked nervously. "Just following the rules, you know. We are supposed to check out the premises."

"Sure," I said, knowing all the boarders kept their rooms locked. "Make yourself at home."

He disappeared up the stairs and I went back to work. He must have ventured all the way to the third floor—to Frost's inner sanctum—and found Frost lying on his bed stark naked surrounded by fluttering birds that he had released from the aviary. Henry, whose room was on the third floor and who happened to be home, heard Frost shout at the fleeing figure, "Come in young man, come in!"

The last I saw of the agent, he was stumbling down the stairs, looking wild-eyed. He tipped his hand to his head as if he were wearing a hat, and rushed out the door, mumbling that he would get in touch with me. He was as good as his word and he sent me a check for the amount claimed on the lost books.

Herb and I had an occasional meal together. He was going through a dark period. He had signed up for courses in the fall. One was on the novels of Dostoevsky, including *The Brothers Karamazov, Crime and Punishment,* and *The Idiot*—a somber list for someone in a depression. After a bout of colitis, he decided to drop out of school that semester but continued to read Dostoevsky and write poetry and occasionally drink too much. He and Janet had a disastrous evening together when they both got drunk. Herb made unwelcome advances, they both got deadly ill, and Janet knocked loudly at my door, asking me to go get Fred in Boston, where he lived. Because it was midnight, I agreed to go only if someone would go with me and the only sober available being was Jerry, so the two of us made our way to St. Botolph Street, where Jerry banged on Fred's door until he woke up and came back with us. While Fred took care of Janet, Herb crawled down the stairs, looking like death, and apologized profusely for the inconvenience. I was annoyed at his handling of the crisis so I accepted his apology curtly. Our relationship did not bloom until later when I got to know him under different circumstances.

I spent Christmas of 1953 with my sister and her family on Long Island. My mother was there, too, and on Christmas Eve we shared the ritual of wrapping presents and filling stockings for Betty's three young children. The household was busy and cheerful but by the time dinner was cooked and cleaned up on Christmas day, my sister and mother were exhausted and I had had enough of family celebrations. Herb and I had exchanged phone numbers; he was spending Christmas with his mother in

Langhorne, Pennsylvania, and both of us agreed that we might want to escape and should try to get together. He called me Christmas Eve and we agreed to go into New York City the next evening. He could get his mother's car and would come and pick me up.

When he arrived at Betty's door, all I could see was a huge dark blue winter coat with massive shoulders—a leftover from Herb's Riverdale School days when he and his friends emulated the New York gangster look. He loved New York and wanted to show me his favorite spots. We drove around and stopped at Rockefeller Plaza and ended up in Hamburger Heaven close to Saint Patrick's Cathedral because we had decided to go to church. After we had tried the famous devil's food cake and finished our coffee, we crossed the street and stood in line waiting to get into church. It was a cold night and I put my hand in Herb's huge coat pocket, simply and naturally, without much thought. Later both of us agreed that the gesture was the beginning of our new relationship.

By the end of the year, our group at Frost's house had broken up. Herb decided not to return to Harvard and moved to Beacon Hill where he took a tiny, dreary room. He was running out of money; his mother had given him a certain sum that was to have covered his Harvard education but that was almost gone. He didn't take a job but he had a brief encounter with secretarial training—a desperate move to prepare him for a job while he worked on his writing. He quit the secretarial school on his second day of attendance after the fearsome teacher shouted at him continually for being absentminded. Abandoning employment for the time being, Herb did some settlement work and read to a blind gentleman who lived in a rooming house for elderly men on Beacon Hill. We spent more and more time together. Sometimes he stayed over in my room, and because we didn't acknowledge publicly that we were sleeping together, he occasionally departed hastily through my window into the garden if someone who was not part of the Frost community knocked on my door in an unexpected visit. We were half in and half out of the bohemian world and we used to laugh about this later.

Nancy Cole, another friend of mine, moved into Herb's room and we began to really clean up the kitchen and dining room and throw candlelight parties using the remains of the beautiful English china and the silver that Frost had abandoned to his boarders. We wondered how much had been taken off by departing roomers. Nancy came to Cambridge to work for the Friends Service but she was interested in the theater and very talented, too. By the end of the spring she had put together a one-woman presentation of Gertrude Stein that was very successful.

With a year of course work at Harvard behind me, I had just one more semester left. It had been a mixed academic experience. I did well but did not find any inspiring mentors. No one in the English department made me feel special, and I no longer had the encouragement of the Radcliffe dean, Wilma Kerby-Miller, who had retired and who, in any case, would not have had much influence in the graduate school although she once taught a course for them. A course in Irish literature with Kelleher was intriguing. A required course in Anglo-Saxon was a disaster. None of the experience was memorable. I intended to go on and finish my doctorate but the semester ahead seemed like drudgery. I began to wonder if graduate school was the right path for me. For the first time, I looked ahead to my future without a sense that something exciting would happen to me, that I would be lifted out of my uninspired life into another world of wonder and romance. My fantasy world was dying.

The atmosphere at Frost's house, which at first seemed so intriguing, now seemed just dreary. Everyone was very self-absorbed and there was an existential gloom amongst us, perhaps seeping in from the outside world —the fears and suspicions of the evolving Cold War. By the end of the spring Nancy went on tour with her show, and in early summer Janet married Fred and the graduate students graduated and moved on. Gregory Corso, the Beat poet, moved in soon after I left in June and a new era began in Frost's house.

In the midst of this, Herb and I turned to each other like two ship-wrecked survivors—he a survivor of family traumas, which I would soon get to know, and I a survivor of false dreams. As we became closer, I became less and less conscious of my disability. It did not seem to play a part in our relationship. It was not that Herb entirely ignored it—he opened doors and parked the car and carried heavy books for me—but we did not talk about it either. Perhaps it was a mistake not to do so, but it gave me a great sense of release. I felt like everyone else and that, apparently, was what I wanted to feel. At the same time, I felt needed because Herb was emotionally needy. One day when I was driving him back to Beacon Hill and he was feeling particularly down, he asked, "Would you stick with me if I had a mental breakdown?"

The question caught me off guard. I don't think I actually answered it but I am sure I had a flashback to my brother Tom, who had not been able to share his depression and anguish with anyone. I felt more committed to Herb then but also a little frightened by what he had said. I had an ashtray in my room, an enameled yellow dish with a design on it by the cartoon-ist Steinberg. It had two stick figures clutching one another and the caption read, "Hold me." That was Herb and I at the time, but it was also a current feeling of the early 1950s and certainly of the intellectual milieu of Cambridge where angst was in.

On the other hand, our relationship was certainly not always gloomy. During my last months at Frost's house we explored Boston together from Scollay Square (which still existed) to the North Shore and joined up with some of his writer friends. One in particular, Gene, was part of the MacLeish writing group at Harvard but as an Irish Catholic Boston boy, he shared Herb's anti-establishment feelings about Harvard, although for different reasons. He was a heavy drinker, and combined a lot of Hemingway machismo with Irish wit and satire. We spent a number of hours in bars where I never learned to like the beer but always enjoyed the black humor.

In spring Herb landed in Massachusetts General Hospital with acute colitis and called me at Frost's house. "I've just been invaded," he said.

"What do you mean?" I was alarmed.

"A roly poly intern in saggy white pants just came into my room with the longest instrument I have ever seen."

"Yes, so . . . ?"

"Well, he proceeded to put it up my ass—as I bent over, of course—and look in it. He must have seen all the way up to my teeth."

I went to visit him and picked him up when he was discharged to a bland diet and no alcohol. His condition improved, but later, after we were married and he was drafted into the army, his colitis kept him out of the service. By June we had decided to get married in the fall. Herb brought it up. "I think we should get married." he said. There were no immediate bells and whistles for me. In fact, I felt a little surprised that I was actually getting a proposal. But it seemed right to me and I was very happy. We designed a lovely engagement ring from diamonds and a sapphire belonging to his father, and I showed it proudly to my family and friends. In the fall Herb planned to return to finish Harvard, using up the last of his education money. I would finish my graduate courses—my mother agreed to continue support for that—and then I would get a job. We decided to get married in Boothbay Harbor, Maine, and chose a date: September 11, 1954.

I wanted our wedding to be simple and unpretentious. I had no intention of competing with my sisters, who had been traditional brides even though they were married during the war. Their formal wedding portraits sat on my mother's living room table. Betty had a small wedding at home in November after my father's funeral in August. Jane, using the same wedding dress, was married the following January when her fiancé, a Royal Canadian Air Force fighter pilot, had a two-week leave from the Battle of

Britain. Their portraits could be ads for wedding photographers—a side view, looking serene and composed, wearing a slim-fitting satin dress with a long train and veil flowing from a satin cap embroidered with seed pearls, their long blonde hair falling stylishly to their shoulders. My mother's table did not display a formal wedding picture of me. Neither Mother nor I ever thought of having one taken, but she presented me with a wedding album with "MSG—HWM, September 11, 1954" embossed in gold on the white leather cover.

My wedding album still makes me feel uncomfortable today. I wore an ankle-length ivory brocade dress with a sweetheart neck, and a small satin hat with a shoulder-length veil. One photograph shows me coming out of the church holding Herb's arm. We posed without my crutches. My two sisters and the best man and two ushers are behind us. The picture reminds me of my "Springtime" costume look at the country club, when I was dressed up like a doll by Mother and my sisters. Other pictures show me cutting the cake and standing in a reception line. There are actually more pictures of my sisters in this album than of me. They are wearing cranberry brocade dresses and matching pumps. They pose first together and then with my mother and again with their husbands. They look glamorous and stand with one foot slightly in front of the other. Even in the traditional pre-wedding photo of "preparing the bride" where I am looking into a mirror and my sisters—one on each side of me—are holding out my veil in a gesture of service, they clearly dominate the scene. As I look through the photos, I wish I had let go of that world and found my own image no matter how damaged or untraditional it might have been.

We invited fifty guests to the wedding: a few of my Radcliffe friends, including Janet, and my roommate, Jean, and Nancy Cole from Frost's house, a few relatives on both sides and some family friends, including the D'Oliers from Moorestown and some other summer friends of Mother's. Our best man was William Alfred, who had been Herb's tutor at Harvard and whom I was later to assist as a teaching fellow. Our uninvited guest was Edna, the biggest hurricane to hit the Maine coast in a decade. The wedding took place at the height of the storm.

When I called the coast guard on Friday before the wedding to ask about the prospects of the storm, the answer was brief. "There'll be no wedding on Ocean Point tomorrow, ma'am," the spokesman said. We had scheduled the ceremony in a little chapel on the outer road of Ocean Point facing the sea. Soon after my call, the coast guard called back to say the Unitarian minister from Fisherman's Island, who was going to marry us, had radioed that he would not be able to come to the mainland anytime in the near future. Herb and I realized we had to make some new plans and after some suggestions from local friends, we were able to engage a Methodist minister and his church in the center of town. Our reception was in an inn in Southport, not far from where my mother rented a cottage on Juniper Point.

The storm added zest to our wedding. No one who made it that day ever forgot the occasion. Some guests, like Herb's half sister Eleanor and her daughters, didn't make it but came to the dinner the night before and to the cocktail party given by Herb's mother at Topside, where she was staying in town. Mildred Mason always gave a fabulous party. She provided food and drink lavishly but she also stirred up a crowd, rather overdramatically my mother thought, but she made it an occasion where there was a definite pitch of excitement and even tension. Herb hated her parties and looked drained, but his reticence only made her more outrageous. She brought along Robert, a tall black man, part Native American, who had been a family retainer to the Masons in Wilmington, Delaware, since Herb was a child. Mildred Mason treated him alternately like an intimate friend and a servant. I could never figure out why he stayed loyal to her, but of course, there were not many career opportunities for black men in Wilmington, although Robert was a part owner of a bar and his wife was a hairdresser. I think part of his loyalty was to Herb; he was almost a father figure to him. (Herb was seven when his father died.) At the party Robert was the bartender and he stood by the table like a sentinel.

The rain was torrential as the hour for the wedding approached. My sisters helped me dress, and as I finished, pinning my hat as securely as I could to withstand passage through the storm, Jane and Betty, who along with my mother were thrilled that I was marrying, gave me last-minute words of encouragement and advice. They asked me if I had been to the doctor to get the proper contraception and added, "You won't want to have children, will you, dear? It would be too difficult for you."

I smiled and nodded but I said nothing because I did not know my own feelings at the time. I might have agreed, accepting my sisters' judgment, that I could not manage a family. I had not thought out my future role as a married woman. I was going to take one step at a time.

I was delivered to the church completely dry, wrapped in a huge plastic bag. After I was unwrapped, my brother-in-law Eddie took me by the arm and we entered the church by the side door because I did not want to make the long walk down the aisle. As I approached the altar, I heard the squish squish of Hugh's shoes coming up the aisle to seat a final guest, and when I looked up at the minister I saw water streaming down the wall behind him. Herb and I exchanged amused glances as if to say that naturally our wedding would be part of some disaster. Despite the wind and water, we completed the ceremony and managed to get to the reception before the worst part of the storm hit. We felt like hearty marooned sailors as we ate our lobster thermidor and made the champagne toasts. My twin cousins, like true daughters of my Aunt Jane, arrived with a great flourish in huge picture hats that had collapsed like flower petals in the rain. Soon after I cut the wedding cake, the caterer announced that we were about to lose the electricity.

Everyone has a story to tell about their departure from my wedding. Trees were falling across the roads and roads were flooding. Herb's cousins, the Lyons, escaped from their jeep as it filled with water, and they had to stay overnight in a farmhouse. Mildred Mason threw another party for those who were stranded in town. Herb and I were saved from electrocution by a fireman who stopped us from driving into a live wire. He pointed the way to the nearest tourist house, where we stayed the night. Our plan had been to go to Christmas Cove on our wedding night and then to go on to Port Clyde to catch the boat for Monhegan Island, where we had rented a housekeeping cottage for a few days. In the days following the wedding, the seas were calm and the skies crystal clear. The storm did not seem like an ill omen then.

I was soon introduced to the myths and drama of the Mason clan and most especially of my mother-in-law, Mildred Mason. My first memory of her was of a large face peering into my car at a gas station near Langhorne, Pennsylvania, where Herb and I were meeting. I was giving him a ride back to Frost's house after the Christmas holidays the year before we married. His mother drove him to our meeting place and came over to my car to greet me. She was a formidable-looking woman—very large, but active and impressive. She dressed professionally, keeping her hair rinsed to its original dark reddish color. She always wore black and liked to decorate her coats and dresses with huge flashy pins. She gave me a pin every Christmas but they were scaled to my small size.

Mildred Mason was very much a presence in Herb's life—not an altogether welcome presence at that. Herb soon filled me in on life with his mother. He and his older sister, Libby, had been overwhelmed by her ever since childhood. They were both quiet, reticent types, perhaps taking after their father even though he had died when they were young. Their mother was a larger-than-life figure and told her children, whom she found wimpy, that she intended to embarrass them at least once every day. And so she did. Herb described many incidents, sharing them with ironic humor clearly touched with pain. Once when they were teenagers, he said, they went to the theater in New York where their seats were in the first row. As soon as they got seated, his mother kicked off her shoes so violently that they landed in the orchestra pit near the percussionist. "Herbert," she said (she always used his full name), "go down and get my shoes before the orchestra starts playing." Herb tried to put her off until intermission, but she would have none of it and, laughing loudly, sent him down to retrieve the shoes. Herb felt as if a huge spotlight were turned on him. He dreaded these public appearances but he also found that the rowdy parties his mother gave for her business associates at home made him even more miserable and angry enough to smash the liquor bottles. In his Riverdale School years his mother's business went into bankruptcy, and they went through a year of avoiding creditors and sneaking valuables out of the house at night. Herb made ten or twelve clandestine trips to New York City, taking furniture, china, and silver to his sister's apartment there.

We first went to Mildred Mason's apartment in Langhorne for the Christmas following our marriage. Like all her settings, her apartment was memorable and unusual. It was part of an immense plantation-style mansion that her landlords had divided into rental units. Her apartment consisted of one huge room with a high ceiling and beautiful floor-length windows looking onto an elegant garden. It had a small Pullman kitchen, a bathroom, and a glassed-in porch, which she had made into a bedroom with partitions and curtains. Later she expanded into two other rooms, and she had a large attic storage space as well.

Displayed prominently in her apartment, on one of the massive pieces of furniture she had kept from her husband's former Boston life—was a bust of Herbert Senior. It was commissioned in Arden, Delaware, a utopian community promoting artisanship and a single tax philosophy, where the couple had settled after marrying. The bust was not a great work of art, but its presence represented the kind of romantic legends she created about her life with Herbert.

It was a romantic tale. A young New Hampshire woman goes to Boston with her younger sister, Maud, to make her fortune. She goes to Katherine Gibbs School and becomes the secretary to a Boston Brahmin businessman and family man, Herbert Warren Mason. Their romance follows. Scandal. Divorce. Possibly an illegitimate child who did not survive. No date or place of a wedding is known. It was the first divorce in the Mason family. The first wife, from a well-connected Maine family, moves with the three daughters to Washington, D.C., to avoid the infamy of being a divorced woman in Boston. The couple breaks off all ties with the Boston life, relocates to Delaware where Herbert buys the Curtis Paper Mill. They live in Arden, pursuing arts and crafts and a utopian ideal. So the story goes until Herbert dies of a heart attack in Alstead, New Hampshire, where they spend their summers in a sprawling New England colonial house by Lake Warren.

Although Mildred Mason talked constantly about the Mason and Warren families and told stories about her married life in Arden, she rarely spoke of the world in which the two children grew up after her husband's death—a world consisting of private schools and clubs for the children, but for her another world of business deals, successes, and failures. She inherited the Curtis Paper Mill after her husband died, but it had been run almost into bankruptcy through the Depression. She managed, with the collaboration of a co-director, to bring the business around and sell it. Then she started another obviously profitable paper company that ultimately failed. When I met her, she was working as a consultant, and had built a very successful line of papers for Patterson Parchment Company. She had her own chemist, and produced and marketed her own product, traveling frequently all over the country.

I don't remember that Mildred Mason asked me much about my disability although I think I told her about Warm Springs and FDR. I am sure she was surprised and probably displeased that Herb did not marry an able-bodied person, but when I asked him what she thought, he claimed she never brought it up. She always treated me with respect, which she did not do for Libby's husband, always implying he was mistreating her daughter. In fact, she was very thoughtful about what was convenient for me. For several summers when our children were very young, she provided us with a cottage on Lake Sebago, right on the water where I could easily swim because the dock was very accessible and close to the house. She also hired someone to come during the day and cook and clean for us while she visited so that we didn't have to do any housework. I could always count on her to try to make my life easier, whenever she chose to focus on us, which was not very often.

8

BEACON HILL AND AFTER

By 1954 I had achieved one agenda that had driven my life unconsciously—I never would have admitted to it consciously. I didn't even think
about it. I had done what my sisters and many of my friends and most "normal women" did: I found an eligible, handsome man and married in my
twenties (I was twenty-six). My aspirations to finish my Ph.D. and teach or
write were put on hold as I lived out the story of a traditional woman of the
1950s even though I obviously did not fit the usual stereotype.

Our first apartment was a tiny place on Buzzwell Street, where if you
were in the tub with the bathroom door open, you could say hello to anyone who came in the front door. It had all the features of a cheap apartment—roaches, uncontrollable heat and/or cold, and peeling paint—but we
liked it. We lived an alley away from Janet, the harpsichordist, and Fred, the
harpsichord maker—they had married—who played poker with us. We also
went to bad movies together and afterwards dined on tough London broil
and mediocre red wine.

Soon after we married we tried to start a summer theater in Rockport
on Cape Ann. Herb previously worked for a theater on Nantucket, and
knew some actors and actresses always looking for work, as well as several
budding playwrights, including himself. An architect I knew worked out
plans for converting Redman's Hall in Rockport into an arena stage, and
we met a Scotsman, Hamish MacEwan, who was a painter and possibly a
stage manager and scenic designer. It was a naive idea because we had no
money and backing. After spending several weeks calling on potential
"angels" in Rockport, including Mr. Filene of Boston's famous Filene's
department stores—he was not impressed with our plans—we realized we
were not going to make it and gave up the venture although our spirits
were unabashed.

A year later we moved to an apartment on Beacon Hill's Myrtle Street.
It was much larger, but it was on the second floor so I had a steep set of

stairs to climb. Furthermore, the stairs and hallway were badly lit because our landlady hated to use electricity. When she heard me open my door she would try to rush out and click on the hall lights before I started down the stairs. She did the same thing when she heard me come in the front door. She was always at home and, it seemed to me, always crouched by her front door ready to spring into action.

My friend Ilona, the Polish novelist, shook her head disapprovingly. "Why are you living on the second floor?" she insisted. "You shouldn't be climbing all those stairs and carrying up groceries, besides."

I shrugged, "It doesn't bother me." I realize now this bravado was part of my denial of my disability. I refused to demand any special accommodations except for the fact that I drove a hand-controlled car. Herb's acceptance of this arrangement was for years part of our relationship. Years later when my physical strength deteriorated and I could no longer master those challenges, the balance of our marriage changed. But for now I insisted on acting as an able-bodied wife in a traditional marriage.

But of course, we were not an ordinary couple. Herb was still an undergraduate at Harvard and I was in my third year of graduate school. When I finished my course work, I had to become the breadwinner. Herb could only manage a few hours a week as an admitting secretary at Massachusetts General Hospital. Because it was the middle of the school year when I started looking for work, I was unable to find a teaching job in a college. My Harvard professors were very little help, and I had not yet chosen a thesis director. The attitude of the English department faculty was typified by my experience in a Renaissance literature seminar I had taken in the summer with Professor Herschel Baker. In the class of twelve students I was one of two women. Baker automatically paired me with the other woman, who was not a Harvard student, but just taking a summer course. She was a disaster to work with—harebrained and pleasant and completely unequipped to do graduate work. I realized to my fury that Baker not only paired us together to present a project but also placed us both in the same category in his mind—female and inconsequential. I knew that no matter what I did, I would not excel in that seminar.

Once again I took a post in a secondary school, the Winsor School for Girls, where a job opened up because someone was ill. The school was located conveniently near us in Boston, but I was getting further and further from my career expectations and I felt cut off from my former life in graduate school and from my friends. I began to feel claustrophobic and once, on an impulse, I left the apartment while Herb was out and walked down Beacon Hill to visit college friends of mine. This was unusual for me;

I rarely took spontaneous walks, particularly on the brick sidewalks of Beacon Hill. Herb had the car, and when he returned and found that I was not there and that I had left no message, he panicked and called all the taxi companies to see if I had used them. I returned in an hour or so and minimized my lack of communication as forgetfulness on my part. I was not aware at the time of the hostility that my impulsiveness implied.

Gradually Herb and I began to build a life together, develop our own group of friends, and share our mutual interests and outlook on the world, and so I felt less isolated. As a couple, we fit somewhere between the 1950s pattern of middle-class wives supporting their husband's education and the world of couples who lived marginalized lives as writers and artists. We were definitely not part of the Beat generation, but we didn't fit into the suburban pattern described later by Betty Friedan in *The Feminine Mystique* either. I found that my college friends who were marrying and settling into a life of home and children did not share many common interests with me at that point.

We continued to see Gene, from Herb's Harvard days, and Ilona, as well as a few people from Harvard's English department, although Herb generally had an aversion to academics. His best man, William Alfred, the playwright and professor, and originally his tutor at Harvard, often had us over to his house on Athens Street in Cambridge. He was a close friend of Robert Lowell's and talked a lot about the literary scene and offered to introduce us, but Herb was wary of a literary discipleship. Visiting Bill Alfred was always a delight. He was a bachelor and a devout Catholic practicing good works as a third order Franciscan. He was also an irreverent anti-establishment Irishman who brought his Irish mother from Brooklyn to preside over his house in the stuffy Cambridge academic community. She cooked and served dinners to his Harvard colleagues and did not hesitate to speak her mind in the evening conversations. She also brought with her an eccentric scruffy dog who protested too much late company by peeing on the leg of one of their Victorian chairs.

Another friend of ours was Jack Kotteman, a fellow graduate student of mine but also assigned to Herb as a senior tutor. Jack was a gentle person of great wit and talent. He came to the university from the Midwest and was one of the favorites of the "old boys" in the department, but he had none of the affectation or arrogance that usually went with being a chosen disciple. We took Jack with us on a number of our picnics. One day we drove to Alstead, New Hampshire, the summer place that Herb's family once owned. We packed a picnic lunch, and when we got there, we borrowed a small rowboat from the owners of an inn next to the old Mason house. We soon discovered that the boat leaked but we dawdled on Lake Warren any-way, eating our cold chicken and drinking our wine. Jack recited T. S. Eliot's "Dry Salvages" lugubriously and mockingly as he bailed the boat, chanting, "In a drifting boat with a slow leakage / The silent listening to the undeni-able / Clamour of the bell of the last annunciation."

I did not know at the time that Jack had Parkinson's disease. He died while we were in France. When I heard the news, I was deeply grieved and I thought back to an evening I had with him in Boston. He knew how much I had loved jazz in Chicago, so when Sarah Vaughan came to Boston, he asked me to go with him and some other friends. He didn't ask Herb to join us, which seemed a little odd, but he made it quite clear that he was just asking me. I had a wonderful time but I noticed a deep melancholy in Jack, although I felt absolutely comfortable and happy with him. We shared the same favorite Sarah Vaughan song, "Poor Butterfly," and heard her sing it to perfection. I was not aware then that he knew he had little time left to live, but I knew the evening was very special. Only years later when talk-ing to Ilona, also a close friend of Jack's, did I fully understand the sadness of that evening. She and I were reminiscing about Jack, and Ilona said, "But you knew, didn't you, that he was in love with you?" I had not known, but in retrospect I could see that the evening was meant to memorialize some-thing between us.

We spent time with people outside academia too—older people that Herb gravitated toward. Herb always felt between generations because his stepsister was older than him by more than twenty years. He still read to his blind friend, and we occasionally had him for dinner. One of our favorite weekend trips was to visit an elderly Quaker lady, Mrs. Rawson, who knew Herb's family and lived in Alstead, New Hampshire. She collected and pub-lished books on early New England tools and household objects, and her house was a museum itself. She kept it as close to the style and condition of the seventeenth century as she could, refusing for years to put in elec-tricity until finally her children insisted. She claimed to have gone down on her knees and apologized to the spirit of the house when the lights went on. Her nearest neighbor was a very old graveyard on top of a hill, which she said gave her great comfort because she felt close to all the departed souls and knew many of their stories—full of local color and sometimes gothic horror. We would often take our picnic to her long tree-filled back-yard and share our food and cider with her while she related New Hampshire tales.

At the end of the year, Herb graduated from Harvard and was immedi-ately drafted into the army. Because we did not know where he would be,

I decided to move to Cambridge where I could more easily access the libraries I would need when studying for my Ph.D. comprehensive exams. I found a room with kitchen privileges in a charming house on Brown Street and Herb moved me in the day he was to report for induction. After he left, I spent a lonely night thinking of the time that stretched ahead without him. I did not feel much enthusiasm for going back to my studies. I had become a wife—a supportive wife—and my own life seemed very bound to another.

In the morning, before I went downstairs to make my breakfast, I heard the telephone ring.

"Mary, it's for you." My landlady, a warm and lively elderly widow, called me to the phone.

It was Herb, gleeful on the other end of the line. "I'm free," he shouted. "I'm 4F!"

I couldn't believe it. "What do you mean? You can come back?"

"Yes, I'll be there in a few hours."

His colitis had exempted him, and we were thrilled. My landlady was very understanding, letting us out of our lease to retrieve our Beacon Hill apartment. In a day or so we moved back and resumed our life on the Hill.

Herb worked in a variety of jobs over the summer and then taught one semester at a technical institute in the fall. I went back to Winsor and did not think about studying for comprehensives. There seemed no time for it, and I had drifted away from my graduate student identity. After teaching, Herb looked around for another job and ended up as a private detective, thinking that would give him experience in the world and material for fiction. As it turned out, the work was inglorious and dull, going after store employees who would pocket small change instead of putting it in the register. Herb spent his mornings driving around with a partner who constantly smoked, stopping at doughnut shops and convenience stores where the perpetrators would be trapped and caught. Not only was this process depressing and boring but it also demanded that Herb eat a huge amount of doughnuts and snacks while posing as a customer. Herb began to develop a pasty look, and in desperation, while sitting in a pay toilet waiting to catch a restroom thief, he wrote a note to Walter Whitehill, one of his Lowell House mentors at Harvard, describing his plight and asking if there was not a better way for a writer to get on in the world. His letter must have tickled the "old boys" at Harvard and the Boston Athenaeum because he found Herb a small grant from a private foundation that supported young writers who wanted to live in Paris.

The Kittredge grant gave us seed money to go to Europe but we still needed a basic income to live on, so I found a job at the American School of Paris teaching high school English. Actually, Herb found the job and wrote the letter of application in my name. When he told me about the job, I was not enthusiastic at first. The thought of teaching expatriate American teenagers did not thrill me. Although I enjoyed the Winsor students, who were bright and college oriented, I was still discontented with secondary school teaching and frustrated with my failure to get on with my degree. My first impulse was one of rebellion. On the other hand, I wanted to go to Europe. We had tried for Fulbright grants to Ireland but had not gotten them, and we felt more alienated from the Eisenhower era after Adlai Stevenson lost the election. So I decided to take the job when it was offered to me. We stored our few pieces of furniture, sold my hand-controlled car, and bought a Renault *quatre chevaux*—the car most driven in France—which was to be delivered to us in Paris. I would no longer be independently mobile because the Renault did not have hand controls. It took me a while to realize how dependent and confined that would make me feel.

My maternal grandparents and their children, circa 1902. Mother is standing between her parents.

Nana Grimley and her grandchildren in 1928: Betty, Tom, me, and Jane (left to right)

Mother and Aunt Jane, 1922

In Ocean City, New Jersey, 1932, before polio

With Tom at Stanwick Avenue, Moorestown, 1932

Family portrait in the 1930s: Mother, me, Tom, Jane, and Betty (left to right)

Refusing to be a poster child, Warm Springs, Georgia, Thanksgiving, 1934

My father returning from Japan when I'm stricken with polio

Thanksgiving dinner sitting next to President Roosevelt in Warm Springs, Georgia, 1934

My family posing for Christmas card picture in 1938

On my scooter at Wheaton College, Massachusetts, 1947

My brother, Tom, holding our nephews, 1948

PART II

THE TRAVELER'S JOURNEY

I traveld thro' a Land of Men
A Land of Men & Women too

—William Blake, "The Mental Traveller"

9

THE FRENCH EXPERIENCE:
MEMORIES OF PARIS 1957–1959

In August of 1957 Herb and I sailed from Boston on the *New York,* a Greek ship with a German crew, spending ten days on the ocean to reach France, where we expected to spend a year but stayed three. My years in Paris were formative, planting the seeds of my future feminism and of my self-identification as a disabled woman with a unique spiritual and intellectual development of my own. However, I did not realize the impact of my experience in France until much later.

The summer we left the country, we had been house-sitting in Cambridge in a large home on Acacia Street. As departure time came, the extra bedrooms filled up with my mother, my mother-in-law, and several friends all of whom came to say good-bye. My mother-in-law added her usual extravagant touch, stuffing three dozen caramel custards, which she had taken a fancy to, into our refrigerator. Ill from my shots, I could not even touch the custartds, and dragged in and out of bed. Herb, meanwhile, became obsessed with taking our cat with us and went out to buy a carrier. Mother was outraged. "Does he think more about the cat than about you?" she queried.

I was too sick to focus, but I didn't think Sybil should go to Paris, as much as I loved her. We had invested a lot of devotion in that cat, curing her of ringworm, which I then contracted, and getting her out of trees that summer in Cambridge when she first discovered the outdoors. Herb's cousins in Holyoke agreed to take her and finally Herb capitulated, but it was so late at that point that his cousin had to fly up to get her in his small private plane. My mother shook her head in disbelief, and even Mildred Mason was stunned.

A large group of well-wishers gathered at the docks and expected to join us in our stateroom with champagne and a cake that said "Bon Voyage," but we discovered that student passage was like a camp excursion—no visitors allowed. Our stateroom was a tiny cabin with just enough room to slide in between the bunk beds and the single dresser. We were not daunted. France and Europe were before us.

The voyage was long. I was able to finish Tolstoy's *Anna Karenina* and start Dostoevsky's *The Idiot*. Our ship, as if to extend the uncertainty of its identity—American, Greek, German—decided not to land at Le Havre as scheduled, but dumped us instead at Southampton, England, where we had to proceed on our own, with two metal footlockers and many bags, to the boat train. Fortunately, English friends cheered us up by appearing in the boarding tender to greet us at Southampton and took us for a meal before we got on the train at night. We arrived in Paris at the end of the next day, and collapsed into our small hotel, the Jean Bart, near the Jardin du Luxembourg. This was our home for several months until we finally found an apartment.

I had a week or two before I had to report to work at the American School, so we decided to go to Mont Saint Michel and a few other spots in Normandy. We were joined by a young Californian, who had that scrubbed fresh-faced look—he always looked as if he had just stepped out of a shower—that we now began to recognize as uniquely American. We drove to the coast in our little Renault and stayed overnight in a bed and breakfast halfway up the endless flights of turning steps that comprise the landscape of Mont Saint Michel. Years later when two of my children went to France and visited the site, they were incredulous that I had climbed all of the stairs to the cathedral at the top of the town. "Mom, how did you do it? All those steps and more than once?" (I had made three visits there while we were in France.)

I have to stop and think about it now. I am not sure how I did it except at the time it didn't seem extraordinary. I was determined to do everything, take in all of the sights and sounds that the world offered. I suppose my father's relentless pressure and my own denial made me even more resolved. I simply did not acknowledge my disability as a barrier to anything. I stopped to rest from time to time as I ascended the steps, but there were shops to visit and views along the way. Our room at the top looked down at the ocean below, and we could watch the tide come in each day and cover the road out to the island. Our American friend, unlike Herb and me, had no fear of heights, and almost made us faint when he jumped on top of the wall outside the cathedral and pointed his camera at the crashing waves below while he teetered on the ledge.

When we returned to Paris, we explored many of the city's tourist spots. We were joined on our night out in Montmartre by Carlos, a

Colombian student we had met on the boat. As we wandered around the streets, we noticed the billboards on the clubs: *"Les nus les plus oses du monde"* (the most daring nudes in the world), one of them said. We finally chose a more modest place that simply said "Striptease." During the performance, which included a tacky chorus line and a couple of pale and tired-looking stripteasers, Carlos became enraged, shouting, "Shame, shame!" He jumped up on the table to scold the performers, who ignored him with supreme indifference. The audience began to shout, *"Taisez-vous!"* (shut up) and other less polite epithets, and a waiter came over to quiet him. But by that time we had decided to leave anyway and we went on to a cafe.

During our first year in Paris it became clear to me that our roles were going to be clearly differentiated. Herb, who had been given a grant to write a version of the Gilgamesh epic—not a modest goal—easily took on and nurtured the role of young poet and seeker of truth. I, on the other hand, had come to a job and brought in a salary. No part of my life, for the moment, was as a student, scholar, or writer. I accepted this at the time because I was excited about the opportunity to be part of this new adventure, but also because in the 1950s I had very few role models of wives who developed their own vocations.

I soon made a place for myself at the American School, which mainly served the American business and diplomatic community and some Anglo-French families that wanted American connections. When it was time for me to appear at the school, Herb drove me over to Boulogne. The headmaster, who had the Dickensian name of Mr. Wedge, was a square stout man with a florid complexion. I later discovered that he could turn purple when he had one of his coughing fits, which made his eyes bulge and his collar buttons pop off. He greeted me warmly. "Dr. Mason, welcome to the American School of Paris!"

No matter how much I protested that year and the next that I was not *Doctor* Mason, that I had not finished my degree, Mr. Wedge insisted on the title. This misplaced promotion annoyed at least one member of the faculty, Douglas McKee, who took almost a year to warm up to me and who would give me mock greetings ("Well, good morning, *Doctor* Mason") or play students off of me ("I don't know the answer. Why don't you ask *Doctor* Mason?"). Douglas had an acid tongue that could subdue the most arrogant teenager. He had been in the army during World War II and stayed in France to teach half-time and to work as a literary agent the rest of the time. He was a handsome lean man with fierce blue eyes that could nail an obnoxious student to the wall, and despite his initial hostility, we eventually became good friends.

It didn't take long to discover that Mr. Wedge had no control over the students, who generally ran amuck unless you took control in the classroom. When there was a serious discipline problem, Mr. Wedge simply brought in the parents for an ineffectual meeting with him, the teacher, and the student, so I soon developed my own disciplinary strategies. Some teachers were more successful than others at keeping the students in order. One teacher who was not always successful was Al Donnelly, one of my favorite people, who later became the godfather of my daughter Cathleen when she was born in Paris in 1960. He was a tall, gentle, ascetic-looking man who married a Frenchwoman during the Second World War and stayed in France because she refused to live in America. When I passed his ninth grade homeroom in the morning, I would glance in and see Al standing in front of his desk, swaying slightly, as if he was buffeted by the waves of noise and chaos that surrounded him. He never raised his voice, but he had a deep resounding delivery when he spoke. Eventually the students would wind down and respond to his enduring presence, and then Al had them. Al was often in a fragile state of health—he had respiratory illnesses and spent winter vacations at spas or in sunnier climates, sometimes with his wife and some of their six children and sometimes alone—but he also had a great resilience that the students responded to.

I became good friends also with three of the women who taught at the school. Rosemarie Clark, a frequent companion on our weekend trips, was Cathleen's godmother. She came from Brooklyn and returned home each summer to visit her mother. She had the sharp wit and ironic humor of a true New Yorker, and she kept a compassionate but determined detachment from her middle school students. She clearly was not intellectually stimulated by her teaching, but she accepted this as a trade-off for staying in Paris so that she could enjoy its culture as well as the less definable French "way of life." During the winter, she became a weekend skier in all of the popular places where young singles congregated. I met a series of her eligible bachelor friends—an American journalist, an Italian businessman, and a Frenchman with whom she had really fallen in love, but who left her to marry a young Frenchwoman, more acceptable to his family. Like many expatriates at that time, she lived in a tiny apartment—housing was scarce even for Parisians—with very few conveniences but a great location on the Left Bank. Rosemarie was one of the first members of the faculty to make me feel at home at the school. No nonsense—she took you as you were, with lots of humor and joie de vivre. On our trips together to Amsterdam or the Loire Valley I noticed that she drank a bit too much, but I was shocked when I learned years after my Paris life that Rosemarie had died of alcoholism.

Cecily Robertson, a tall gangling Scotswoman, who looked straight out of a British movie on girls' boarding schools, lived with her mother in an artist's studio on Rue Danton. Her mother, once a well-known Australian actress (so she said), was always as ready as her daughter to have a party or take a trip—we met once in Belgium at Bruges for the weekend. Sometimes we would go to a film together and I remember being amazed the first time I realized that Cecily had a trick knee, which caused her to suddenly rise from her seat in the theater, all six feet of her, and stand briefly at attention before sinking back into her chair. It was a startling event until you became accustomed to it. Her atelier was always cold, heated only by a coal stove, and her elderly mother would wrap herself in blankets to serve us proper English tea and biscuits. Cecily taught history and tried to assist Wedge in his administrative duties. I don't think she was more efficient than he was but she never missed a day of work and was always ready for the fray. I liked to think of her in retirement in her English cottage in Devon—her mother died while Cecily was still teaching. I am sure her house was cold and damp, but I imagine her in the garden, digging in her flower beds, or serving tea to the vicar.

My third friend was Annemarie Calvet, who had taught at the school since it opened after the war. She was a handsome Frenchwoman with black hair pulled back into a generous twist. Offputting at first because of her short temper and cutting dismissal of anyone she considered a fool (Mr. Wedge was frequently her target), she was by far the most interesting and well-educated member of the faculty. She read widely in many languages, traveled all over the world, had taught a few years at a private school near Boston, and kept up with all the literary and cultural events of Paris. She lived in a spacious inherited apartment on Rue Sarrette with her elderly cook, who had served her family for at least two generations. Annemarie was particularly fond of Rosemarie, and frequently invited her to dinner with us for a delicious French meal. She rarely spoke about the war but I gathered that the family had suffered many kinds of losses. At first I wondered if the war had been responsible for her not marrying, but her sister, who was living and working at that time in Ethiopia, had stayed single also. When I got to know Annemarie better, I realized that she probably had not married by choice. She and her sister were both very independent women and might have rejected the typical bourgeois married life. Every summer Annemarie took passage on a freighter and traveled to different parts of the world. She told me with great glee that on a trip to Morocco, a young boy at one of the villages she visited was so worried about her single status that he promised to arrange a marriage for her. I admired Annemarie and enjoyed her acerbic wit, but at the time, I found that her fierce independence and sharp tongue kept me from developing a very close relationship.

Other members of the faculty came from all over the United States and occasionally England, Scotland, and Ireland, and made up a strange but fascinating community. Students remember the school vividly. Years later, whenever former graduates reappeared in my life, they would speak of missing the camaraderie we had at the school. We were all foreigners together, and they had felt uprooted, taken from their basketball games and their local high school culture. They never recovered, they said, and often felt like foreigners when they went back to the United States to go to college and to live.

I never felt that my disability made much difference to my students. The American School building had no elevator so they would pass me daily going up and down the stairs to my classes and to the faculty lunchroom, but I don't remember feeling that I slowed traffic or that anyone had to get out of my way. The parents were more obviously surprised to find me on the faculty, but I only saw them at our yearly parents' receptions, which were generously supplied with French wines and champagne, and my recollection of most of the parents is that they fortified themselves heavily and were slapping Mr. Wedge on the back or stumbling around trying to find the bathrooms.

At Christmas time and at the end of the school year, the faculty gathered for a magnificent banquet, prepared by our French chef and given to us by the board of directors to soften the impact of our tiny salaries and the scars of doing battle with undisciplined teenagers. The meal, always six or seven courses with accompanying wines, mellowed even Douglas McKee and Annemarie Calvet and brought to their knees the Scotsman, Mr. Durning, and his landlady (who, we figured, was something more than that), Madame Dubus, a member of the French department.

It was still postwar France in 1957 when we arrived in Paris. The city was pinched and gray and wracked by the war experience. (When Frenchmen met it took them less than ten minutes to discover from each other what each one had done during the war.) Housing was scarce. Consumer goods were not plentiful and "conveniences" that the United States had already taken on as a religion were not available; we had no refrigerator or appliances. These hardships made friendships more precious. The passionate pursuit of the spiritual and moral questions of the day replaced, to some extent, the material commodities that North Americans were indulging in so eagerly. There was an air in our lives that anything unexpected could happen. We could meet the great minds of Europe or witness miracles or revolutions. But in fact, the Algerian war was tearing France apart and almost created a civil war. Starting in the fall of 1954, the Algerian revolutionary movement had begun a fight to end Algeria's colonial relationship to France. The conflict did not end until July 1962 when Algeria won its full independence. During our years in Paris, we witnessed a bitter struggle between those who insisted that Algeria be kept as an integral part of France and those who recognized that independence was inevitable. President Charles de Gaulle led the government from open hostililty and fighting to peace and the final settlement, infuriating the army officers and the French settlers, who felt betrayed. During our second year, de Gaulle had to quell an army revolt of the paratroopers that threatened to take over Paris and depose his government.

My other life in Paris—outside the American School—was the one I shared with Herb. I shared his enthusiasm for travel and exploration of France and Italy, and I also became part of his discovery of the world of Catholic writers and scholars. I was fascinated at the time, and I did not realize until years later how peripheral I felt in this world. We were invited into homes and salons that were usually closed to Americans. Partly through chance and partly through self-confidence and an undaunted curiosity, Herb was introduced to some of the major Catholic intellectu-als—François Mauriac, Gabriel Marcel, Jean Daniélou, Louis Massignon, and others. He had been drawn to the Catholic Church for some time, and soon he made the decision to convert and started his instruction with a priest at the American Catholic Church of Paris. His imminent conversion sparked interest and even a kind of rivalry among his new French mentors, who each wanted to claim him as one of the enlightened. We were adopted as an innocent pair from the New World whom the French felt might be worth shaping into something. The focus was on Herb, the young poet and convert, and I was the supportive wife. I think my disability made us even more interesting as a couple to some. The fact that Herb had chosen to marry someone disabled fit into the self-sacrificing spirituality that charac-terized the Catholic Church we knew then. Although no one explicitly stated it, I got the feeling we represented a model Christian couple, partic-ularly if I, too, converted. My feelings about all of this were confused, but I certainly considered the possibility of a conversion.

Many of our trips became half pilgrimages. Our Catholic friends insisted that we must see this special cathedral or that unique monastery. One weekend we went with friends to the Benedictine monastery at St. Anselm in Normandy to hear Gregorian chant sung. Our group included Rosemarie Clark and two young men, Albrecht Smit, a South African

diplomat and an aristocrat with a long German lineage who was also converting to Catholicism, and his friend, perhaps lover, a beautiful dark-eyed
Englishman named David. At the monastery, Rosemarie and I were treated
differently from the men. They were hustled to a special audience with the
presiding head of the monastery and a visiting bishop, while we were left
to walk in the gardens of the cloister. Albrecht later confided that he was
very nervous about how to approach the clerics and whether or not he
should kiss the bishop's ring. The service was glorious, and as I sat at the
back of the chapel where Rosemarie and I had been placed, I experienced
conflicting emotions that would become an increasing part of my life. On the
one hand, I was captivated by Gregorian chant, by the ascetic beauty of the
music as well as of the monastery and indeed of much of the ritual of the
Catholic Church. On the other hand, I felt that I was being engulfed and
pressured into an institution that gave me second class status, where a woman
could never be a priest and where she would often sit on the sidelines.
Changes would come to the church after Vatican II, the ecumenical council
convened in 1962 by Pope John XXIII that helped move the church into the
modern world, giving more participation to the laiety. However, in the chapel
at St. Anselm, I felt the power and exclusiveness of the patriarchal world that
the church had so effectively nurtured since the Middle Ages.

We stayed that night in a little inn, the only one in St. Anselm. Our host
was delighted to have a party of five people and he served a magnificent
meal of six courses accompanied by several excellent local wines. We sat for
hours in front of a huge fireplace, which, we later discovered when we
went to bed, was the chief source of heat in the inn. (We were given hot
bricks to warm our beds.) After cheese and fruit, we cracked nuts and
sipped brandy and speculated on what it would have been like to live in the
past during some of the glorious days of the monastery. David was sure he
would have had a good life, because he would have been part of the aristocracy. Albrecht concurred. But the rest of us were not sure.

Among our literary encounters soon after we had settled into our Paris
life was a meeting with Alice Toklas, Gertrude Stein's partner. Bill Alfred
supplied us with a letter of introduction because he had become friends
with them on his trip abroad after the war. As a young soldier in World
War II, he sent them his own care packages when he heard that they were
living poorly in the country outside of Paris. They welcomed him warmly
when he came to visit them later. Even though I had seen pictures of Stein
and Toklas in their later years, I was still stunned when the tiny figure of
Alice Toklas opened the door of her apartment for us at 27 Rue de
Fleurus. She was quite bent over with arthritis, but her bright dark eyes

still looked out sharply through the bangs of that familiar short bob of hair.

"So you are the friends of William Alfred," she said. "Come in, come in." She had invited us for tea and showed us through a foyer and through the salon to a couch and some chairs near a small coal stove that barely warmed the chilly dark rooms. There was a table set for tea, that she served along with rather dry biscuits. I tried not to look around too obviously for famous paintings, but I couldn't help noticing that there were some still hanging on the walls. As Alice Toklas explained later, most of the Picassos and other treasures were now in museums. She told us how the Germans at the end of the war had packed and crated all of the art collection in the apartment, preparing to take it with them in retreat. She and Stein were living in the country, but they heard that the concierge had diverted the Germans. When they returned, they found all the crates still there packed for removal. As I sat by the grate with my tea, listening to her talk of the famous artists and writers who passed through those rooms and how she was often left to entertain the wives, I was struck by her fatigue. How tired she must be of reciting the legends of the 1920s for a never-ending stream of young Americans! Her sharp wit and memories were vivid, but her conversation was also interlaced with the concerns of the elderly—living in a cold, postwar Paris on very modest means. She had difficulty getting the coal delivered, she said, and the fire kept going out, and she could no longer count on her *femme de ménage* to keep the large apartment in order and to do her shopping. The daily anxieties and difficulties of old age outweighed the glories of the past. I could understand her fondness for Bill Alfred because he always addressed the immediate human needs of a person no matter how famous or obscure. In fact, it was Bill who influenced Alice Toklas's decision a few years later to spend her last days in a convent in Italy, in the care of the same order of nuns who had nursed Bernard Berenson, the art historian and famous collector, before he died.

After our visit, Herb tried to offer his services to deliver coal or tend to her stove, but he was given a cool response. She said proudly that she could manage on her own. She did read one of Herb's plays and wrote him an enthusiastic and detailed commentary on his work, suggesting possible producers to contact. Her literary criticism was sharp and relevant.

Sometimes, moving between my daily world of the American School, with its long days of teaching, correcting papers, and preparing classes, and Herb's heady intellectual world, I felt schizophrenic. My teaching world was prosaic but demanding. My other world was stimulating, but one in which I was an observer only. I was feeling the absence of any creative or unique work of my own, and I resolved then that secondary school teaching—though often engaging—was not where I wished to develop a career. In addition, I began to feel confined because I could not drive, which made me completely dependent on Herb when I wanted to go anywhere. Ever since I got my first car the year I transferred to Radcliffe College, I treasured my mobility and freedom. Now they were disappearing.

By the end of November, the dampness of our hotel and the gray climate of Paris afflicted me with a sinus infection, and so during Christmas vacation we went in search of the sun in Spain. After driving to Barcelona, we took a boat to Majorca, triggering my first and only experience with seasickness. We started off innocently, unaware of what lay ahead. Joining a group of people for lunch, we found the conversation, mostly in English and French, very lively. However, I soon began to notice that one by one our companions rose from the table abruptly and excused themselves. The last person to leave before us was a German gentleman who clicked his heels and strode rapidly out of the dining room. Soon after, Herb and I looked at each other and realized we had better get to our cabin. When we went below, we discovered the halls and bathroom were a war zone. People were strewn all over, and we soon followed in deathly seasickness. When we arrived in Majorca, all of us tottered onto land looking white and drawn, barely able to acknowledge each other in farewells.

The rest of our vacation did not get much better. It rained almost every day, and the town was crowded with American sailors on leave. Our hotel was huge and quite elegant, but built for sunny weather. We spent Christmas Eve attending mass in a cavernous church with no pews, and on Christmas Day—still rainy—we ate our holiday dinner in an almost empty restaurant. I felt quite homesick. However, the next day we went to visit an elderly painter, a friend of Alice Toklas's, who showed us many of his paintings and reminisced about his Paris days and his friendship with Stein and her group. He seemed grateful that we had come to see him and had shown interest in his work. I began to have a warmer feeling about Majorca.

The next day, the sun came out and we drove around the island through the narrow streets, noticing that a shabby outer wall or series of buildings often hid a beautiful inner garden with an elegant house just visible through the gateway. We also drove up to the mountain town where George Sand and Chopin had lived. Their villa was not impressive—we wondered why Chopin went to this rainy spot for a tuberculosis cure—but the experience of driving up and down the steep mountain road, which was very narrow and lacked guardrails, was thrilling and even terrifying. One of the pleasant memories I have of Majorca was the taste and scent of Spanish oranges; the roads were strewn with orange peels wherever you drove. Another familiar sight were the military patrols, consisting of two soldiers who strolled along the roads with no apparent function except to keep down unemployment.

The big event of our life in Paris that winter was that we found an apartment. We had previously moved from the Jean Bart to a housekeeping hotel in the fifteenth arrondissement, which had some minimal cooking facilities and our own bathroom, but it was noisy and dreary and frequented by many American soldiers. In February, Herb's half sister, Persis, whose husband was in the diplomatic service in Paris, called us about an apartment that was available. It was owned by a friend of theirs, Sophie, who belonged to the White Russian community. The apartment was on 20 Rue Thiers in Boulogne-sur-Seine, not far from the American School, so it was perfect for us. We eagerly arranged to meet her at the apartment to look it over.

Sophie, a handsome blonde woman in her thirties, greeted us at the door in a friendly but rather arrogant manner, as if she were bestowing royal favors upon us. Behind her, in the shadows of the apartment, was a slim, rather worn looking woman with her hair tied up in a scarf. Her features were delicate and her posture and demeanor dignified and reticent. Sophie did not introduce her to us, but as she showed us through the rooms—there were four rooms including the kitchen—her companion followed behind her silently. Finally, after we had eagerly agreed to rent the place and were about to leave, Sophie turned to the woman. "This is Olga Lebedeff. She has been the *femme de ménage* here and can continue to come if you wish." I shook her hand and said I would be very happy if she would come and help me in the apartment. Sophie looked a bit scornful at my friendliness. Madame Lebedeff, as I was to going to call her, smiled and nodded her head nervously.

Madame Lebedeff became my friend, although she was always reserved and anxious to fulfill her role as a servant with exactitude. I gradually got to know her story. She had come from aristocracy in Russia, and one day she brought an album filled with pictures of her early life before exile. Her husband had been a military officer, and she was born into a wealthy landowning family, portrayed in the photographs sitting in the gardens among fountains and carefully pruned flower beds. She and the other little girls in her fading pictures wore white dresses and tied their long hair back with large silk bows. They sat for their photographs with hands crossed demurely in their laps. The boys stood behind them in white sailor suits. Madame Lebedeff's husband had been killed along with many others in her family, and their lands, of course, had been confiscated.

Sometimes, after Madame had finished the sweeping and dusting and cleaning in the apartment, we would have tea and *patisserie* together if I was at home. Once she played the piano for me—a lovely Chopin prelude. She shook her head in dismay at her rough and stiff fingers. "I practiced and practiced as a child and my father was so proud of me. I would perform for the whole family," she sighed. She still gave lessons to children in her *quartier* to supplement her income as a *femme de ménage*. I had never seen such frugality and dignified poverty before, a way of life common to those in exile and others, too, in Europe in that postwar decade. One day she brought me a yogurt culture so that I could make my own yogurt, an everyday French staple that was very cheap to buy. When I returned home to the United States, I could not adjust to the waste and plenty of the American way, and found myself storing up dozens of paper bags and bits of string and thinking of Olga Lebedeff.

Before we left Paris, Madame Lebedeff made her first visit back to Russia since she left in exile. She had a daughter who was married to a French-Russian engineer, who arranged her trip. The daughter lived in Algeria, and Madame visited her every summer. The Russian visit was thrilling to her, and she told me how she found a nephew living in the basement of one of the family mansions in Moscow. The house had been taken over as a government building.

As spring came, we took more trips out of Paris on weekends. Unscheduled and ready for the unexpected, we would head off with a friend, often a colleague from the American School. We drove to Normandy, to Bruges and Brussels, and once all the way up to Amsterdam on Saturday, just in time to see the Rembrandts in the museum before it closed, and all the way back to Paris on Sunday, when I would prepare for my next day of teaching. We covered the chateaux country in the Loire Valley and we especially loved Burgundy and the hill town of Vezelay. This was where we met Douglas McKee's friends, Dorothy and Lesley Adams, who lived in an eighteenth-century villa, built out over the valley, looking from its terrace over the village wall onto rolling Burgundy countryside. The brother and sister had been living there for five years. Lesley, an architect, came to France first and established himself professionally, and then bought a villa and brought over Dorothy, who was in a wheelchair from polio, which she had contracted later in her life. By profession, she was a writer, but her hobby was cooking and she served us many gourmet meals on our visits to the villa.

I first saw their home after we were introduced to them by Douglas in a cafe where we had stopped after a visit to Vezelay's Romanesque cathedral, which sits above the winding streets at the top of the hill town. As Herb and I sat down at one of the small outside tables, we were hailed by Douglas, and we moved over to join the three of them. Lesley, a tall thin dark-haired man, rose and introduced us to Dorothy, who was sitting in her wheelchair at the table. You could tell the two were brother and sister, but Dorothy had sandy-colored hair and an almost quizzical look as she talked. They were both friendly and immediately ordered espressos and pastry for everyone. After we had talked for a while and discussed the sound and light show that we just watched at the cathedral, Dorothy insisted that we come to see their villa, which was down the street about halfway between the cathedral and our hotel. We gladly accepted, having heard Douglas describe the beauty of their place.

I walked down the cobbled street to their gates beside Dorothy, who was maneuvering her wheelchair, carefully guided by Lesley. The going was rough for both crutches and wheelchair but we managed. No one commented on our precipitous journey. Douglas and Herb walked in front of us, talking but ready to assist if needed. We entered a rather ordinary courtyard that in no way prepared me for the grandeur and beauty of the villa— a house on one floor with spacious rooms looking onto a terra cotta terrace, where you could see the entire valley. The rooms were furnished with elegant eighteenth-century antiques, although Dorothy proudly showed us her completely modernized kitchen. There was a large basement level that included a wine cellar and remnants of corridors that had once connected the villa to other houses in the village.

Our visit was the first of many. Dorothy seemed happiest when she was preparing one of her elegant meals and when she was in the middle of the conversation and gossip that went on for hours at the table with guests— traveling Americans, neighboring French villa owners, or fellow American expatriates, many of whom had established themselves in their own villas in the hill towns of Burgundy. Although committed to living in France, the expatriates liked to complain about the conditions in their adopted country and at the same time romanticize the America they abandoned.

Meeting Dorothy was the first time I had a chance to know someone else who had polio. I felt that I was confronting myself, although Dorothy was ten or fifteen years older than I and far less mobile. She rarely got out of her wheelchair, and even then she took steps with the greatest of difficulty. We never discussed our physical condition in any detail. Somewhat to my surprise, I wanted to talk about our disabilities and to share our different experiences. I had not had a conversation with my fleeing roommate at Tanglewood, who had disappeared as soon as she saw me, obviously not wishing to identify with another disabled person. And I, too, had been relieved to get a different roommate. But now I was in a different situation. Dorothy and I were friends, or at least acquaintances, and I was ready to have a relationship with someone who shared my disability. I made several attempts to bring up the subject, but Dorothy cut me off with vague generalizations. "Oh, I got this later in my life," or "Lesley saved me from a boring life with my parents." I gather she came from a wealthy family and that she did not go back home very often and did not plan to return to the United States to live. Lesley spoke of her writing, but I never learned what she wrote or spoke with her about her life as a writer.

Dorothy did seem to have a sense of bitterness about her life, which was privileged but very circumscribed. She always kept a barrier of ironic commentary between herself and all others, and rarely spoke about personal matters. I wonder if she resented the fact that I was married. The last weekend we spent with the Adamses was after I was pregnant. It was also the last weekend I tried to ride in our little Renault in my very uncomfortable condition. I was clearly having difficulty getting my body around, and Dorothy was very sympathetic and considerate, offering me extra pillows and the most comfortable chairs. Yet she did not ask me anything about the actual imminent birth or about my becoming a mother or how I planned to manage a child. Perhaps the obviously domestic turn my life was taking made it more difficult for us to relate. I knew that I had something to learn from her, but I was unable to make the connection.

About ten years after we left France, we received a formal announcement from Lesley of Dorothy's death. No explanation of the cause. Her untimely death seemed ominous, and I felt again the regret of not having known her better as if, in some way, that would have helped me know myself.

Summer was a welcome relief from the demands of the American School. We planned a trip to Italy through the Alps in our little Renault, relying on the pre-tourist season in June to provide us with inexpensive reservations. Herb had a genius for finding luxurious hotels with cheap off-season rates in out-of-the-way places. Travel was his element. He loved to explore, to connect with people we had been told about—many of them from his new Catholic connections.

The highlight of our trip for me was Florence and the hill towns of Tuscany. I had been to Europe once before—after my graduation on a whirlwind trip through Venice, Florence, and Rome with my mother. I was overwhelmed and awestruck by the numbers of great works: the grandeur of Michelangelo's statues in Florence and his frescoes in the Sistine Chapel in Rome, and the Raphaels and Rubens and Titians and countless other treasures in all the palaces and churches in the cities. But this time in Florence we were able to spend several days, and I discovered the wholeness of the city's beauty. I no longer saw just a dizzying number of monuments and paintings and sculptures, but rather a living museum in the city itself, from the shops on the Ponte Vecchio to the great bronze doors of Ghiberti and to the Piazzale Michelangelo and its noble statue of David. We even attended an exhibition soccer game presented as a spectacle with all the players dressed in Renaissance costumes, looking as if they stepped out of paintings in the galleries. I also discovered the monastery of San Marco for the first time, and found in the frescoes of Fra Angelico new images that lasted with me longer than any other Italian works of art. We drove to Assisi to see the Giotto frescoes and to the hill towns of San Gimignano and Siena, where we sat in a cafe facing the cathedral and ate what seemed to us then the most superb lasagna and the most perfect wine we had ever tasted.

Unfortunately our good eating eventually got to Herb, who was stricken with a severe bout of colitis when we returned to Florence. We were staying in a small pensione where no one spoke English, but after trying as much Italian as I could muster, I managed to get the name of a local doctor. He came to the pensione and gave Herb a quick examination and prescribed some pills and a diet of rice. After he left, I realized I had to walk across the Ponte Vecchio in the high noonday sun to get to the pharmacy to buy the medication. I was suddenly faced with my vulnerability. Herb was sick. I could not drive, and although I knew I could get a taxi if I had to, I wanted to walk there myself as a kind of test, I suppose, of my strength and independence. I started out cheerfully, stopping at little shops along the way, but I did not realize what the noonday sun can do to your energy. By the time I found the pharmacy and bought the pills and started across the bridge again, I was flushed and exhausted and my heart was pounding with exertion. When I reached the pensione, my face had turned scarlet and I felt that I might collapse. Herb, who was looking as pale as a ghost, noticed my color. "Are you okay?" he asked.

"I'm fine," I lied. I didn't want to admit even to myself that I'd been so vulnerable. "But," I conceded, "I should not have gone out at high noon."

Perhaps the episode in Florence had a sobering effect on me. In any case, our stay in Rome was a mixed experience. On the one hand, we saw wonderful sights. We saw the city at night from a horse-drawn carriage, the Colosseum in moonlight, and the lights on the fountains at Tivoli. We went to excavations underneath San Giovanni e Paulo and at San Clemente, and we saw Michelangelo's Moses in San Paulo e Vinculo and the Fra Angelico chapel in the Vatican. At the catacombs we were guided by a monk who addressed the graffiti of former tourists with a sigh and remark, "We are all seeking immortality."

Another day we went to visit Father Bernard, the secretary of his order in Rome and one of the clergy Herb was told to contact. We drove up one afternoon to his monastery on one of Rome's hills, and we were greeted by him in the cloister. Father Bernard was a sandy-haired and tonsured cleric who seemed to me to be the quintessential smiling monk of the movies or picture books. He showed us around the ancient buildings and took us to the site of an excavation of two ancient towns discovered under the monastery. When we expressed surprise and admiration at the archaeological finds, he sighed a little. "Oh yes," he said, "they are always looking for new places to dig." Then he put his finger to his lips and whispered, "One of the brothers found some artifacts in the vegetable garden last summer." Looking around slyly, he continued, "but we have put them away and we'll say nothing about it. We must save the garden," he concluded, with his eyes twinkling.

Yet for all of its beauty and wonder, Rome made me feel sad. We had a pensione in the Piazza San Ignazio very near the Pantheon in a room with a balcony above a cafe. At night there was music—mandolins, guitars, I am not sure which—but I was overcome by waves of sadness even though the music and atmosphere was celebratory and gay. The contrast of the music and my inexplicable sadness filled me with a strange longing, and the feeling persisted throughout our stay. I think my reaction had something to do with the oppression of time and history. I heard ghosts in the Colosseum and thought of Byron's poem "Childe Harold" and the image of the dying Gaul killed by the Roman gladiator for the Romans' entertainment. I saw fading pageants in the churches. The triumphal Roman ruins and the modern versions built by Mussolini both seemed to me oppressive.

I was glad to get back to Paris, but I was stiff from sitting in our little Renault, which humiliated us going over the Swiss Alps by letting a Citroen—the smallest and cheapest car in France with only two horsepower to our four—pass us. On our arrival back, Herb landed in the American hospital with another attack of colitis. This time he had to stay in bed several days and keep to a strict bland diet. I took taxis to the hospital to see him, but I felt more in control here in Paris, with our familiar neighborhood and friends I could call on.

The next big event in our lives was Herb's confirmation in the Catholic Church. He and Albrecht Smit, our South African friend, were confirmed by Cardinal Marella, the papal nunzio in Paris, in an impressive ceremony at the American Catholic church in Paris. By that time our circle of French friends had enlarged. Herb had sought out the writer Robert Rochefort (his pen name), after reading a book of his, and we were taken into his family hospitably. We were also introduced to Madame Abeille, a collector of well-known writers, scholars, and priests. Herb particularly became part of her coterie and I, too, was often included. Most of these people represented the somewhat fanatic postwar spirituality of French Catholicism that I found difficult to embrace. I felt a subtle pressure to convert, partly from Herb—although he did not say so explicitly—but also because I felt I was missing something. Herb was a zealous convert, practicing acts of charity conscientiously. He would stop the car to help a clochard off the street or bring home foreign visitors to Paris whom he met in church and who needed assistance. I was moved by his dedication to good works, but at the same time, I resisted the notion of conversion for reasons about which I was not clear until years later. I often felt conflicted and I even tried to put myself in a state of readiness for conversion, learning some Catholic prayers and being particularly attentive at mass. But I did not have a revelation. I needed something that definite, and it never came, so I finally rejected the idea of joining the church. In time, I would see that my decision was partly due to my desire to hold on to my own identity, which seemed eroded by my dependence on Herb and by the interruption of my own intellectual pursuits. Although a conversion would make me part of the group, it would also be a capitulation of sorts. And so I stayed the observer.

Even more important than Herb's confirmation was his introduction in 1959 to Louis Massignon, an Orientalist and professor at the College de France. This meeting deeply affected our lives, particularly Herb's, because Massignon was responsible for his choosing a totally new field of study that would eventually lead him to a doctorate in Middle Eastern language and literature. Yvonne Chauffin, a novelist from Brittany, introduced Herb to Massignon as a poet and seeker of the spiritual way and as one who was interested in the ancient world and the Gilgamesh story. Almost immediately Massignon became the lost father, the seer, the guide, and the mentor that Herb had been seeking.

I first saw the professor outside of a church where Herb and I were going to attend a special service. He was white-haired, somberly dressed in black, and he carried himself erectly like a soldier (he had been in the military) except that the tilt of his head, particularly as he greeted you, was humble and slightly bowed and gave you the feeling of a medieval knight of courtesy who might offer to go on a quest to save your life.

He took my hand in both of his: "Madame, I am honored to make your acquaintance." He spoke in English—he was fluent in many languages including Arabic and Hebrew—but often used phrases that were translations from French, thus reminding you that he was a Frenchman above all else. His smile as he bowed his head slightly was gentle and self-effacing, but his eyes were piercingly blue and his glance direct.

I accompanied Herb to Massignon's apartment on Rue Monsieur many times, and listened with rapt attention to his stories of spiritual correspondences and encounters with people all over the world, particularly the Middle East, which was his scholarly field but also his life's passion. His wife, who would sometimes join us in their salon for tea after we sat alone with him in his study, was a rather awkward and angular woman, but very down-to-earth. She often would interrupt her husband's spellbinding stories of physical and spiritual and intellectual quests, in order to correct his facts and to downplay the drama of his narrative. Once she insisted, for instance, when he was relating a story in which he was ill in Turkey and facing imminent death, that he was not that ill at all and by no means on his deathbed. He stopped and shrugged a little impatiently, but then went on with his story. The contrast of man and wife—scholar and mystic and practical housewife—was striking and even amusing. I can still recall the fascination of those encounters with Massignon. It was a completely new world to me, but not one that I felt part of. Massignon's significance in my own spiritual and intellectual journey was not clear until much later.

10

FINAL DAYS, NEW BEGINNINGS: 1959–1960

The summer of 1959 was a climactic one for me. We went on a pilgrimage in July to Brittany, where Massignon had a country home that had been in his family for generations. Driving through Brittany was like returning to the ancient world, with landscapes dotted with pre-Christian dolmens and ancient towns huddling on the rocky coast. When we arrived at Massignon's large weather-beaten house, we were greeted by Madame Massignon, who was keeping track of the many visitors arriving from Paris and all over France—writers, professors, government officials, North African workers, and many different students. The purpose of the pilgrimage was to pray for reconciliation between Christians and Muslims, who had been torn apart by the French-Algerian war. Massignon had acted repeatedly on behalf of justice for the Algerians, and had used his personal influence with de Gaulle to plead for a settlement of the war, but that summer peace was not in sight and the bringing together of Muslims and Christians—of Algerians and French citizens—was certainly dangerous. Nevertheless, several hundred people came, some risking their safety.

The site of the pilgrimage was a small medieval church, the Chapel of the Seven Saints, in Vieux Marche near Plouaret, which was built on a dolmen connected with the story of the Seven Sleepers, a legend of a miracle that was shared by Christians and Moslems. The service was dedicated to peace and reconciliation, and Massignon arranged for representatives of both the Muslim and Christian faiths to be present at the mass, an unprecedented event in that church and probably any Catholic church.

Before the service, many people, including many local villagers, gathered in the courtyard to witness the strange procession of pilgrims joining together to worship. We sat on a stone wall with Massignon outside the church waiting for the service to begin, and I listened with admiration as he spoke to the villagers, using their Breton dialect and explaining how their ancient language connected with the history of the church and with the dolmen on which it had been built.

During the service, which included a recitation of some verses from the Qur'an in the dolmen crypt below the Chapel of the Seven Saints, I felt awed by the power that these great religious traditions had in shaping history, and by the amazing continuity of human spirituality. I did not, however, feel committed to one particular faith, and again I felt as if I were a guest in someone else's house.

At the end of mass and as the afternoon began to turn to dusk, the crowd became a procession and walked to a bonfire, where an ancient Breton epic was recited telling of the building of the chapel. The next day after a visit to the "holy spring" (with seven sources), we walked to a nearby meadow where long tables had been set up and where we all shared a meal of lamb and couscous. Herb and I sat next to two Algerian men who exchanged halting French with us (ours was better than theirs but not fluent) and also with Yvonne Chauffin, who had come to the pilgrimage with four bright-eyed little grandsons. One of her sons was serving in the French army in Algeria, a situation that represented the kind of personal agony many French families faced who were against the war in Algeria. The priest who officiated at the service represented a very small minority of clergy who would support such a pilgrimage, and we were told that he was taking a great risk by being there.

I was very moved by the pilgrimage but I was also going through a more personal trauma at the time. I discovered in late spring, after experiencing some terrible morning sickness, that I was pregnant. It was not a planned pregnancy, and my first reaction was one of panic. I had no idea what a pregnancy would mean to me physically—how difficult it might be to carry or to deliver a baby. The doctor, a French obstetrician with no talent for relating to pregnant women, suggested I should have an X-ray during labor to see if I had any anatomical condition that would make a natural delivery dangerous, although he did not anticipate any problem. Actually, what seemed even more frightening to me was how we were going to survive without my working at the school. Even though the French were very generous with maternity leave—and I qualified for French social benefits because I was paid in francs, not dollars—I knew that I couldn't manage teaching at the American school while I was pregnant.

My mother saved my letter to her announcing the news, and I am amazed today by how calm and pleased and together I sounded, but the truth is I felt nothing of the kind. I was sick and very anxious. How would I manage to care for an infant? How could we afford to live? Herb had used up his small grant the first year we were in France, and his tutoring did not constitute a livable salary. He was euphoric about having a child but did not seem to be facing our real financial situation. I thought seriously of going home alone to my mother's house in New Jersey, but I wondered what would happen to our marriage. My sister Betty returned home to have her first child when I was in high school, because her husband was doing an internship at New York Hospital. I am sure it was not easy for her to live at home, but at least she saw her husband frequently on his weekends off. I decided I would see it through in Paris.

As it turned out, the most difficult part of my pregnancy was the isolation I felt from people who could talk to me about what to expect in the months ahead, advise me on what I would need for a layette, or share with me the experience of having your first child. Our French friends were excited and thrilled, but they were mostly priests, scholars, single men and women, and older couples. Almost no one we knew had young children, so I had no network of young mothers to call upon and certainly no one who was disabled and had a child. My only shared experience was with Yvonne Wasilewski, a young Frenchwoman married to an American major, who lived with their three-year-old daughter in an apartment across the street from us in Boulogne-sur-Seine.

We met the Wasilewskis that spring before I learned I was pregnant. I didn't know Stan had a wife at first. When the concierge from the apartment across the street came to us for help with *l'Americain*, it was in desperation. The American major had been drinking for six or seven days without stop and was growing more and more unapproachable, shouting and yelling periodically so that he could be heard even on our side of the street. Herb went over to see Stan cautiously at first, but he had managed to make contact and eventually he persuaded him to go into the hospital for treatment because he was in very serious physical condition, especially for a man in his late forties. When Stan was discharged from the hospital, Yvonne was in their apartment and had with her their three-year-old daughter, Michelle.

As it turned out, Stan had two wives—one in Boston, a Polish American woman, and a common-law wife, Yvonne, in Paris. I met Yvonne for the first time when Stan insisted that we come for dinner; he wanted to thank us for pulling him through his latest drinking bout. Yvonne was about twenty at most, a thin pale French girl with upswept hair and large eyes that rarely looked at you directly. She alternately embraced and rebuked her little girl. She was not abusive to her, but scolded her in a rapid patois French, almost a nervous habit. At supper that night, she served us all before she sat down with Michelle, helping the child to spoon her food. I did not notice her eating anything herself. The television set was on while we ate, placed prominently beside the table facing Stan. There was only one channel on French television at that time, and the selection was poor. Stan and Herb exchanged news about the Boston Red Sox, and we talked in general about our common Boston memories. The meal was delicious, Yvonne's French cooking with a touch of American in the onions, which Stan claimed were the potatoes of Poland. We didn't talk much of his past, but he told Herb that he had been in the Second World War and then the Korean War before he was posted back to France somewhere in the northern provinces, at a base near Yvonne's home village. Stan glanced at Yvonne—we were speaking in English, which apparently she did not understand very well. "She doesn't feel at home here in the city," he said. "She has no one to talk to and Michelle has no playmates." Yvonne looked over at the mention of Michelle's name. I wasn't sure whether Yvonne understood his reference to her or not. It made me a little uncomfortable. Our conversation continued in the general area of mutual reminiscences— a familiar pattern among Americans who have a fairly casual relationship with each other abroad.

As we were leaving, Stan walked us to the door and stopped for a moment outside. He addressed himself to me now. "I sure would appreciate it if you could invite Yvonne over some time to talk. Your French is good, isn't it? Probably better than mine." He went on to explain that she wanted to go home to her village to visit, but he did not want her to go. He was afraid she might not come back. I said I'd be glad to have her over, and suggested she come the next Saturday afternoon, when I would be home alone.

On Saturday morning I went to the Prix Unic and bought some paper and crayons for Michelle to play with, as I had very few things for children around the apartment. They arrived promptly at the agreed hour, entering the apartment shyly. Michelle was a sunny child with a smiling round face and bright curious eyes, an almost comic contrast to the rather sharp and delicate features of her mother. When I remarked on how much she looked like Stan, Yvonne smiled and pinched her little girl's cheek gently. "*Surement*—indeed—she is the daughter of her papa," she said.

We talked rather awkwardly at first, of weather and shopping. My colloquial French was really quite limited. All of a sudden Yvonne broke into a new subject. "Is it a nice place, this Boston?" she asked.

I told her a little about the city and answered her questions about America. She began to talk about her life with Stan—how they had met at the army base outside of her town. She was very young, she said, and it was exciting to know an American major. They met at the bar and cafe where her mother worked and where Yvonne sometimes helped serve, too. Stan brought them luxuries from the PX—nylon stockings, instant coffee, American cigarettes. Sometimes he came for her in an army jeep. They dated and he did not tell her that he was married.

Her account was very unsentimental, almost brutally matter-of-fact. When she became pregnant, he promised to divorce his wife and to take her to America, but he never did either of these things. The people in her village looked on her with increasing disapproval. Her mother told her that she had better leave him, because without a marriage license, she would get no money for child support. Instead, after Michelle was born, Yvonne went and lived with him somewhere off the army base, away from the unfriendly army wives. His drinking bouts, which he kept hidden at first, got much worse; he began to get physically abusive, violent and frightening to the child. She would leave him periodically, and he would call her at the cafe and beg her forgiveness and make promises he didn't keep. Her mother would answer the phone and shout at him to go home to America. When the doctor called from the American hospital, Yvonne's mother tried to conceal the message from her, but the proprietor of the cafe told Yvonne of the call, which had also come through the local police station.

Her story came out in a quiet but continual stream of French. I followed her clearly because she was talking less rapidly and energetically than was usual for most Parisians.

"He loves Michelle very much," she said at one point, turning to her little girl who was busily drawing, "but he has another daughter in America." She shrugged with an inscrutable French gesture of fatalism.

"If he goes back to America, he will surely send you support for Michelle, won't he?" I realized as I spoke that I was saying something quite inappropriate. Her reply was angry and cut through our quiet exchange with bitterness.

"I hope he goes back—soon," she said in a flash. "It would be better if he would leave us alone." But then she continued, looking at Michelle lying on her stomach on the floor absorbed in making streaks of red, yellow, and green on her paper. "Michelle misses him *tellement* when we are apart. She cries for him when we go back to the village."

I felt very inadequate in my responses. A whole world of experience and pain lay between us, although I was at least nine or ten years older than Yvonne. I said something bland about hoping things would work out for all of them. She smiled briefly and made her departure with one of those useful

French social exchanges that relieves you of finding the right words to say.

After that afternoon, I did not see Yvonne again until the next fall when I was five months pregnant and home alone a lot. Herb took over my job at the American School, solving our financial problem for the year but leaving me without any sense of community. I felt lonely in a way I could not have imagined to be possible a few months before. The apartment, which seemed such a treasure when we found it, began to seem dreary and confining and very characterless except for a few nostalgic mementos of the Russian exiles who owned it—a heavy brass samovar or an embroidered shawl thrown over the worn couch. Other than these items, the apartment held only the anonymous belongings of those who don't feel they belong.

Since I stopped teaching, my days seemed long and tedious. My daily social contacts included greetings with the concierge, the people in the local stores where one shopped for daily food, and my neighbor across the hall—a middle-aged Frenchwoman with pale orange hair who traveled from health spa to health spa in the south of France, seeking cures for the many ailments she described to me when she returned home. I also had a regular monthly visit from the French social worker assigned to me. She was very business-like and told me of all my rights and privileges—and there were many—as a prospective mother in France, including an allowance for baby clothes and equipment, and compensation payments because my health did not permit me to work. Not even these visits seemed to make the approaching event any more concrete to me, and my anxieties grew as my own physical complaints increased. I wanted to share my fears with someone intimately and to ask a thousand questions about little details and real and imagined problems.

Finally, in desperation, I decided to ask Yvonne to come over. She had apparently just returned home after another stormy separation from Stan. Her voice was a little uncertain when I telephoned her, a little hesitant in accepting the invitation, I thought. But she came. I bought a book for Michelle, and the little girl took it eagerly and sat on the stool reading it. Our conversation opened up quickly. My condition made an obvious topic.

"Do you suffer much with carrying the child?" Yvonne asked after scanning me quickly to assess the stage of my pregnancy. I mentioned a few of my complaints, back trouble and others, and Yvonne shook her head back and forth, making a rapid clucking noise of sympathy.

"Oh, Madame," she said, "I suffered so many things with Michelle." Then she began a long account of all the difficulties of her pregnancy, and of her sister's pregnancy, too. The two of them made a case history of disasters— blood poisoning, overweight and loss of weight, phlebitis, infections of the kidney, and finally, for Yvonne, a premature delivery with a difficult labor ending in a cesarean section. She recounted her recollections with urgency. I grew more and more uneasy, finding that I was not ready to hear all this detail at once. I felt almost victimized by my young visitor's intense narration. I got up to get the tea and cups, hoping to break the conversation.

Suddenly, Michelle tugged at her mother's arm for attention and Yvonne looked at her with a mixture of recognition and annoyance. *"Petite Americaine, quoi tu?"* She didn't use her child's name and there was a flash of hostility in the response to her daughter's demand for attention. I passed the cake and poured the tea for us and juice for Michelle. The little girl immediately turned her attention to the pleasures of food. Her mother gazed at her silently, twisting in her fingers the hair ribbon that had fallen out of the child's hair and that Michelle had brought to be retied.

"I am leaving tomorrow—for good," she said. "Stan does not know." She was still looking at Michelle. "The little one will go with me. She will have to forget him. Soon, he will be sent back to America for retirement, to his *real* family." She said the latter with a sharp anger that contrasted with her rather pale, unemotional face. She reached out and pulled Michelle into her arms and smoothed her hair and retied the hair ribbon, holding her now on her lap.

"I have brought for you Michelle's baby clothes," she said, leaning down with her free hand and taking out a package wrapped in a piece of tissue paper and tied with a white ribbon. She opened it and spread out some little nightgowns, a pink sweater, two pairs of booties, and a knitted pink cap. They were all handmade in the French style, not from the American PX's ample supply of mass-produced baby fashions. Michelle leaned down to pick up the little clothes with delight.

"Take them," Yvonne said, gathering them back into the paper and pushing them toward me.

"Oh, but I can't." I said. "You'll need them some day." I picked up the clothes uncertainly, embarrassed at my response.

She laughed at my clumsy remark. "I don't need them," she said and got up to go, taking Michelle's hand and going to the door. She looked at me steadily for a minute, a rare open gaze for her. "Don't tell Stan that I am going," she said. Our glances met and we exchanged confidences.

"I won't," I replied. And I knew that she believed me.

"Bon sante, Madame!" she said, and embraced me in the formal French manner. Michelle gave me a hug and skipped down the hall beside her mother. I waved good-bye and lingered beside the staircase as they descended, feeling close to tears. Yvonne was half-chiding, half-cajoling

Michelle for stopping rapturously to pat the concierge's huge orange cat, who had been sitting on the banister in mysterious omnipotence.

"*A demain!*" I said, without thinking of the inappropriateness of my farewell. I looked down at the next landing and waved the package. "Thank you!" I called, not noticing that I spoke in English. Both of them looked up and smiled and waved. I watched them until they disappeared, and then I returned to the empty apartment and opened the package again, spreading out the little clothes on the table.

A month or so later, the apartment across the street was empty. The concierge said that the major had gone back to America. The wife and child left several weeks before, she said. None of them left a forwarding address. My own loneliness and fears had not disappeared, but I felt that I shared another kind of anguish with Yvonne, one that was far worse than my own.

Although I began to feel physically uncomfortable by the end of the fall—I had backaches and I was almost too clumsy to get into our little Renault and enjoy weekend trips—I began a plan of reading in French literature and was regularly dropped off at the Bibliothèque nationale de France for a few hours. Getting back to literature gave me a sense of recovering my own work. I had decided that I would focus on the 1880s and 1890s in England, the period of transition from Victorianism to Modernism, one which had always interested me for its sensibility of spiritual doubt and its ambivalence between the religions of art and faith. Later I would choose Walter Pater, a mentor of Oscar Wilde, as my dissertation topic because he seemed to embody this sensibility and also because he developed the poetic prose of autobiography, a genre that had interested me ever since I read Wordsworth's autobiographical poem, *The Prelude*. This period also had correspondences with French literary movements, so my reading of Baudelaire, Mallarmé, Gautier, and Huysmans gave me material for a chapter of my dissertation. I also read Sartre and Camus, but I did not know of Simone de Beauvoir's *The Second Sex*.

It was Massignon who introduced me to the work of J. K. Huysmans, once a spiritual brother of his. Huysmans was a French novelist, whose literary path took him through the naturalism of Zola, the symbolism of Baudelaire and Mallarmé, to his place in the decadent movement with his novel *Là-Bas* (Against Nature). This novel, an exhaustive depiction of a temperament devoted exclusively to aesthetic experience, had a great influence on Oscar Wilde's aesthetics, but had led Huysmans from spiritual nihilism to a conversion to Catholicism. Subsequently, he wrote conversion narratives, the history of Chartres, and saints' lives, returning to the dogmatism of the Catholic renascence of the 1890s. He died of throat cancer after long months of illness during which he offered his suffering as "substitution" for his own sins and the suffering of others. Although he was a fascinating figure to me and I would use him as a contrast to Pater, his spirituality, with its emphasis on the transformative power of suffering, troubled me.

As my due date approached, my mother announced her plan to come over to help me when the baby was due, much to my joy and gratitude. I began to count the days till I would feel able to move around without such difficulty, and I collected the layette and equipment that family and friends began to send. We bought a small refrigerator for the kitchen and set up one of the two front rooms as a nursery.

The birth itself, on January 31, 1960, was a natural childbirth—not by choice, really, but because the doctor was not there to give me medication beforehand. Fortunately the midwife was prepared to handle everything. I had taken a few classes in breathing, which helped me through a long labor. After I was X-rayed during the labor, I went to the delivery room and was trying to give the final push when the doctor arrived. He gave me a whiff of something that dulled the pain and in the following confusion I heard the first infant cry and the nurse showed me Cathleen, throwing open the receiving blanket as she said, *"C'est une fille!"* We named her Cathleen Marie Mason: Cathleen after *The Countess Cathleen* by Yeats, which I had been reading, and Marie for her French connection. I experienced both joy and terror those first few days of Cathleen's life. I was thrilled to have this lovely baby girl, but I was overwhelmed with fatigue and worry about taking care of her. Even though I was able to stay in the hospital for several days, I had an impulse to ask the nurses to keep her for a while—until I felt stronger—and then I would come back for her!

The day did arrive for departure from the hospital. My mother was with us and brought in a small pink outfit for Cathleen's trip home. Our arrival at Rue Thiers was recognized with great celebration from our whole neighborhood. Several of the local tradespeople gathered at the entrance of the apartment building when we got out of the car. The florist handed me a bouquet of flowers. Madame from the *boulangerie* ran out with a little package of *patisserie* and everyone exclaimed over Cathleen. *"Quelle enfant!" "Comme elle est belle!"* It was if they had never seen a newborn baby before! But I learned that this was normal in France. The French really love babies and make children welcome when they enter their society. I did not experience the same enthusiasm and love from casual acquaintances when my two other children were born in America.

Even with such support, the first three months were difficult. For about two weeks I was provided with a French baby nurse by the state social services and everything seemed to run smoothly. We were even able to go out with my mother for a celebratory meal—the first in months. However, soon after the nurse left and my mother returned to America, Cathleen developed colic and cried continually. She also had an intolerance for her formula and since France had not yet developed any of the canned substitutes such as soy milk, we had to concoct, at the doctor's direction, a daily bouillon from fresh vegetables to which we added a powdered thickening. The process was a nightmare. One of us would hold the screaming baby while the other tried to punch a hole in the bottle's nipple so that the formula would run through smoothly. In our panic, we went through two doctors—the American doctor from the hospital and then a French woman doctor, a professor, who eventually gave up on us because we called her in the evening once too often. Finally we found Dr. Malartre, a wonderful Frenchman, who was patient with us and suggested that Cathleen was suffering from prickly heat among other things. She had been snugly swaddled in the French fashion and kept too warm in our well-heated apartment.

In the middle of the intensity of these first weeks, I got a call one morning from Sophie, our landlady. "Mary, this is Sophie de Enden. I am afraid I have some bad news for you. I'm going to need the apartment again and as soon as possible."

I wondered if I had heard her correctly. "I've just had a baby, Sophie. We can't move right away." She barely acknowledged my comments and kept insisting.

"Well, I am sure you can find something else. I do need the apartment."

We were *bouleversé,* as the French say. Herb had also gotten a call at the school from his half sister, and for the next several weeks we were constantly pressured to move. Housing was still impossible in Paris unless you had a salary in American dollars, which we did not. We looked at a few dreadful places—a room or two in someone's apartment usually—and then decided to take our French friends' advice. "Stay put," they laughed. "No French judge is going to evict a mother and her newborn infant from an apartment."

But, of course, we felt uncomfortable in the position of squatters and we began to think about going home. I was ready to go. I could see that motherhood for me would be easier with some of the conveniences of the United States. Further, I did not want to go on teaching at the American School. Herb would have liked to stay another year even if he had to continue teaching, but he, too, began to realize that we needed to go back and decide where our life was going. His Catholic French mentors advised him to take on the responsibility of the good Catholic father, so we began to plan to return in the summer.

Meanwhile I began to establish some control over my routine. I worked out a changing table that I could use and a method of moving Cathleen around in the bassinet and the stroller. Madame Guerin, whom we hired to supplement Madame Lebedeff's housework (I could not bring myself to tell Olga that I needed someone to do more demanding work), came almost every day to help me make the formula and to boil the diapers in a huge pot on the stove—we had no washing machine—and hang them in the bathroom. Herb did lots of carrying and changing of diapers when he was at home and we began to join other parents in the park with Cathleen in her carriage.

We had one more event before our stay was over: Cathleen's baptism, which took place at the American Catholic Church in May 1960. We had a reception at our apartment afterward and brought together all our French acquaintances as well as godparents and friends from the American School community. Cathleen wore a white eyelet dress with a pink under-slip, a dress that her own infant daughters wore for their baptisms more than thirty years later. The event was a high point in our French experience. I was feeling strong again and happy that we had resolved to go back to the United States. Yet I also felt sad, as I realized the intensity and importance of our three years in Paris. I had gone through many experiences that I would not thoroughly process for many years. I was leaving some very good friends. I had met some extraordinary people. The celebration also marked a moment of reconciliation between our two friends, Louis Massignon and Robert Rochefort, whose family we had come to know well. The two men were personal and ideological antagonists. The personal rift had grown from some miscommunication following the tragic death of the Rocheforts' son, when Massignon had offered the grieving father some spiritual advice. The ideological conflict was real. Massignon, the renowned Orientalist and friend of the Middle Eastern world, stood for justice for the Algerians and a settlement of the Algerian-French war that would leave the North Africans independent and end French colonial rule. Rochefort belonged to the rightist French political wing and believed in the necessity of keeping the French empire. As inspector of prisons for the government, Rochefort had denied the charges of torture of Algerian prisoners, charges which Massignon had personally verified, often giving sanctuary and assistance to some of the torture victims. The two men had not spoken to each other for some time, but on the day of Cathleen's baptism they met outside the church and clasped each other's hands. We all felt at the party afterward that we were celebrating friendship and reconciliation. Cathleen sat propped against pillows on the couch in her French christening dress, smiling and content, but unaware of her role of great importance.

We sailed from Le Havre in June for New York, on an Italian ship this time. We sailed back to the New World. Herb returned with his spiritual journey complete although he had yet to begin the new career it ordained for him. I returned with many questions unsettled—not even surfaced in some cases. My understanding of the French experience was going to take years to unravel.

REFLECTIONS ON A MEMOIR:
THE MAKING OF A FEMINIST

My reflections on my French experience are based on memory and the letters to my mother that I sent during those three years. The letters, which my mother saved, helped to reestablish certain facts and names and to document the details of my daily life, my domestic conditions, and my travels. I did not, however, keep a personal journal. Herb, on the other hand, kept extensive diaries and journals on the experience, and published a book about it, *Memoir to a Friend: Louis Massignon 1883–1962*. It is a portrait of Louis Massignon and an account of the main themes of the French Catholic Orientalist's thought, but it is also Herb's account of his spiritual journey, much in the tradition of other romantic tales of self-discovery. He portrayed himself as a solitary young poet, who humbly came to listen and sit at the feet of great men, ready to take the mantle of wisdom and experience should it be passed to him. I am not in it. Nor is our daughter Cathleen.

My reaction to Herb's memoir was at first disbelief and then anger that I had no part in his account of our life in France. Much later, I realized that the book uncovered more clearly my own intellectual and spiritual journey during those years and also the foundation of my feminism. What has become clear to me is that when I first experienced many of the significant intellectual and spiritual encounters that we had in France, I did not completely understand my own reactions to them. In fact, it was not until I read Herb's account that I recognized the vast difference in our journeys. Mine is a woman's story, initially of a wife accompanying her husband and becoming the observer of a patriarchal drama of father and sons and of the bonding of men. My story includes the drama of motherhood, particularly of a disabled woman who is isolated from the comforts of a community of women. It also is the account of becoming engulfed in a religious conversion that was not mine and which had to be resisted, no matter how alluring, in order to ensure my own spiritual integrity. What follows is a comment on Herb's memoir and how it illuminated my own journey.

In his encounter with Louis Massignon, Herb found the father figure he had been seeking and also his wise man, his mentor. He made his own spiritual journey coalesce with Massignon's lifelong discipleship to al-Hallaj, the tenth-century Muslim poet and mystic who was martyred in 922, and whose life was about love—love in fraternal friendship as well as spiritual and paternal love—about grief, and about transcendence through "crossing over" into another mind, another culture. Herb was to narrate his own version of these themes through his poetic rendering of the epic of Gilgamesh.

As I record these words about these powerful myths, these overwhelmingly riveting stories—divine and secular—about father and son, about fraternal friendships that demand unequivocal loyalty and love, I feel erased. Yet I recapture some of the moments and feelings of my days in Paris in the presence of these intense friendships and alliances.

Did I listen as I sat in the study of Massignon's apartment on Rue Monsieur, watching him bend toward me courteously to include me in the conversation? Did I listen in the Left Bank living room of Gabriel Marcel, the Catholic philosopher? Did I listen to Robert Rochefort in his tiny study in his apartment in Neuilly before the family meal when Rochefort spoke so intensely, trying to win, as it were, the spiritual contest that was taking place over Herb, the young *American?* Did I listen in the elegant Breton country estate of Yvonne Chauffin, the Catholic woman novelist who orchestrated Herb's meeting with Massignon, as she stood with Herb near the window gesturing and talking, while I sat silent, irrelevant to their conversation?

Yes, I listened, and what I heard were the great Western myths of man, the heroic struggles of the fathers and the sons and the anguished conflicts of the brothers who both hated and loved one another. The stories were told in a certain time, and in a certain setting—postwar France's Catholic renascence and the beginning of an important chapter in the conflict between the Western world and the Middle Eastern world reflected in the Algerian-French (Muslim-Christian) war. Two great belief systems and empires of the past were beginning to face off, and Massignon was dedicating his life trying to bring them together. I was witnessing the bestowing of the wisdom of the Old World by the ancient seer, Massignon, on the young hero-poet, Herb. I listened and I tried to hear my own voice composing a counterpart, but I had no seer to tell me a story. I was not empowered to go off on a journey carrying the sacred emblems.

I realize now that I *was* given a place in this world: the role of the sufferer and victim—pure and humble and enduring. This was the major theme of the role of women by the French Catholic writers at that time—in the plays of Claudel and Bernanos and in the novels of the women writers such as Yvonne Chauffin. I am reminded of a whole series of images of women that I heard about and saw during my French experience: saints, like Saint Lydwine, Saint Therese of Lisieux, or Saint Catherine of Siena; fictional characters in the plays of Claudel and Bernanos; depictions of the Virgin Mary. All of these images described women as victims and patient sufferers, sometimes creatures of darkness and mysterious primal strength, sometimes of delicate sensibilities exquisitely tortured, but always as creatures where the body prevailed over the mind. In a letter to Herb from Thomas Merton from the Trappist monastery in Kentucky (quoted in Herb's memoir), a photograph was enclosed and was described as a statue of the Blessed Virgin made in Ecuador. The context is Merton's reference to Massignon's belief in the spiritual power of suffering and the idea that salvation comes from the most afflicted and despised. Merton's comments on the photo provide another version of the Catholic image of women that I encountered at that time. He writes, "The Holy Mother is the Indian woman of the Andes, the representative of all that is most abject, forgotten, despised and put aside. . . . [T]he face of the Madonna is terrific. It has precisely the kind of blindness, the withdrawnness in a great mystery of poverty and darkness and strength."

Here the worship of the abject and the despised becomes an idol in itself, an idolatry that has happened many times in religious history. I knew then instinctively that there is, after all, no "great mystery of poverty"; it is simply a misery that should be changed, and it is not necessarily conducive to holiness. The fact that women so often provide the symbols of mankind's suffering simply supports the systems that keep women in positions of poverty and oppression. The icons of the martyrs of men, like al-Hallaj, stand for intellectual, political, and social change. The icons of women witness passive suffering and the placing of their bodies at God's disposal. They rarely represent the heroic characteristics of the male tradition.

Massignon's "chivalric respect" for women and his reverence for the Virgin Mary, which was at the heart of his spirituality, represented the best of Catholic thought, but also the basis for the fatal dualism of that thought. In his memoir, Herb describes Massignon's perception of the Virgin Mary as "the emblem of humility and purity," and he goes on to further describe it as "a symbolic prism reflecting the hearts of women whom he believed to retain virginal centers regardless of their exploitations and violations by men." The problem with this idealistic view is, of course, that this emblem can so easily be flipped to the other side—to the image of Eve represented so often in Western Christian history, as the emblem not of purity, endurance, and suffering but rather of sensuality and the corrupting evils of the body.

Suffering was, of course, a major focus of postwar France, still trying to figure out the horrors of the occupation, the Holocaust, the betrayals, and the sacrifices. In Massignon's thought, suffering is given legitimacy through the power of mystical substitution of a few witnesses or substitutes, "a spiritual elite" who are given a special grace that translates their sufferings into spiritual power. The "crossing over," as Herb described it in his memoir, occurred through the powerful source of patriarchal friendship, a tradition of male bonding characterized by the spiritual values of "bravery, fidelity, and honor." It includes, finally, a friendship and identification with God.

The story of the journey of woman, who provides the vessel for this God-created creature, does not include these heroic friendships or spiritual values. She is denied the tradition of bonding and correspondence that would lead directly to a bonding with God. She is honored through the passive role of bodily suffering and through the spiritual values of purity, patience, and endurance.

This was the story that I heard as I listened during my French sojourn. Years later I would read critiques of this system in the writings of women theologians such as Mary Daly and Rosemary Ruether. In Paris, I listened, but what I heard were puzzling snatches, like bars of music that played and then disappeared. For a long time afterward I was consciously trying to put the song together, but it would not play for me. I realized that I had listened but the song did not include me, and the snatches that I heard had no counterpart in my own reality. Virginia Woolf, writing in *Moments of Being* about how art is a "token of some real thing behind appearances," said, "There is no Shakespeare, there is no Beethoven; certainly and emphatically there is no God; we are the words; we are the music; we are the thing itself." To me she was writing about the perception of being erased from the world of great art and culture and from human consciousness and finding, as I had found, that there is only your own words, your own music. In "Diving into the Wreck" Adrienne Rich describes the search for her own story, a woman's story. She writes, "The thing I came for: / the wreck and not the story of the wreck / the thing itself and not the myth."

My immediate reaction to the troubling images of women that I encountered during my years in France was to feel uneasy. I listened to the opera *Les Dialogues des Carmélites* and felt indefinably depressed. I walked out of the second act of Claudel's *Soulier de Satin* and was not quite sure of the source of my anger. I did try to accommodate myself to my role, but never felt suited to it. Particularly during my pregnancy, during which I suffered much discomfort, I felt cast in the role of the woman whose body was the instrument of a divine will. Meanwhile, trying to grasp something of my own, I began my course of reading at the Bibliothèque nationale de France and when I showed interest in Huysmans, Massignon responded warmly to my research. He provided me with personal recollections from his own life when Huysmans had been a friend of his father's, and he put me in touch with Huysmans's biographer, Robert Baldick, and introduced me to another of his biographers, Helen Trudgian, an English scholar who had studied in France. Massignon also suggested that I translate the life of Saint Lydwine, Huysmans's hagiography of the medieval expiatory victim of mystical substitution. The book graphically describes the saint's horrible physical sufferings and how they were a substitution for the sins of the fourteenth- and fifteenth-century Europe. I began to translate the book, and years later, discovering this translation in my filing cabinet, I was amazed that I could have worked on it and tolerated the kind of interpretation of a saint's life that glorified, in this case, a woman's suffering.

For many years, I tried to reconcile the stories and wisdom of the great men in France whose work touched my life during those years with my own sense of its irrelevance to my life. I examined the lives of women who dedicated themselves to those heroic themes of mankind's political and economic and spiritual suffering. Dorothy Day, for instance, was a strong figure in my consciousness in the 1960s. Day, once a radical journalist and compatriot of the political and artistic leftists of the 1930s, was converted to Catholicism and started *The Catholic Worker* newspaper and the Catholic Worker Movement in New York with her friend and mentor, the French peasant, Peter Maurin. She, more that anyone I know, tried to deal with the danger of romanticizing poverty and suffering. Her soup kitchen and hospitality houses, her agrarian movement and open forums for intellectual discussion, her retreats and her political demonstrations, all addressed with immediacy the issues to which she was dedicated. When I met Dorothy Day, who visited us once in our Cambridge apartment, I was awed by her serenity and strength and singleness of purpose, but I was put off by something that I later identified as a blindness to (or denial of) the systemic flaws of elitism and sexism in the church she so wholeheartedly embraced. Later, when I wrote an essay on her autobiographical writings, I concluded that she had actually lost all sense of her solidarity with women's issues as she became involved in the church. She was an inspiration in so many ways, but a disappointment in this one personal and important dimension for me.

My experience in France wakened me to the great themes of Western culture: the quest for "bravery, fidelity, and honor" and the attempt to reconcile the suffering of wars, disease, poverty, and oppression with a belief in a benevolent deity. I was also enlightened, however, by how much and how often the great intellectual and spiritual debates of the world excluded the experience of my world and of women in general—or if not excluding them, co-opting them into a narrow, deforming role. This perception laid the groundwork for me to seek my own version of the stories and my own reality as a disabled person—to seek, as Adrienne Rich writes, "the thing itself / and not the myth."

PART III

AFTERSHOCKS

Through writing her body woman
may reclaim the deed to her dwelling.

Nancy Mairs, *Remembering the Bone House*

12

A MAINE IDYLL

When I waved to Herb and saw him disappear out the front door, my heart sank a little as I realized that Cathleen and I were trapped in the second-floor apartment until he returned again that day at about three o'clock. His teaching schedule was four days a week, but he could get back fairly early most days.

We had finally found a two-bedroom apartment in a farmhouse outside of Gorham at the end of September after looking all around the Portland area and finding nothing that was both affordable and decent. Many places we looked at had no central heating—surprising in a cold northern city, but apparently not many people rented apartments. After returning from Paris that summer, we had stayed in my mother's house in Boothbay Harbor, Maine, until Herb found the job teaching English literature at Saint Joseph's College on Lake Sebago. Thomas Merton had promised him a job at a Catholic college near Merton's Trappist monastery, Gethsemane, but the position had not materialized. Actually, I felt relieved. It would have been too isolated in a parochial Catholic world for me and even for Herb, despite his religious enthusiasm.

Our house was on the main road into town. The road showed a few landmarks of small town progress: a tire supply company, a tackle and bait shop, and the basement of an incipient church—Jehovah's Witness—which promised salvation as well as a more substantial worldly structure in the near future. When we explored the town we found, much to our surprise, that Herb had family connections there. His great-grandmother, Sarah Warren Mason, was buried in the local graveyard in the center of the town. She had been abandoned by her husband, John Mason from Ireland, after he married into her prosperous mill-owning family. Herb's father had been the treasurer of the family's company, S. D. Warren of Westbrook, before his divorce.

I turned to Cathleen, who was banging her rattle on the side of the stroller and looking expectantly up at me. Poor little one, she would have to be content to go from stroller to playpen to crib to changing table to her eating table. That was about the range that I could manage to lift her from one place to another. I could also put her on the floor—she was beginning to crawl and to pull herself up—and fortunately, she was not hyperactive and could not get away from me easily. I wondered if a child's activeness was the result of nurture, not nature. I did have a high school girl come three afternoons a week to take Cathleen out in her carriage, but the walk was only down the adjacent street of small ranch houses decorated with pink plastic swans or other cartoon lawn animals. There were no blue and white Virgin Marys on those determinedly Protestant yards. The local Catholic church was a movie house, and the parish priest a Sunday visitor. In the nearby town of Westbrook, however, a large French Canadian population had created a Catholic community.

The day loomed rather long ahead, but my thoughts were interrupted by my neighbor, Estelle, from the downstairs apartment. She and her husband owned the house. She came up to tell me that the contractor was coming to fix our kitchen ceiling, which had fallen down the day before, barely missing Cathleen and me as I fed her lunch. The ceiling, which must have been weak, apparently collapsed after a sonic boom from an airplane flying overhead.

"Did you have any more trouble with the ceiling?" Estelle asked when I let her in and she'd gone to the kitchen to check for further damage. I had called her after the accident and she had come up immediately and helped me clean up the debris. She brought her three-year-old boy and new baby girl with her, and they had amused Cathleen while we worked. Estelle and Dan, her husband, shared a touch of Down East fatalism, which made them react to all events calmly—disasters and ordinary happenings were treated with equal respect. "A-yah. That's the way things are," they seemed to say. They were good people, and like most of the residents on the outskirts of Gorham, they were struggling to make ends meet.

"Connie Sherman down the road asked me to see if you could come to her coffee party Wednesday evening. I thought your husband would be home then so you probably could come if you want to. She's going to call you about it later."

"That sounds very nice." I was astonished at the amount of involvement Estelle's invitation suggested. She must have discussed my schedule with her friend. She was usually very pleasant but detached.

Later Connie did call me, and I did go to the coffee party at seven o'clock. It was in one of the little ranch houses down the road. There were about ten other young women there. Everyone was dressed up in a print dress and pearls or a skirt and frilly blouse. I had put on a skirt and blouse after much debate about what would be appropriate. Herb put Cathleen to bed so that I could get ready. I was nervous about the event, never having been to any ladies' parties before except for an occasional bridal shower for college friends.

We were introduced as we came in, and coffee and cake was served by the hostess from a table formally set with flowers and candles. After the cups and plates were passed and I had found a place to sit and balance my coffee and dessert, I decided to initiate a conversation with the young woman beside me. As I turned to introduce myself the hostess stood up and seemed to be about to make a speech. "I am so glad you could all be here tonight," she said, and then suddenly turning to an attractive woman in a silk dress and high heels, she continued, "And I have great pleasure of introducing to you Blanche Rogers, your Tupperware hostess tonight."

Mystified, I watched while another table was brought out, a cloth was laid, and the new hostess began displaying a series of dishes and pots and other kitchenware, talking excitedly about all the wonderful ways we could use our Tupperware to make our home more efficient and hospitable. I had, I later discovered, gone to my first (and last) "Tupperware party" and before the evening was over I realized that I would have to choose something to buy before I left. Because we were living on a very lean budget, I picked out the simplest item I could—a small mixing bowl—and then I escaped home without having shared more than a few words with any of my fellow guests.

Our other social contacts came from the college where Herb was teaching. The Sisters of Mercy at St. Joseph's made us very welcome. In fact, they doted on Herb with his newly minted religious enthusiasm and his interesting stories about Massignon and Merton and others. The head of the English department, Sister Stephanie, attached herself to him as if he were a life preserver. She was going through a personal crisis that would eventually make her decide to leave the college and then the order. She found the politics of the order and the lack of intellectual stimulation in the college too much to bear and she welcomed a sympathetic listener in Herb. Most of the teaching was done by nuns, so the students also found Herb, one of the few male faculty members, a thrill. We would occasionally have them for tea on Sunday afternoons and they would listen wide-eyed and attentive to his every word. I felt a twinge of jealousy, or perhaps envy, that I was not the one who had students listening to me. The role of the quiet wife and mother did not come easily to me.

One of the most striking male figures on the campus was Father Clancy. I noticed him when we went to the opening reception in the fall. He was a handsome man, an Irishman with raven black hair, a slightly ruddy but not flushed face, a strong and athletic build, and the bluest, coldest eyes I have ever seen in a face. His smile was Mephistophelian, and indeed as we got to know him, he seemed to me extremely cynical, using the college and the sisters for his own purposes and aggrandizement. He was bored with his assignment on Lake Sebago and spent much of his time in Cambridge and Boston with academic friends and clergy who were close to Cardinal Cushing. We were a slight diversion for him, too, although I think he was simply amused at Herb's earnest involvement in the church, while genuinely intrigued by his contacts in the Catholic world. I felt that he had a complete contempt for women—students, nuns, myself included. He recognized Sister Stephanie's talents, so he had her writing, editing, and *typing* his articles. He had very few academic obligations—a class in theology, I think, and the chaplaincy, which he took lightly although he made a handsome sight at the altar when he said mass.

Sometime in the fall term Herb came home with an invitation to dinner from Father Clancy. Sister Stephanie from the college had also been asked to go. "How come Sister Stephanie is invited?" I asked. "I thought Bill disdained to socialize with nuns?"

"Stephanie is dean of the college. That gives her status, I guess." Herb laughed. "Bill needs a co-host."

When we arrived at Father Clancy's attractive apartment on the college campus, we found that he had also invited the college's doctor and the Thaxters, a prominent Catholic couple from Portland. Our host was most gracious and served us drinks and then a tasty dinner of beef bourguignon. He served from the kitchen and let none of his guests help him except Sister Stephanie. I noticed through the kitchen door that another nun was there. Perhaps she had even cooked the dinner, although I doubted that Bill would have put his French menu into the hands of the plain Irish nuns at Saint Joseph's. Dressing and tossing the salad at the table, he had muttered with annoyance about "nuns who don't know that you are not supposed to wash a salad bowl with soap and water."

My mornings with Cathleen always followed much the same routine. We listened to records and I sang a lot of songs I thought I had forgotten. We read books and laughed a lot; she was very responsive when you made faces. After lunch when she took a nap, I tried to read or do something to use my mind. I was thrilled to get a letter from Miss Trudgian, the Huysmans scholar. I had written her to ask advice about my dissertation subject, and her reply, which gave me many concrete suggestions, was like a lifeline to my intellectual life. I had begun to feel that I was losing both my capacity to think and the opportunity to do anything about it. I read the letter many times and thought about how I could get back to work. The first obstacle, I realized, was not being able to drive. My mother arranged to have a Ford station wagon equipped with hand controls ready for me when we returned from France, but I had not gotten around to taking a driving test, my license having expired while I was out of the country. I brought up the subject that night.

Herb was aware of my feelings of isolation and very supportive of trying to help me get back into action. So we went to the registry the next afternoon, got the forms and the test booklet, and made an appointment for the next week. As we drove up to the registry for the test, Cathleen on my lap (there were no mandatory infant seats then), I suddenly panicked. I had not driven for more than three years and had hardly practiced at all. I felt very incompetent. The state trooper was a taciturn middle-aged man who looked at me with some disbelief. I had my old license that proved I had been a driver and had a specially equipped car. We took off around the block and into traffic. At the first left turn I had to take across oncoming traffic, I froze and let the light turn red again. Then when it turned green, I started to turn too soon.

My examiner spoke sharply: "You can't do that." I stopped again but managed to make the turn before the next light. I knew, however, that I was in trouble. My judge sat beside me in silence and I felt condemned. Still I had done everything else right up until that point and I tried to maintain an air of authority and control. I would show him how well I could stop and start on a hill. I had had lots of practice on Beacon Hill. And my parallel parking was superb. I learned that in Chicago along the Midway.

The officer pointed to the street where the registry of motor vehicles was. "Turn in there," he said firmly. I was surprised. Was that all? Was the test over? I began to feel worried. When I pulled over and stopped, he jotted something in his notes and without looking at me said, "You haven't passed the test. You'll need more practice." I was devastated and could not even form a response before he left the car and nodded to Herb, who was standing at the curb. I felt I was being handed over like a child to her parent.

Herb tried to joke about it but it seemed to me that I had just lost my last chance of survival. I felt incredibly inadequate and depressed. I didn't want to think about it again and refused to talk about making another appointment or even practicing driving. Perhaps I had some form of agoraphobia—fear of going into the world. I tried to console myself with a kind of numb acceptance. I would just let things happen. There was nothing I could do about it. Besides, wasn't I doing what was normal in my family? I was a wife and a mother and I could take care of a child. I had proved all that. Herb had a job and was the breadwinner. My family had hinted more than once in the past that they did not approve of my providing the primary income, as I had while he finished college and then again in our first two years in France. We were living on a tiny income but we would no doubt find a way to do better. I made curtains for the apartment and cookies for the students who came to tea. I once again took up the translation of Huysmans's life of Saint Lydwine in all its grisly detail and promptly related my martyrdom to hers.

By sheer luck we heard of an apartment available in the center of town, and we moved the next summer to a lovely white colonial built in the eighteenth century. It was a first-floor apartment with inside shutters, handsome wainscoting, a fireplace, and, going up the stairs to our landlady's apartment, a rare mural painted by an itinerant nineteenth-century artist as compensation for rent. We were hardly settled in the apartment before our lives were disrupted again; I had discovered myself pregnant that spring. We thought it would be a good idea for Cathleen to have a companion although we actually had not expected it to happen so soon. The clumsy Catholic rhythm method that the college doctor prescribed was hopelessly inaccurate, so I was soon experiencing my second bout of morning sickness. My mother was supportive but she sounded concerned. "How will you manage, dear?" I did not really know. I felt anxious.

On the other hand, our lives had improved a lot since we first arrived in Maine. Cathleen was walking, so it was easier for me to take her out to the yard and take care of her during the day. Herb was a doting father, taking her for walks around town and into the local bookstore and gift shop where the proprietress gave her balloons and lollipops. Holding on to her father, she walked along the stone wall of the graveyard across the street, looking over Sarah Warren Mason's tombstone. Like many first children, Cathleen did not have many playmates, but she enjoyed being part of our life. She would sit with us in the living room in her own small chair, and as we talked, she would pretend to read—out loud—from a miniature book, imitating our conversation. When the endless winter snows came, Herb built her a snowman in the yard, and once when she had a cold and could not go outside, he clowned outside the living room window, making prints in the snow by throwing himself down and bouncing back up covered in white from head to toe while Cathleen laughed in glee at his antics. He came back in red-faced from the frost and had to thaw out with cinnamon tea and brandy.

Our life in Maine brought us close to nature. The winters were long but very beautiful with the snow pristine white without city grime. The spring was muddy, but when the summer flowers finally came they seemed brighter and fresher than any we'd ever seen. We could go to my mother's house in Boothbay on weekends as soon as the water was turned on in May, and we would stop in Brunswick to have tea with Herb's uncle, who was blind and a professor of philosophy at Bowdoin College. He had been part of the philosophy department at Harvard when George Santayana and Josiah Royce were there, but when his sight began to fail, he decided to seek a less pressured life and moved to Bowdoin in the quiet town of Brunswick, Maine.

Uncle Phillips lived in a unassuming but spacious house on a side street in Brunswick. It was an entirely Victorian world, with oriental rugs, dark massive furniture, and glass cabinets filled with books. Phillips was the eldest of the many Mason sons. As a young philosophy scholar, Phillips married the daughter of his mentor and professor from Germany—a frail sad woman, much displaced, who served us tea from Royal Doulton cups with hands that shook as she passed the tea around. Her husband, being blind, seemed unaware of her nervousness. When the imposing grandfather's clock struck nearby, he would take out his gold pocket watch to check the time that he could not see. Our visits were formal and gracious and like a ritual dance, but the impression I had after each occasion was that I had experienced an episode from a gothic tale. In fact, Gretchen, his wife, had been often hospitalized for mental breakdowns and had once, it was said, strung a wire across the bottom of the stairs before her husband descended. His son discovered it in time. Their story was dramatized by Herb in a play, the one Alice Toklas read in Paris and liked.

Before Paul, our second child, was born, Herb and I talked about our future plans. I don't think either of us wanted to admit to the other that we were unhappy. I was determined to be the good mother. He was determined to be the good Catholic father, but it was clear that he did not want to go on teaching literature at Saint Joseph's College, and it was clear to me that I should be teaching literature somewhere. Herb kept a very intense correspondence going with Massignon, who wanted him to translate his lifework on Hallaj. That would take going into the field of Middle Eastern studies, learning Arabic, going to graduate school. Herb also saw himself as a writer—poet, dramatist, novelist—and so he was conflicted about his future. I knew that I wanted to finish my degree, but was not sure how to do it while caring for our children. Finally, we decided to do something concrete. After making some contacts at Harvard, we drove to Cambridge, where Herb went to talk to some of Massignon's friends at the Center for

Middle Eastern Studies and I went to the Harvard English department. We left Cathleen with a baby-sitter for the day, the first time we had done something so daring.

As I approached Warren House, the inner sanctum of the English department, I felt a wave of panic. I had not been part of the academic world for five years and I was almost seven months pregnant and walked with even less grace than usual. Furthermore, I had done what Professor Herschel Baker, who was the second reader of my undergraduate honors thesis and who was memorable for being able to have a whole conversation without moving a muscle in his face, expected women to do—quit their careers to go have babies. Although I had done well in graduate school, I had not carved a place for myself in the male hierarchy; as a result, I felt tolerated but not embraced. I hesitated at the door and thought about retreating, but then I felt angry. Why should I apologize for living a life? I would not let some pedantic stuffed shirt keep me out.

When I went in the door I was grateful to see Miss Jones, the department secretary, still at her desk in the outer office. She was one of the many faithful women at Harvard who worked for very little money and provided the glue that held the department together. Miss Jones also added a much needed human touch in a very dry world. Everyone counted on her to know the answers and solve the problems. She walked with a decided limp (I never knew what her disability was), and she never talked about herself or her life, but it was clear that much of her life was Warren House and the English department.

"Mary, how are you?" she greeted me warmly when I came in. "Bill Alfred told me you were coming to Cambridge and that you have a baby girl! Congratulations! Professor Bate will see you in a minute."

I felt revived at least temporarily and sat down gratefully on the edge of a chair—the last months of my pregnancy made me move with great difficulty—and asked about Cambridge and department news and told her about France and more immediately about the expected birth. She smiled and clapped her hands enthusiastically—a considerable display of emotion even for her and certainly unusual in the usually hushed and controlled atmosphere of the office. In a few minutes Walter Jackson Bate, the current chairman of the department, popped his head out of his office and Miss Jones told me to go in. Bate was a little grayer than I remembered but he still jumped up from his chair as if he was a puppet dangling on a string and when he sat down after shaking hands, he twisted constantly in his chair as I remembered him doing when he lectured. He was a very courteous man, but as an aging gay bachelor with no connections with pregnant women—

certainly not disabled pregnant women—he clearly found it difficult to relate to me. He looked rather alarmed at my condition and watched anxiously to see if I could negotiate settling into a chair. "So you think you want to come back for more, do you?" he said with forced jocularity.

"Yes. I want to schedule a time for taking my comprehensives and then get on with writing a thesis." I tried to sound as confident and forceful as possible although I felt my self-esteem beginning to slip away.

We talked about my exam and who might be on my committee. I gave him a brief idea of the area of my dissertation interests and he suggested a nineteenth-century specialist who might be my committee chairman. As our conversation came to an end, I realized that I needed to secure a teaching fellowship to help pay for my tuition. I had not found any mentor in my year and a half of graduate courses to whom I could now turn for help and I could not bring myself to ask Bate for suggestions. Anyway, that was not the way it was done. You really had to establish your contacts and keep them going. I left the office feeling pretty discouraged, not knowing how we were going to finance both Herb's and my graduate study. After his interviews, Herb was still in the preliminary stages of his inquiries.

When I returned from Cambridge I was engulfed in daily life. After living in the town of Gorham for more than a year, we were almost accepted as real residents although we knew that it would take generations to be accepted as natives. Our landlady, Miss Fox, had kept her distance when we first moved in, but she gradually became more communicative and she really opened up to us after I brought Paul, our second child, home from Mercy Hospital in a snowstorm.

The snow was falling heavily when Paul and I arrived from the hospital. It was Christmas Eve and my mother had arrived the day before to take care of Cathleen. She greeted us at the door with the news that there was no heat—the furnace had gone off. Cathleen had on her fleece sleeper and a sweater and we all gathered around the fire, putting Paul's bassinet near enough to keep him warm. Mother and Herb fixed a little supper, which we ate wrapped in sweaters.

Miss Fox made her first appearance as we sat around the fire eating supper. We heard her hallooing as she came down the stairs. "I've brought you some hot soup," she called loudly as she brought in a large tureen of split pea soup. A tall woman with an angular face, and white hair pulled into bun but often escaping in wisps, she reminded me of the Margaret Rutherford headmistresses in many British films about girls' boarding schools.

Her appearance was the first of many that night; each time she brought something else—more blankets, wood, molasses cookies—until finally about midnight, the service man arrived and Miss Fox bounded down the stairs to let him in and show him to the basement. An hour later the furnace started again. The next day we did our best to celebrate Christmas. Mother had bought special breakfast buns and Cathleen was given a stocking with toys. I took care of Paul. We had invited one of Herb's students for dinner—a young Chinese woman who was alone for the holidays—so Herb had to drive to the college to get her. When we finally got everything on the table—the turkey and sweet potatoes and vegetables and cranberry sauce—I was so tired that after everyone was served and we were about to make a toast, I found myself sitting there with tears running down my face uncontrollably. It was not from grief but from sheer fatigue.

Finding someone to help me with child care was harder than I expected. I thought that surely some woman would be looking for part-time work. You only had to drive a few miles out of Gorham to see the extent of the rural poverty in the area. Houses were literally made out of scraps—different kinds of board and wood, pieces of metal, oddly shaped pieces of plastic. However, the visiting nurse told me that women were very reluctant to do any domestic work, feeling it would not be dignified. Finally we found Mrs. Giles, and after Paul was born and my mother left, she came four mornings a week and helped me with baby care and all of the household tasks.

Mrs. Giles was a gray-haired lady with short bobbed hair and very blue eyes. She bounced a bit when she walked and she had no trouble working with our very basic household equipment—an old soapstone sink in the kitchen, a gas stove with a heating unit in it that did not work efficiently so the kitchen was generally cold, and no washing machine or dishwasher or any of the modern conveniences. Mrs. Giles had raised two boys who were now off trying to make a living. She and her husband owned a small house a few miles out of town up a steep country road with no neighbors in sight. She kept a garden and her house and property were very neat, not like many of the houses along the road that were strewn with decapitated or gutted old cars, assorted machines and miscellaneous collections, and usually a sign out front advertising an astonishing range of goods for sale: bait, chicken coops, jam, mattresses, and any number of unrelated items. Mrs. Giles described her neighbors "of that sort" in very scathing terms— "common," "lazy," and "good for nothing." Her husband did many different kinds of work, from fixing cars to collecting trash. Their life had been hard, and at one point when there was no work, they were hired as a matron and caretaker in the state reformatory in Thomaston. She had done cooking and housekeeping and he had done the janitorial services. It was a good living, she said, but a confining routine and a depressing atmosphere.

All of this information and a great deal more was told to me every morning. Mrs. Giles started her narrative as soon as she had given a cheerful morning greeting and she did not stop until she walked out of the door in the afternoon when her husband came to pick her up. I was aware of a constant stream of noise, like a hum or maybe a drill, invading my brain all day. We were locked together in the daily tasks of housework and lunches and changes of clothes and outings. I tried to develop a deaf ear because she did not often pause for a response. I knew that she had come to this state from the isolation of her life in her little house at the top of the winding road, and I saw her monologue as a warning of what could happen if you stayed alone too much.

Actually it was Mrs. Giles who gave me the extra push I needed to change my life and to work out a return to graduate school. I was offered a part-time job at the local teacher's college where Herb had been moonlighting, teaching a night class. I turned down the job, feeling I could not get myself or my head together to do it. I mentioned it to Mrs. Giles and she shook her head. "You should have taken that," she said, "a smart woman like you with all your education. You should do something for yourself." I was shocked by her frank remarks, but I realized she had sized up my life accurately and had drawn the right conclusions.

We began to make plans to spend the next summer in Cambridge. Herb was going to take a class in Arabic. I was going to start reading for my comprehensives and begin planning my thesis topic. Everything began to come together. We contacted Mrs. Wilson, whose house we had stayed in before we went to France, and found that she wanted a housesitter for the summer. We hired a summer live-in baby-sitter. Herb got a tuition grant and I was given financial aid from the new president of Radcliffe College, Mary Ingraham Bunting, who was committed to helping women "retread" and get back to their interrupted careers. Mrs. Giles helped us pack up our things for the summer, and in a nonstop commentary, she expressed her strong approval. I was—and am still—very grateful to her.

13

CAMBRIDGE DAYS

It was a hot sticky July day in 1962 when I answered the phone and heard a Swiss gentleman announce that Michelle Dupres was waiting for us at the Kennedy International Airport. I was stunned. Michelle, the daughter of our *femme de ménage* in Paris, was supposed to arrive in the fall to be a live-in baby-sitter for us after we moved to Cambridge. Our friend Annemarie Calvet, having misunderstood our plans for Michelle and thinking she was being helpful, paid her passage and put her on the plane. At the moment we had with us a baby-sitter from Maine. Herb was traumatized by his first encounter with learning Arabic, and I was spending hot days in a Widener Library stall trying to write something on George Moore, later to be a chapter of my dissertation. Our Maine sitter was an overweight depressed teenager who lacked energy and enthusiasm but she managed to handle both Cathleen and Paul while I was out. I knew she would not be able to get along with Michelle, who spoke no English and was not a country girl.

"Could you see that Michelle gets on a shuttle to Logan?" I asked. "We shall meet her there." I tried to briefly explain what had happened to our plans.

As I expected, the two baby-sitters did not get along, but fortunately we were able to send Michelle to my mother's house in Boothbay Harbor for the summer to help my sister Jane with her new baby. Michelle came with us in the fall when we moved into the house on Green Street, where we would spend the next six years. It was a two-floor (plus attic room for Michelle), two-family house with a large yard, a garage, lilac bushes, and many trees, just a few minutes from Harvard Yard. It seemed like a palace to me although we were still without a washing machine and dryer. We almost took an apartment in someone's house, but Mildred Mason had appeared and urged us to look further for a larger place. The house on Green Street was more than we could afford, but she insisted on paying part of the rent so we took it.

Michelle was one of the first of a number of child care providers that I had over the next fifteen years or so. Child care was one of the most important parts of my life at the time because peace of mind depended on having responsible people with the children. I was not quite ready for a teenage daughter when Michelle arrived, but she was steady and she put in many hours taking care of Cathleen and Paul while Herb and I juggled studying with grants and loans and teaching. She took English classes in the evenings, where she made friends, and while her English became fluent our French diminished. Michelle was followed by another au pair French girl, who turned out to be a disaster. Despite letters back and forth in French describing the job, Monique came to us completely misunderstanding what to expect. She was from a French military family that belonged to a small group of Royalists in France. Unlike her brothers, she had not been sent to university but had come out as a debutante (or the French equivalent), and after not immediately marrying like her sisters, she was looking for something new in her life, which I soon discovered did not include taking care of children. She arrived with plans to spend weekends in Chicago, Miami, Phoenix, and other distant places, having no apparent sense of American geography or of our agreement about alternate weekends off. She was an attractive young woman but very melancholy and obsessed with a small scar on her left cheek, which she said came from her brother's rapier when he tried to teach her to fence. I could tell in a week or so that our arrangement would not work out and told her so. She stayed on for a month while she looked for another job, and I hired another person, a woman who was the first of a series of wonderfully supportive mature women who came in by the day and solved my day care problem for the years ahead.

One of the first things I did when we got to Cambridge was to get my license renewed. This time my driving test gave me no problem. I seemed to have regained my confidence, and as soon as I could drive myself again, I felt in control of my life and able to tackle anything.

My return to graduate school to study for my comprehensives was the best part of my Ph.D. program up to the dissertation. Most of my graduate courses were uninspiring, and like most graduate students, I spent most of my time worrying about how to get an A in my courses. I had not been mentored by any of the male faculty, so I had not been given much encouragement despite my good record. Now I was on my own and I was able to read for hours in the library, thoroughly enjoying the world of literature. My only other obligation was to attend the lectures for the English literature survey course in which I was teaching a section. I did not get one of the sections in the freshman writing course—which paid quite well—when I applied for it, although Herb did, reminding me that "the boys" still got the goodies at Harvard. However, I was rescued by Bill Alfred, who taught the survey course with David Perkins and hired me as a teaching fellow. He and Perkins provided me with two different models of pedagogy: Bill was very informal—anecdotal and narrative, spiced with Irish humor—and Perkins gave finely crafted informative lectures. Since the graduate school gave its students no clues about how to teach, assuming that teaching was intuitive or irrelevant, I was grateful for the chance to watch them and then once a week try out my own version of their methods in my section. My students were challenging but rewarding to teach. Many of them would soon join the busloads of young people who traveled to the South in the voter registration drive of the Civil Rights Movement. A few were worried their grades, fearing the limbo of academic probation.

I really looked forward to my days at Widener Library. I arrived at about nine o'clock in the morning and parked my car inside the Yard. Harvard was still giving me parking privileges as it had when I was an undergraduate. This would change when the demand for disabled parking began to grow. I was still a rarity on campus.

The elderly guard inside the back door at Widener always greeted me with a familiar "good morning." I showed my pass and entered the stacks and took the elevator to my desk on the fifth floor, where I settled down beside my window and looked out at the Yard and then at the row of books I was going to read in preparation for my comprehensives. I had begun with my special topic, which was the works of George Eliot, and I luxuriated in the idea that I could simply sit and read for a number of hours every day with no paper to write and no deadline to meet; the exam seemed a very distant distraction. One morning after reading for an hour or so, I glanced out my window and saw a charming scene below me in the Yard. A young dark-haired woman was pushing a baby stroller carrying a small boy in a blue snowsuit and a red scarf. A little girl in a pink snowsuit—about three years old—was walking beside the carriage holding on to a white fluffy toy animal. I looked again and saw that they were Michelle, Cathleen, and Paul. I got ready to wave but soon realized they wouldn't look up and see me—I was too far above them—and so I relaxed back into my books knowing that they were safe and reasonably content.

When I returned home each afternoon, my serene scholarly life ended. I was the primary caretaker so I was immediately swamped with making up lost time with the children, organizing and cooking dinner, putting

Cathleen and Paul to bed with stories, and then catching up on miscellaneous household tasks before I started to prepare my weekly class or correct papers. Herb was taking a full program in graduate school as well as
teaching, so he was under a lot of pressure but helped out when he could.
We were also active in a number of community groups, including the
Riverside Association, a neighborhood organization that brought together
the black community, the Catholic parish, and the academic community of
graduate students that included a large Harvard graduate student apartment
complex down the street from us. By 1963 the tensions and challenges of
the Civil Rights Movement had begun. I remember the first night that the
meeting of the association was at our house. We had recently joined the
group and were eager to participate. After I put the children to bed, I set
out the store-bought cakes and made the coffee. Herb got out the cups and
plates.

The first person to arrive was Father Collins from Saint Paul's parish.
This was the first time he had come to a Riverside meeting and one of the
few times he had met any of the black leaders from the neighborhood
around Putnam Avenue and Central Square. He was a florid-faced bulky
man with a jolly voice and a twinkling eye—the perfect Santa Claus figure.

"Mary, how are you?" He put his arm around me like a visiting uncle
or cousin. "Are you giving those *Haavad* students a *haad* time?" His Boston
accent resonated as the next guests arrived: Dave Taylor, one of the association's black leaders; two of the local black clergymen from churches in
Central Square; a fellow Harvard graduate student who lived on our street;
and Mr. McCafferty, a policeman, and his wife, both Green Street residents
and members of Saint Paul's parish.

We served the cake, coffee, and tea and started on the agenda for the
evening, which included the deteriorating condition of the local housing
project—there was vandalism and a growing threat of drug dealers, the
grass was uncut, the halls unlit and littered with refuse and feces, and no
police patrols went near it—a recent racial confrontation on River Street;
and finally, the ever present concern of local residents that Harvard and
MIT and other powerful landlords were going to swallow up the neighborhood and force out the residents.

There was a good deal of tension as the discussion began. We were not
yet familiar with each other and we came from very different backgrounds,
but as the evening went on, we found common ground. We drew up some
plans of action. Mr. McCafferty was going to contact his precinct about
having a member of the black community ride with a police officer during night patrols. Father Collins was going to contact one of his former

parishioners, now head of public housing in Cambridge, and demand better lighting and maintenance at the projects and also regular police patrols. Someone would call on our local city councilor about the city's plans for building expansion.

As the evening went on, Father Collins became more and more pleased with our progress and with his new sense of ecumenism. "I tell you," he exclaimed, "this is wonderful. You know, I see great things happening in our community." His words expressed a common feeling. I think all of us—our black neighbors and our white neighbors—felt, probably for the first time, that we were getting to know each other in a community that had been living separately although side by side. We continued to work together in the association over many projects, including a "sweep in" at the local elementary school when we discovered it was going to open in the fall with a school yard full of glass and rubbish. While we were members, the association became involved in a long dispute with the school committee over the proper relocation of children during the construction of the new elementary school building, which was named the Martin Luther King School in 1968. Cathleen and Paul started school before the construction began. Their classes had a slightly larger number of black students than white so they had an opportunity to learn and play in an integrated setting.

In the spring of 1963 I took my comprehensive oral examination. My mother agreed to take the children and Michelle for a long weekend, so Herb drove them to New Jersey and I had three days to cram and prepare my mind for the event.

My committee was a lackluster group, which I felt had been put together carelessly. Hal Martin, my chairman, was not really in the field of my specialty—Victorian literature—and his questions showed it. John Kelleher, whom I had studied with, came in late and asked three questions that fellow graduate students predicted he would ask. In short, I felt was not taken very seriously. Although I passed the exam competently and was duly congratulated, I had no feeling of triumph or great accomplishment.

My exam was over about two o'clock in the afternoon, and Herb and I left almost immediately for New Jersey, where my mother was happy to turn over the responsibility of the children to me. Resuming the daily routine of my life so quickly reinforced the anticlimactic feelings I experienced after the exam itself.

It was not until the fall, when I found my thesis advisor, that I finally engaged in a significant intellectual exchange with Harvard faculty in graduate school. My thesis director, Reuben Brower, was stimulating and he was enthusiastic about my thesis topic on Walter Pater's autobiographical fiction—its indebtedness to Wordsworth's autobiographical poetry and its influence on the development of modern fiction. He encouraged me to include a chapter on Huysmans—a French parallel—so that I could use the research I had done in France. I was still a long way from discovering my real interest in women authors, but I had identified autobiographical writing as a focus for future research.

Meanwhile my daily life on Green Street was demanding but engrossing. On weekends when the baby-sitters were gone, I took over. Herb started teaching a course at Simmons College in addition to his Harvard freshman course, and he was still struggling with Arabic, which he had to master in order to go into the doctoral program. He spent most of Saturday in the library. I developed a repertoire of activities for the children: the theater at the Children's Museum, the Science Museum, folksong concerts, the children's room at the Cambridge library, and so on. On Sundays Herb was part of the team and we had picnics at Fresh Pond park or took rides out of town for ice cream cones; sometimes we joined other families at the Harvard athletic fields where the fathers played softball and the children ran around while the wives talked about the children.

I rarely thought of myself as disabled at this time. I was negotiating a two-floor apartment, taking care of the housekeeping and the children, and teaching and studying. I was married. I was not alone. I was passing as able-bodied and I did not have to go to social gatherings where I would be reminded that I was not able-bodied and have to battle the instinct to turn tail and run.

Cambridge in the 1960s was an expansive, exciting place to be. From the extremes of Timothy Leary's LSD regime and Harvard Square hippies to the inspirational idealism of student activism and community solidarity, the atmosphere was one of inclusiveness, experimentation, and commitment. Our colleagues and peers in our political and social groups came together over common causes: cleaning up the neighborhood schools, working for better racial relations, or civil rights questions and antiwar protests. In our professional groups, status had not yet been established. People were on their way up and had not joined the academic pecking orders. At the yearly fundraising fair at Cathleen and Paul's cooperative nursery school, future Harvard celebrities and those who would not make it to the top raised money together for new playground equipment and took their turns on parent participation days. We were all insiders so I did not feel like an outsider.

While in France, a small but persistent voice in my head began to question and reevaluate my own perceptions of the life that Herb was more or less shaping for us. In Cambridge, however, this voice became submerged in the dailiness of our lives and the stimulation of my work and the relevance of the issues of the time. Nevertheless, the voice was still there, buried deeply perhaps, but offering a dialogue. On the one hand, I longed for the certainty and almost dogmatic commitment that Herb showed in his work and his religious life. I wished I could be so certain. On the other hand, a voice kept asking, "What are your real feelings? Who are you?"

I started to attend Saint Paul's with Herb and sometimes we took Cathleen and Paul, because the comfortable cavernous church provided room for the children to crawl around on the pews or the floor. Herb was active in the parish and we both joined a Cambridge discussion group interested in matters related to Vatican II. There were discussions and sometimes arguments about the vernacularization of the liturgy, and everyone was excited about the dialogue that had been opened to other Christian churches and to the Judaic and Muslim traditions as a result of the council. The post-Vatican developments had a particularly big impact on Saint Paul's, a local parish but also the parish for the academic community at Harvard.

Caught up in the enthusiasm of the changes and the ongoing dialogues, I made another go at trying to join the church. I felt outside the glow of warm belief and belonging, and I prayed in church, "Help me in my disbelief," but nothing happened. I felt like a failure but I was waiting to be struck from my horse like Saint Paul. Furthermore, I objected to the church's impossible attitude toward sexuality, particularly birth control. I was aware that Herb would rather have followed the church's teaching about contraception, but I was anxious about the physical consequences for me of another pregnancy. Herb suggested I go see one of the parish priests. *What would he know about it,* I wondered? *But, okay,* I decided, *I will try.* I called and made an appointment.

The parish house was across the street from the church on Mount Auburn Street. I found a place to park and nervously rang the bell. A young priest answered the door and showed me into a comfortable office where Father Noonan sat in a leather swivel chair. He rose as I came in, shook my hand, and fussed over where I would be most comfortable. He had a young thin face even though he was balding. He was very lean and ascetic-looking but mild mannered, almost ingratiating.

"You are Mrs. Mason," he said when he took my hand. "Your husband is a fine man, a great asset to the parish." When I was settled in a chair he asked, "What can I do for you?" He sat down again and crossed his legs and folded his hands in his lap.

What can I say? I wondered. *I can't join your church because of its attitude toward birth control? I'm worried about surviving another pregnancy?* I managed to get out something about my concern about limiting my family.

Father Noonan looked sympathetic and nodded. "Yes," he said, "it is harder to raise families nowadays." He leaned forward in his chair and warmed to the subject. "When I was growing up families were large and we just coped—helped one another out. We didn't seem to need so many things. Large families were desirable. It was much easier."

Oh sure, I thought. *Much easier for whom? The mothers? But anyway, what are you talking about? What has that got to do with my life?* I realized he was going to be useless. He was not even considering that I was a disabled person, that I took special physical risks in pregnancies. I listened to him natter on about Catholic families. I mumbled a few platitudes, not even able to acknowledge the anger I felt for his insensitivity.

"I'll pray for you. God bless you." He looked benign and held my hand a moment as we shook hands. I managed a frozen smile and went toward the door clumsily, not caring if I knocked over his papers as I brushed past his desk.

Despite my problems with the church, Father Collins, our parish priest, was a good friend and contact. He heard about a job at Emmanuel College, which I took in 1965. Herb and I needed one of us to be earning a regular salary. I was interviewed by Sister Barbara Gill, a bright woman whose field was medieval literature. She seemed pleased to have me in the department, which was made up almost entirely of nuns except for a large group of young women who taught freshman composition and were peripheral to the regular English program. It was a full-time job and I taught literature courses in my own field. My students were bright Catholic girls, who at that time were guided into Catholic women's colleges while their brothers were permitted to explore a wider range of secular institutions. That situation would change in the 1970s.

While I was teaching at Emmanuel College, I helped our Austrian friend Charlotte Teuber get a position there, too, and we both stayed at that institution far longer than we expected. Charlotte Teuber Weckersdorff was one of the most important persons to come into my life in Cambridge. Our house was often full of international students, whom we were drawn to because of our experience abroad. Through the Harvard Host Family Program, we entertained and hosted several foreign students, including them in our holiday celebrations at Thanksgiving and Christmas and helping them adjust to American life. Herb was always hopeful that he would find graduate students who spoke Arabic, but we were rarely assigned one, though we finally connected with Kojiro, a Japanese student, who actually was studying Arabic at Harvard.

Charlotte met Herb when they both were taking Arabic at the summer school in 1962, and after that she seemed to become part of our family until she moved back to Vienna permanently in 1981. In the 1960s she applied for a Fulbright to study art history at Princeton but had been sent to Harvard, where she eventually took a degree in political science, specializing in non-aligned countries and particularly in the Arabic-speaking world. At Emmanuel she taught political science.

Our friendship had an element of the absurd because she was over six feet tall and held herself very erect with regal bearing. I, on the other hand, was four feet eleven at most. Charlotte was a fiercely loyal friend, very unforgiving of people who did not keep vows—priests and nuns who left their vocation, or men and women who left their marriage vows (although she accepted infidelities as part of the human condition). She had converted from the Lutheran Church earlier in her life and became an avid Latinist and traditionalist in all things Catholic, but she was a radical in all things political.

Charlotte's past was as colorful as her present. She was a masterful storyteller. Her linguistic ability was extraordinary; her English, French, German, and Italian were all idiomatic and spoken like a native speaker. Her descriptions were full of metaphor—pinpointing a face, a personality, an event with a devastatingly accurate phrase. However, you could not count on her facts being entirely accurate although she had total recall in memory. She preferred to embellish, to manipulate reality slightly, and if she got caught in a fabrication of events, she would tough it out. Her stories had an element of conspiracy. In fact, she loved to talk about the strategies and conspiracies of the European aristocracy, of which she counted herself a member, and she loved to describe the excesses of the church and its saints and martyrs. One of her favorite texts was the *Legenda Aurea,* a medieval text relating the lives and deaths of saints and martyrs in grisly detail. She kept a very large collection of relics from all over the world.

Not surprisingly, Charlotte's stories from the Second World War were grim. She herself had been dragged off a truckload of Jewish detainees being taken to a camp. She had thrown herself on the truck in despair and was barely saved by a companion. Her flattened thumbnails attested to the thumbscrews used in her interrogation by the Gestapo, who had taken her into custody on suspicion of helping Jews escape. She said that her family was divided between Nazis and Social Democrats and that her brother's Jewish wife had to be legally adopted by her family to save her. Near the end of the war, Charlotte went to a hospital in search of a friend of her brother's who had been a prisoner of war of the Russians. According to her account, the sisters who ran the hospital gave her a uniform when she arrived, put her immediately to work, and detained her there until the war was over.

I had never before met a person who was so absolutely fearless as Charlotte. She had no sense of limitations on what she could do or where she could go. She was not really a mentor to me because our interests and talents were so very different, but she became a kind of superwoman figure in my pantheon of outstanding women. She also was a devoted friend when needed, and helped me through some very difficult times.

Although I could never be the kind of superwoman Charlotte was, I found myself part of a superwoman syndrome in Cambridge among my peers in the 1960s. As wives, graduate students, academics, and parents of young school children, the women I knew were following a certain pattern: we were employed full- or part-time, we were pursuing a graduate degree, we were political activists, and we had two children. In addition, it was expected that we would bake our own bread, make our own birthday party favors for our two- to four-year-olds and of course, their Halloween costumes. Last but not least, we cooked gourmet meals for Saturday night dinner parties using the recipes from Julia Child's newly published cookbook. My next-door neighbor, Ellen Berg, illustrated the strains and demands of the superwoman syndrome.

It was early Saturday afternoon and I was very grateful that I was not giving a dinner party that night. It was Ellen's turn. We shared a wall in our side-by-side two-family house. I could hear the whole agonizing process of preparing for the party, managing two boys, ages one and three, and doing weekend shopping and laundry, among other things.

"Eliot!" I heard Ellen's voice clearly through the wall. Eliot was her husband. He was being summoned to go to Chinatown or some other distant place to find the special mushrooms for Julia Child's recipe. Two piercing screams followed. Adam had hit Zachary and Eliot was angry. There was a lot of running up and down the stairs and some crying. Ellen's voice was shrill. Eliot slammed the front door to go on his mission.

My phone rang. "Would Cathleen and Paul like to play out in the sandbox with Adam and Zachary?" I said yes although I knew that meant I would have to watch them but I empathized with Ellen. Herb and I had planned to take the children to the supermarket to do the weekend shopping, but Herb could do that himself when he got back from the library.

Late afternoon. Next door there was a lot more running up and down the stairs, which were directly opposite ours through the wall so it sounded as if someone was running up our stairs. I had fed Cathleen and Paul and was running their bath. I was happy that all I had to do after I put the children to bed was get dressed for dinner. The baby-sitter was coming at seven.

"Eliot!" Ellen's voice was very loud. Apparently there was not enough tonic and soda water. Eliot left again and I heard the car start.

Herb and I were ready at seven o'clock. I gave instructions to Cathy, the baby-sitter. She lived just two blocks away so Herb didn't have to go get her, but he would drive her home later. We walked out our front door and down the street and into the Bergs' entrance next door.

Eliot answered the door. He was wearing an African print shirt, slacks, and sandals. (Both he and Ellen were in African studies. They had already lived in Kenya for a year.) He wore glasses and had very little hair left on top of his head. He was very calm and cordial. "Come on in! The Myers are here. Ellen is just putting the boys to bed. She'll be right down."

In fact, as he spoke, Ellen was just appearing at the top of the stairs. She wore a bright purple and gold African sheath dress that came to her feet, sandals, and a pendant necklace of ivory. She swayed a little at the edge of the steps. "Hi there!" For the first time that day, her voice was not loud or shrill. It seemed distant. She descended the stairs and we all went into the living room, where Eliot was fixing drinks from a side table. After taking care of the guests—another couple had arrived—he handed Ellen a gin and tonic and she sank into one of those uncomfortable canvas chairs that were popular at the time.

"Here's to everyone!" Ellen raised her glass and drank down most of its contents. The doorbell rang again for the final guest, and we were now all talking in pairs or threes. I looked over to where Ellen sat and saw her hand hanging loosely over the chair, her glass standing empty on the floor. I looked more closely. Her head was reclining on the back of the chair and she was fast asleep.

The sight of Ellen's exhaustion stirred me to change our superwoman ways, and soon after that evening my mentor from Wheaton, Mrs. Boas, paid me a visit and confirmed my decision. She always renewed my own sense of self when we met. We kept in touch and she often called me when she returned to Boston from her long visits to England and to California, where her son lived. She arrived at the house dressed in one of the many silk dresses she had had made for her in Hong Kong (another one of her frequent travel destinations). She was more bent than ever—her head seemed to grow out of her shoulders—but her eyes were bright and her gaze penetrating. I could tell that she was surveying my house and my situation carefully. When I showed her the kitchen, she sized it up quickly. "Mary, you have no dishwasher! You are too busy not to have a dishwasher!" Fortunately, we had finally purchased a washing machine and dryer, which she checked out in the back pantry.

She brought with her a black leather tote bag—the one she carried her books and notes in to classes at Wheaton—out of which she took a box of sterling silver knives and forks and spoons and a number of articles and documents on Shelley, who had been one of her scholarly interests. First she handed me the silver. "I am trying to get rid of excess baggage," she said. "I have no use for all this silverware. I hope you can use it." Then she flipped through the Shelley material. It included a photograph of the gravestone of Shelley's daughter Ianthe from his marriage to Harriet Westbrook. "My friend Edwin Blunden wants me to write a biographical essay on the life of Ianthe, but I am passing on these tasks to others now. Perhaps you are interested?"

I was flattered by her suggestion. I took the picture and articles and said I'd consider it someday. After she saw the children, whom I was leaving with my baby-sitter, we went off to the Harvard Faculty Club for lunch. When we got to the club, we both tugged at the heavy door as several people passed on by.

"Did you ever notice how rude people are here?" Mrs. Boas remarked sharply. She had a penetrating voice and I winced a little but at the same time I admired her lack of self-consciousness. She went on to exclaim that it was only recently that the club had opened the front door to women. "Can you imagine that?" she said. "When my husband was a member here, I had to go in a side door." She added wryly, "I don't think Harvard's mentality has changed that much, do you?" She stopped and peered at me, pinning me down to an answer. I nodded my head in agreement even as I saw several familiar professors glancing at us.

Our lunch was lively with conversation and Mrs. Boas got me talking about my research and my work. Her visits were restorative. She believed in literature, in revolutionary causes for humanity, and in the rights of women, and she left me believing in my own significance in the scheme of things. Soon afterwards, I bought a secondhand dishwasher and put away my copy of Julia Child's cookbook.

By 1966, Herb and I had joined antiwar demonstrations and heard Daniel Berrigan, the Jesuit priest, and his brother Philip, also a priest, start their long crusades against war and armaments and particularly against the Vietnam War. We had also become involved in local school politics. Cathleen had gone to a private kindergarten in Cambridge but we had decided that it was too full of parents who were frantically adopting the mandatory rules of the upper class intelligentsia in Cambridge, preparing their children to become intellectual snobs, and giving them every after school lesson you could imagine and taking them on African safaris for vacations. We had neither the money nor the inclination to follow that route so we sent Cathleen to first grade in the neighborhood public school and Paul to the kindergarten there as well, after he had finished his two years at the Cambridge Nursery School. Herb would often transport him to nursery school on his bike, sitting him in the little child's seat behind— a familiar Cambridge sight.

The public school turned out to be a good experience for the children. Cathleen learned to walk to school with a friend after we were told by her first grade teacher that it was time we stopped overprotecting her. Herb had accompanied her down Putnam Avenue, a busy thoroughfare, every morning, and someone always met her at the end of the day. I don't think we would send young children alone if we lived there today. Dangers have increased, but at the time, the neighborhood was close-knit and the mayor of Cambridge and his twin sons, who were in Cathleen's class, lived two houses down from us. Cathleen's teacher, Miss Dow, was a genius at managing a large group of children from mixed racial and economic backgrounds, shaping them into a community. She walked the class around the neighborhood, identifying each child's home, and she also took them all over Cambridge—to libraries, museums, and other sights, trailing them behind her, two by two. Paul was not as fortunate in his teacher. Faced with a large class of five-year-olds who, on the whole, had never been to nursery school, she spent most of her time trying to keep them in their chairs. Her only strategy seemed to be to shout at them. However, Paul and his inseparable friend, Matt, who shared his preschool experience, were not fazed. They built a little world of their own, full of action drama. They bided their time in school and then when they returned home (they were neighbors) they costumed themselves in towel capes and tee shirts with huge paper S's for Superman pinned on front. They lost themselves in fantastic scenarios of feats of heroism, swinging between the jungle gym and the trees or riding their plastic cars on the sidewalks.

At the end of my first year of teaching at Emmanuel College, I discovered I was pregnant. This third pregnancy made me keenly aware of the limitations my disability imposed on me. I gave up my teaching job for the year, knowing how restricted and disabled I had been in my second pregnancy, and I planned to finish writing my thesis, which kept being shelved for other priorities although I would try, without much success, to work on it in the summer. I was soon so plagued with muscle strain that even working on a typewriter became an agony, but I managed to finish it just before Sarah was born on January 24, 1967, and I proofread it in the maternity ward of the Boston Lying-In Hospital.

When I came home from the hospital with Sarah, I sat down in my bedroom chair and found that I could not move. Cathleen, who was thrilled with the baby—she had prayed for a sister—had gone downstairs with Paul to play Chutes and Ladders, the game I had bought them as a present. Herb was helping my mother fix dinner in the kitchen. I was in such severe pain that I shouted at the top of my lungs and everyone came running. I was suffering from a complete muscle collapse from the strain of the pregnancy and I could neither sit up, stand up, or lie down. After a hectic few hours when we called my obstetrician and my orthopedic doctor, our family doctor finally came and administered morphine and ordered a home nurse for several weeks because I could not hold Sarah in my arms to feed her. My mother stayed on for a few more days but the house was crowded—she was in with Cathleen and Sarah; Herb was using the attic room, which had become his study; and Sarah was with me, her bassinet replacing the typing table. I had a daytime baby-sitter and nurse so Mother felt that there was not much more she could do. Considering the orderliness of her own life, she did well to put up with the chaos of our life at that point. Moreover, she had just visited my sister in Montreal and I could tell by her descriptions of their very solid way of life that I fell more under the category of social welfare work

Sarah's arrival—despite my temporary physical collapse—brought a lot of joy to the family. Cathleen, playing the surrogate mother, would hold her and show her to all of her friends. Paul entertained her as soon as she could sit up, getting into her playpen to arrange her toys. She became a playmate to him, a relationship that they kept while growing up. Her presence seemed to distract Paul and Cathleen from their own rivalry as they began to fight for their own turf in the family. After I recovered from my muscle collapse, I decided to take my birth control dilemma into my own hands. After trying the Pill and finding it had bad side effects, I consulted my doctor and eventually had a tubal ligation.

In June I received my Ph.D. but I did not attend the ceremony. I didn't give this omission much thought at the time because our life at that point seemed very stressful and distracting. Looking back, however, I realize it was another example of my inability to demand more recognition of the stages and achievements of my own career. Our financial situation was very grim. Because I had given up my job, we had lost our major source of income, and to make matters worse, Herb lost one of his grants that spring. We were at one of the lowest ebbs of fortune, but once again Herb's mother came to the rescue. I went in April with the three children to stay with her in her apartment in Langhorne, Pennsylvania, so that Herb could be alone for two weeks to prepare for his comprehensive exam, which had been scheduled earlier than he expected. My mother was in England for a family wedding.

I didn't expect to spend more than a week with Mildred Mason. I had planned to move on to Herb's sister's in Swarthmore, but soon after our arrival in Langhorne, Cathleen came down with the mumps. I found myself quarantined for over two weeks in the apartment. A daytime helper came to care for Sarah but I had to entertain Cathleen and Paul day after day. I had no car and it rained continually so we could not even go out in the yard. Mildred Mason left early in the morning and came back about seven at night. She provided me with reams of colored paper, paints, crayons, books, cutouts, and anything else I could think of. I used every iota of creativity I had as well as the television. We even played school.

Despite my feeling of being incarcerated, I remember my evenings with Mildred Mason with pleasure. Ordinarily, she would return home from work late, after I had fed the children and put them to bed. We would sit together over drinks and afterwards have a late dinner. We talked in a way we had not done before—a kind of leveling with each other and a communication between women that was rare for her, I think, because she lived almost exclusively in a man's world and considered most women as rivals or as not worth much.

My pleasure was overshadowed by the knowledge that I was going to have to ask for financial help. We did not have enough money to pay the rent and buy food for the months ahead before our grants came through in the fall. We had hit rock bottom and Herb was absorbed in his studying and seemed unable to deal with the immediate crisis. I knew it was up to me. Much to my relief, Mildred brought up the subject herself. "I know you and Herbert are in a financial crisis," she said as we sat down with our drinks, "and I want to see what I can do to help. Things are tight for me right now but I might be able to approach my sister Maud."

"I wish we didn't have to ask you," I said. She had been generous to us in the last few years and I hated to ask her for more. "I'll be on a grant next year but that won't start until the fall. Hopefully Herb's other grants will come through by then, too."

She went on to tell me about how she lived on a tiny budget when she and Maud first came to Cambridge and how they had watched every penny. I knew she was telling me a cautionary tale, but I also knew that after she married Herbert Mason Senior she had gone through money like water.

"I don't think Herbert has been good at planning," she confided. "You must make him be more responsible. He can't always just do what he wants without thinking of the consequences. Try to bring him down to reality."

I couldn't say exactly what was on my mind—that she had been somewhat responsible for giving him a sense of entitlement, making him feel he deserved to get what he wanted—but her frankness and intimacy were comforting. We had another drink together, like women meeting in a different time zone, away from the world of men and their foibles.

Actually, it *was* Aunt Maud who bailed us out. Maud was like an alter ego to her sister—a small, rather stupid version of her dynamic other half, she provided some of the missing characteristics of their composite personality. She was domestic, affectionate (unless told to be otherwise), trivial, and companionable. They had known each other's secrets for so long that they almost had become part of each other. Maud had more money than she could spend, but she was constrained by her lawyers and trust officers. However, Mildred always managed to help her defy her financial keepers.

Mildred talked to Maud that night for at least an hour or more on the phone. The next morning before she went to work, she came into the adjoining rooms where she had put me and the children. "Maud is going to help you out. She can sell some stock and send you the money in about two weeks." I admired her strength and energy in dealing with a crisis. I was also grateful that she did not make me feel guilty or indebted. During the last days of our visit, she never mentioned the money again.

In retrospect, I was glad to have had the opportunity to be alone with Mildred Mason. Unfortunately, she did not have an open and honest relationship with either of her children although she often came through for them.

Her last years were terribly sad. Against better advice, she invested all her retirement funds with her company, Patterson Parchment, and when it went bankrupt, she was left with nothing after having been a major source of its profits. She moved to a house in Swarthmore that Maud picked out for her. It had small rooms and was totally alien to Mildred's style. She developed a paranoia about safety and barred all the doors with some of her heavy Victorian pieces of furniture. After she left the house and moved to an apartment, she became more disoriented and alienated and was eventually put in a nursing home because she could not take care of herself. It was a sad irony that a woman who had achieved so much success and control in her life was now so helpless and alone. She was a person who was very different from me but I think that ultimately we had a respect for each other, recognizing each other as fellow survivors.

One of the positive events of that difficult spring was my discovery of the Radcliffe Institute, founded by Mary Ingraham (Polly) Bunting, the president of Radcliffe, to help women get back into their careers. I was successful in getting a fellowship and spent two years there, starting in the fall of 1967. Although the institute stipends were small at that time—baby-sitting money really—the two years were a godsend to me as I got back my strength and mobility before returning to full-time teaching. I transformed my thesis into a book and published an article from it. Looking back I see that I was not ready to embrace the feminist consciousness of the late 1960s—most of my colleagues there were not yet active in the Women's Movement—but later, in the 1980s, I reconnected with the institute, becoming the president of the Society of Fellows, the alumnae organization, and then I experienced the fellowship and exchange so characteristic of that phase of the Women's Movement and so valuable to my work as well as my sense of identity. Meanwhile, my two years with my mornings free at my own desk in my own office were precious and renewing. My former mentor, Dean Kerby-Miller, came to my presentation on Wordsworth and Pater and told me it was the best she had heard. I felt my confidence and self-esteem rise—just as Polly Bunting's vision had foreseen.

After Sarah's arrival, we were bursting out of our little house. Because we knew we could not afford Cambridge real estate, we began to look for a house in the suburbs and bought one in the neighboring town of Belmont with my mother's financial help. We moved in August of 1968, after Herb got his first job as a translator of Massignon's work on Hallaj for the Bollingen Foundation.

THE SUBURBAN SEVENTIES

Sitting on the floor of the living room of our new house in Belmont before the movers arrived with all our belongings, Herb and I surveyed the empty space that seemed to stretch in all directions. "Let's send the movers away and never unload the stuff," I said, luxuriating in the emptiness and lack of complexity it seemed to represent. We had sent the children to my mother's house in Maine for a few days while we moved.

The movers did arrive—strong and handsome French Canadians who put a box of books on each shoulder and took them to Herb's third-floor study as if the boxes were weightless. The children returned and we settled in and began to squirrel away our treasures for the next eighteen years.

We had a comfortable white clapboard house next to a reservoir on a hill near public transportation and within walking distance of the elementary school, trading in our diverse Cambridge community for the chance to own a home. On the first day of school when Paul came back from first grade he asked, "Where are all the black kids?" There were none and we missed the neighborhood association and the sense of a common purpose. Leaving behind the tumultuous events of the first half of 1968—the assassination of Robert Kennedy and Martin Luther King, Jr., and the growing despair over the Vietnam War—we gradually adapted ourselves to a comfortable though uninspiring middle-class life. Looking back, I see that my Cambridge experience was one of the most vital periods of my life despite its stress and financial difficulties. I became absorbed in my new life, but I never felt deeply attached to Belmont.

After my second year at the Radcliffe Institute, I began looking for a teaching position, thinking that I would probably move on to an institution different from Emmanuel, but I soon found that it was difficult to get a job. I am sure that my disability played a role in my not landing the jobs for which I applied. During the interviews, I did not confront the issue of my disability and so it was not discussed. But of course, I knew it was not ignored. I could sense the nervous but patronizing reactions of the male chairmen of the departments, who were very polite but not really listening to what I had to offer as a teacher or scholar. I was about to take a job at Wheelock College, where I had been recommended by the director of the institute, when I had a knock on my office door one afternoon and was greeted by an attractive older woman dressed in a handsome suit and high heels. After my first reaction to this stranger, I realized that she was Sister Barbara Gill from Emmanuel College, no longer in the black nun's habit of two years earlier. The sisters had abandoned their traditional dress in the spirit of Vatican II. Sister Barbara came to ask me to return to the college— a full-time position had opened up—and since it was a more attractive offer professionally, I accepted it.

I was now back into a full-time academic career of teaching and scholarship. In 1970 I had the opportunity with a small Kittredge grant to go to Oxford University to look at an unpublished Pater manuscript in the possession of John Sparrow, master of All Soul's College and a friend of Reuben Brower, my thesis director. Herb was going on a trip to France and North Africa so I arranged to meet him in Paris. I left Cathleen, Paul, and Sarah with my mother in her summer house in Boothbay Harbor, along with two baby-sitters. With some anxiety, I boarded a TWA flight to take my first trip abroad away from my children.

The trip began eventfully. Friends took me to the airport in Boston after giving me a bountiful dinner, but when we arrived at Logan I discovered my flight was delayed an hour because of a stopover in New York to pick up Princess Grace of Monaco and her two small children. As a result of the inconvenience, I was given a first class seat and I enjoyed a comfortable flight seated behind the princess herself. I was concerned about the change of time, however, and indeed at Orly Airport I was deposited with my bags but found no one there to meet me. After a disconcerting half hour or so, I suddenly heard a French voice shouting, *"Elle est là, monsieur. Elle est là,"* and Herb appeared with our bespectacled Dutch friend, Jacques, running wildly toward me, directed by a French porter. Herb had been caught in an airline strike in Morocco and then he and Jacques almost missed their plane in Amsterdam, making it only because the taxi driver drove through the congested city on the sidewalks. When they arrived in Paris, they were directed to the wrong gate for my arrival. We all hugged and laughed and talked at the same time and after a day of revisiting our life in Paris, we had dinner with Jacques and I fell asleep at the table.

After a few days in Paris, we went to London and then on to Oxford.

John Sparrow was not in residence but he had left me the manuscript, and when I went to the college I was shown to his chambers, which were all I imagined they would be—full of dark mahogany, graceful ornaments, pictures, and many books. I was directed to a desk where the papers were laid out and ready for me. I spent the better part of the day reading and taking notes (photocopying was not available then) in absolute quiet and serenity, feeling, however, that I had entered a forbidden world that might vanish from me as in a dream. The next day I met a young tutor, Richard Griffith—a connection through Massignon's network of friends—for afternoon sherry at Brasenose College, where Walter Pater had resided. Griffith was working on a Festschrift for Pierre Lambert, a Huysmans scholar and president of the Huysmans Society, and had asked me to contribute an article. I approached the impressive college courtyard feeling like an intruder. As I walked through one of the arched entrances, I stopped to read an inscription on one of the memorial plaques. It was for a former servant of the college who was commended for performing his duties "according to his station." After I found my host in charming but austere rooms, we had sherry and conversed about our respective interests in Huysmans and his relevance to French and English literature. My visit gave me the opportunity to feel the incredible graciousness of the Oxford system along with the equally overwhelming sense as a woman of not belonging to that system except "according to my station." Later I discovered Virginia Woolf's eloquent description of this same feeling about Cambridge University in her feminist manifesto, *A Room of One's Own*. Although even Pater felt an outsider at Oxford because he never got a full university appointment—there was some question about his sincerity in signing the prescribed Thirty-Nine Articles of the Anglican church—I knew that a woman in his time (and in Virginia Woolf's) would have had a complete sense of exclusion, some of which I felt even to that day.

My second literary pilgrimage on this trip was to visit Helen Trudgian, the British Huysmans scholar and friend of Massignon, with whom I had corresponded for several years. She had helped me locate an area of research for my dissertation that combined my interest in the French decadent movement with my interest in the corresponding English literary movements. Most of our correspondence took place while I was living in Maine, feeling very isolated from the academic or intellectual community, and Miss Trudgian's letters to me, which simply assumed that I was going to continue my scholarship—while at the same time congratulatory and sympathetic about my role as a mother—were important anchors to grab on to at that time.

We called Miss Trudgian from London and arranged to meet for tea at her house in Cornwall, expecting to spend a night in Devon after a few literary pilgrimages to places such as Bath and East Coker (T. S. Eliot's burial place). Unfortunately, our trip to Cornwall fell on the first day of a national holiday and the roads were solidly packed from one end of England to the other. We arrived after tea time but Miss Trudgian graciously let us in, heated up the tea, and brought out the biscuits. She was a tall, stately woman. She never married and she inherited her family home in the seacoast resort town. Her father, she said, had the house built when there was virtually no one else living in the neighborhood. When we saw it, it was one of hundreds of houses pressed into narrow streets, now teeming with vacationers. In her retirement, after a long career in teaching and travel and scholarship, she must have been astonished at what happened to her retreat in the summer months.

I understood more clearly her connection with Huysmans when she told us that as a student in France, she converted to Catholicism, which was, in fact, the ancient religion of her family. She was part of a very old Catholic aristocratic family in England (she explained the Celtic origins of her name), which had been deprived of its baronetcy and its property during the reign of Henry VIII. When we met her she was totally absorbed in the study of her own genealogy and, in particular, in the search for the precious relics and family altar pieces, which, she claimed, had been buried and then spirited to Rome to escape confiscation. Her tales were fascinating but I had come, obviously, at a time when her interest in French and English literature was fading for these more pressing spiritual matters. She was generous, however, with her knowledge, and she presented me with some interesting personal correspondence that related to Huysmans and to other French writers. She was, perhaps, the second woman scholar whom I could identify as a role model, despite our different allegiances and life circumstances. The other role model was Mrs. Boas from my undergraduate days.

After integrating the material I found in Oxford into my book, I concentrated on finding a publisher for it, but this turned into a frustrating exercise. I no longer had the advice and help of Reuben Brower, who had died unexpectedly. After trying one or two publishers in the United States, I placed the manuscript with a European publishing house, only to have the company become bankrupt soon after it was accepted. When the company recovered, I resubmitted the manuscript and was accepted again. However, the publishers now asked for a subvention to defray some of the costs. Herb and I discussed the matter and decided we could not afford it. It never occurred to me then that time or resources for my own advancement should be a priority. The second reader of my thesis was unfortunately no help. In fact, he had told me that he did not agree with the main thesis of my dissertation, but soon after I received my degree, he telephoned me one evening. I was surprised to get a call from him and wondered what he could have to say. After a brief exchange of pleasantries he told me his new book on autobiography was coming out. "It seems," he said, "as if we both have the same idea about Wordsworth's influence on Pater."

"Oh really," I answered, trying to grasp why he was telling me this.

"Yes, you'll see it in my chapter on Pater," he continued. "I just wanted to let you know."

Of course, I was unable to respond as I should have. A Harvard professor was telling me something, so I accepted it without question. My sense of outrage did not come until later when I grasped the point—he was acknowledging that he had taken my idea but that he was not going to give me any credit for it. What a difference it would have made to me if he, a professor at Harvard, had given me a footnote of acknowledgment, even a patronizing one! I was to learn later in my work on women writers that fellow women scholars in the 1970s and 1980s would bend over backwards to show their indebtedness and connections to their students and colleagues. But I was experiencing the world of the establishment and only special disciples—usually male—were acknowledged. I did manage some time later to get another publisher interested in my book, but at that point my marriage was falling apart and I could not generate the time and interest to go back to that subject matter, which seemed to belong to another part of my life.

During the early 1970s I felt pulled and stretched between two equally demanding commitments. On the one hand, I needed to pursue my career and make my way up the tenure ladder at my institution. On the other hand, the management of house and children was my responsibility and also very demanding. I would rush home from Boston as early as possible to replace the baby-sitters and take on the late afternoon activities and the dinner hour. Cathleen and Paul started their teenage years and got more independent, but still needed strong support for their progress in school and some taxiing to after-school and weekend events. Sarah was still young enough to be overseen by a baby-sitter but she, too, had her ballet lessons and Brownies to attend. Herb did a lot on the weekends, particularly with Paul's sports events, but he was becoming more and more immersed in the demands of his career. I found less and less time to work on my scholarly writing or to go to academic conferences and do the necessary networking for professional advancement.

Nevertheless, I did make my way through promotions at Emmanuel, and between 1973 and 1978 I took my first turn as English department chairperson (no longer referred to as chairman by then). Sister Barbara bestowed the title on me as the first lay chair of the department when she left the college because she could not accept teaching the less selective body of students that the 1970s were bringing in. When I returned to the campus in 1969 from my years at the Radcliffe Institute, the students looked different. It was before the exodus of many of them in the seventies to secular colleges or to the newly coed Boston College, but they had been transformed. I remembered the students conservatively dressed in skirts and sweaters and stockings. When I returned I found them in blue jeans, cowboy boots, and fatigue jackets. They had become demonstrators and protesters. One morning the quad was full of students drawn up in formation wearing blue jeans and shirts and jackets with armbands that gave their blood type and their telephone number, both in case they were detained by the police or wounded in the demonstration. They were organized by student leaders with walkie-talkies, and they waited to march onto the Fenway and join hundreds of other students from Simmons College, Northeastern University, Boston University, and many other institutions in the area. Their demonstration was a rally at MIT to protest the Vietnam War. I was struck by their discipline, solidarity, and intensity.

In the early 1970s when we lost some students to the newly coed Catholic colleges and others to non-Catholic institutions, my job as chairperson included pacifying the sisters in the department, who were stunned by the diminishing number of eager English majors. During one of the college registration days when students ordinarily lined up to get into courses, Sister Anne Cyril, a popular and forceful figure in the department, turned to me accusingly and said, "What have you done with my students?" Indeed, we all were feeling the changes and adapting was not easy. However, the diversity of students that were coming in—adult learners, minority inner-city students, first-generation college students, and foreign students—made an interesting academic community with new kinds of challenges.

Although I was fully engaged in my career, Herb's career was really flourishing. He got a contract with the Bollingen Foundation to translate Massignon's work on Hallaj—a long arduous task of translating, editing, and scholarship—and he successfully published in 1970 his verse translation of the Gilgamesh epic, which was nominated for a National Book Award. Soon after he was hired at Boston University part-time in the University Professor's Program, which had been started by President John Silber, and then he became part of Silber's team, moving directly into the department of religion as a full professor and working on some of Silber's grand schemes for the university. His job was consuming and heady and we were often visited by Silber's private limousine service, sent to deliver messages and documents. There was a feeling of empire building in the air although I certainly did not feel a part of it. In my busy suburban life I felt an undercurrent of discontent that I was not using my own creative and intellectual power to the full and that Herb and I were drifting apart.

My mother's house on McKown Point in Boothbay Harbor, Maine, became the center for me and the three children for several weeks each summer. My sisters and I took turns staying there and sometimes we overlapped a day or two so the cousins could enjoy being together even though they were almost a generation apart. I usually went in July and Herb would come up on weekends. Sometimes we would take a cottage in the area and stay on while he took his vacation. At other times we took a family trip, up to Moosehead Lake or to Quebec or Montreal.

The children looked forward to their stay at "Nana's house." Even rainy days were not necessarily disastrous there. The long attic that stretched above the seven little bedrooms on the second floor could become a haunted house, transformed with sheets and flashlights and a maze that led around dark corners with scary faces popping out from nowhere or strange howls and shrieks startling the visitors who were lured from neighboring houses to come to the show. On one occasion when Paul and Sarah had set up a particularly spooky event, a small boy from the cottage next door had to be rescued when he became terrified halfway through the maze. I reminded Paul, who masterminded the inventions, that he had to monitor his visitors more carefully.

The world of McKown and Juniper Points was my world and yet it was not. There was a certain comfort in being among familiar Wasp faces where I did not feel that I had to apologize for occasionally looking like a Peck and Peck (now Talbots) Wasp. At the same time this summer group was not my group. They had certain expectations of what I should be, and I did not fit the mold. I did not play tennis religiously—or at all—and we did not go to yacht club dances or cocktail parties. Our boat, a small Boston Whaler, barely qualified us to go to the island picnics. On the other hand, occasionally one of the summer commodore types would adopt us. One summer, Mr. Foote, who had actually made his fortune in shoes in Minnesota, lent us his miniature tugboat, *The Little Bear,* that he had had custom made for picnics when his children were small. It had wide decks, a head, and a slow steady pace. In it we navigated up and down the coast and forgot that we often felt like poor relations in this affluent business community.

During the week I was on my own. I drove back and forth to Fresh Pond where swimming lessons and Red Cross lifesaving tests were given as part of the yacht club program. I sat on one of the logs on the perimeter of the beach, where the other mothers waited for their children to finish life-saving classes. My sisters were at ease with these women, but I found it difficult to pursue a conversation. The mothers rushed from their own tennis matches to their children's sailing races and swimming lessons, and they shopped for and entertained huge crowds of people on the weekends. I didn't have much to say to them. When I saw someone I knew from Belmont, perhaps a mother of one of the children's classmates, we would talk about the coming fall and the school and teachers.

Once in a while my vigil was interrupted by a startling image, reminding me that there were more unusual vacationers. One day two watery figures rose up out of the pond carrying a kayak between them. It was Mrs. Nutt, the national kayak champion, and her son. She and her husband, a professor of geology at Dartmouth College, had a cottage on the point. She looked like a Nordic goddess, her short blonde hair slicked back and dripping. Her son was about her height (six feet), bronzed and lean. They were an incongruous sight among the rest of us, sitting in our plaid shorts or skirts and matching tee shirts. They passed by with a nod and walked up the road to their car. I felt as if I had just been visited by Olympians, but Sarah brought me back to reality when she came shivering out of the water and wrapped herself in a towel and we drove home.

My mother was definitely the matriarch in the summer. She both provided generously and ruled autocratically. I usually planned and produced her July 3rd birthday party. It was combined with the annual Fourth of July celebration and the town fireworks as well as two other concurrent family birthdays. The climax of the parties was my mother's seventy-fifth birthday celebration in 1974. It was also the twenty-fifth anniversary of her coming to the point in the summer. My sisters and I planned a huge family celebration.

The party marked a watershed in my life. First it was the beginning of a temporary decline in mother's mental and physical health. Her two older sisters, Mabel and Edith, had just gone into their respective nursing homes, and although my mother often patronized them as spinster aunts, she nevertheless was deeply attached to them and even dependent on their authority and strength of character. Their disappearance from the scene of active life was a devastating blow to her—a sign for her, no doubt, of her own mortality—and she became discontent and depressed. In addition, the party marked a serious deterioration in my marriage, which in turn strained my relationship to my mother. As Herb became less and less involved in our vacations at the point, the burden of planning our activities fell more and more on me.

The birthday celebration was on the surface a great success. All of Nana's children and grandchildren were there and so were all of her friends from the point. We had the party catered, including a special cake decorated with "Happy Birthday 75 Years." The grandchildren wrote and recited poems to Nana and one grandson composed a song in her honor and played his guitar while everyone sang. Through it all Mother seemed distracted. She complained about little details and could not relax. Her behavior was a forecast of things to come. The following year she experienced a severe depression.

My own feelings at the party were an eerie parallel to my mother's mood, although for very different reasons. Herb's life at the university had taken priority over family life and I felt the strain of a loss of sharing and intimacy that had been so much a part of our relationship. Self-doubt and self-pity mixed with anger began to haunt me though I could not yet foresee the terrible challenges that I would face as I entered my fifties. At Mother's party I struggled to appear enthusiastic and cheerful, but I felt otherwise. We had a cottage nearby, but Herb spent hardly any time with us, staying at home and claiming to be too busy to take time off. When he came up for the special weekend, he arrived late in the afternoon and was very unenthusiastic about going to the party. He was barely civil during the event and left early on his own when I said I was going to stay longer with the children.

After he left—I angrily told him to leave the car for me—I suddenly looked around the room at all of the guests: Dick Roberts in his dark blue blazer and white slacks; his wife Sally, the artist and entrepreneur of the point; Debbie Sewall, fresh from the women's tennis tournament; and Kay Witten, part of the Rubicom clan that brought a number of New York advertising executives to summer there. I thought, *What am I doing here all dressed up in a fancy outfit among these tanned and robust people?* I looked around at the young people dancing and singing and I felt that I must not move from my chair and be exposed. It was as if a mask had been ripped from me and my true identity had been revealed. I thought, *I am a fake. I can not pretend to pass in the world of these able-bodied people.* These sensations lasted for only a minute or two, but I was shaken and could not throw off my melancholy mood the rest of the evening. I realized later on that I was unable to acknowledge the anger I was feeling towards Herb's withdrawal and my mother's decline, and I internalized it, blaming myself and my disability.

My mother did go into a further decline, and she battled depression for several years. The next summer I wrote about her in my journal after a difficult visit to the point when she complained to me and my sister about everything. We tried to maintain the house as she expected. She had lost her boundless energy but not her demands for her housekeeping standards. We never seemed to be able to satisfy her. Jane and I met tearfully in the kitchen at the end of the day and compared put-downs: the plates had not been warmed before serving dinner, the porches were not swept, the children had dropped wet suits, and so on. I wrote, "She is morose, self-pitying, almost totally locked in the world of her house. . . . My sister Jane can bring her out of herself somewhat. I cannot."

The next summer I drove up to Boothbay with Sarah. Cathleen and Paul had other plans—soccer camp for Paul and arts camp for Cathleen. Both of them had also taken summer jobs. When I got out of the car and walked toward the house, I was startled to see a halting, frail old woman standing at the steps. It was my mother and I could hardly believe it. She came toward me unsteadily, hardly able to walk, but she smiled very sweetly—she had not smiled much that year—and she moved right up close to me and looked at me intently. "You're so pretty, dear. You're so pretty," she said.

I don't think my mother had ever said that to me before. I was shocked but so touched that tears came to my eyes as I embraced her. In the next few days she weakened even more. She shook uncontrollably and could no longer walk. She was frightened and confused and I sat beside her bed and rubbed her back and arms trying to soothe her. I stayed until I had to leave for the cottage we had taken that summer for two weeks on Orrs Island. Herb did not want to stay around Boothbay Harbor, expressing an increasing hostility to everything about my family. I kept in close touch with my sister by phone. We called Mother's doctor and he prescribed more medication. The local doctor believed she had Parkinson's disease. Finally, she had a complete collapse of all her bodily functions and my sister and her husband had to send her in an ambulance to her own medical facility at her retirement community—from Maine to New Jersey. They followed soon after, and with the care of a specialist and other doctors, they discovered that she did not have Parkinson's disease and that she had been improperly medicated for a long period of time, which caused her collapse. She recovered almost completely.

After her illness I realized that my relationship to my mother had changed. I had felt alienated and resentful toward her at times over the years, perhaps because of my own unconscious guilt of being a burden as a disabled child. I was unable to be as affectionate, open, and giving as I wanted to be, although our close ties were always there. Now that I had helped care for her and comfort her, I was able to acknowledge the affection I had for her. Five years later, after a divorce and many hard times, I identified even more with my mother, recording a brief note in my journal at the time: "I think back to her losses and shocks and I empathize truly for the first time. I grieve for her illness and frailty (though she is well again) but, perhaps, as a premonition of her death and the great loneliness I shall feel."

15

DARK PASSAGES

Times were troubled in general in the second half of the 1970s. Inflation caught most of us in the academic world. Our salaries did not keep up with it, and either our standard of living had to drop or we had to go into debt. We started to do the latter, and instead of facing the problem together, Herb and I avoided it—similar perhaps to Gerald Ford's evasive reaction to the economic problem, which was to issue WIN buttons: Whip Inflation Now. President Carter, when he was elected in 1976, could not seem to rally us back to the old American spirit of self-reliance, and Vietnam and Watergate had left us all discouraged and cynical about the political process.

I found this general malaise creeping into my life. I missed the engaging activism of the 1960s. My own work—outside of my teaching—seemed to me uninspired, and I felt a growing alienation in my marriage. My instinct at this time was to return to my own writing. I started to keep a journal and began to record my search for topics that genuinely interested me and to return to myself as a writer of fiction. I realized that I had lost my real voice somewhere in graduate school and with it the creativity and confidence I had had in my writing as an undergraduate. Gone was the energizing blessing of Mrs. Boas and Mr. Earle, who pronounced me brilliant. What stuck in my head were the seductive words of Frank O'Connor that I would make "the perfect wife of a writer." In my journal of July 1975, I wrote, "How much have I become over the last decade the appreciator of my husband's work, interpreter of his needs, his moods and those of my children?" How many other women were asking those questions at that time? But I did not yet know that.

Herb left home a year or so before I wrote that journal entry. He moved to an apartment in Boston. He was having an affair with a student—the first affair in our marriage. He pleaded that he needed this other person in his life but that the children and I were still most important to him and that somehow we could go on with our lives as usual. "I'll spend Christmas here," he said, "and some weekends and other times."

I was crushed but clear-headed. "Oh no you won't," I maintained firmly. He returned a few months later after the student had transferred from the university and he had taken a trip to the Middle East. He said that keeping the family together was the most important thing to him, but we did not really talk about our own relationship and the boundary lines of our lives became more and more blurred. Since he showed little interest in our going for counseling together to try to work out our problems, I realized I would have to do something for myself.

We had been going with the children to the Paulist Fathers' church on Park Street for the last two years and so in a spur-of-the-moment decision I made an appointment to see Father Young, a beautiful man with compassionate eyes who served mass regularly on Sundays and who was known for his controversial views on divorced couples in the Catholic Church. When I went into his reception room upstairs, I met another woman, about my age, coming out with tear-stained eyes, and I almost bolted for the elevator, picturing myself as part of a long line of suppliants who came at half-hour intervals to be loved. But a strong undercurrent of longing kept me there and I went in. I managed to tell my story without too many breakdowns, realizing as I went along that I did not quite know what I was going to ask of him. "I just feel for the first time in my life that I don't know how to get through the next day," I said.

The young priest talked to me about sorrow and about transitional periods of life and the need for community. He was simple and dignified, but when he suggested I read the autobiography of Eugene McCarthy's ex-wife, I was put off. I felt no connection with senators' wives who wrote forgiving memoirs of husbands who left them. I had come to talk about solutions and hope and despair.

"I'm going to put you in touch with one of our priests who is a little outside of our regular community right now. He does counseling on his own." Father Young's sculpted hands, strong but delicate, took out a little pad of paper and jotted down an address for me. I particularly noticed his hands, and the next Sunday when I went to church, I noted their expressive quality in his gestures during his sermon and in his grasp when he came down the aisle and reached across to me at the interruption in the mass for the sign of peace, when the priest and the congregation exchange greetings. His eyes sought mine as we shook hands and I forced a little smile.

I made an appointment with "Father Bob," the counselor whom Father

Young recommended, and found myself sitting across from a priest dressed in a sports shirt and slacks in his apartment on Marlboro Street. *So this is grief,* I thought, looking at Father Bob, whose eyes were rather hard and at times, I thought, almost blank. I could not say much else because every time I tried to speak, I had uncontrollable fits of crying. I seemed to be talking to myself most of the time when I was not crying. The priest would wait patiently while I blew my nose and then he would encourage me to go on. "Take your time," he would say. "I know it's hard."

But does he know how hard it is? I wondered as I stuffed my used tissue back into my pocketbook. I began to spend more time wondering about Father Bob's life than attending to my own. Often when I rang the bell in the foyer of the converted townhouse, the priest's voice would come on the intercom and ask me to wait a few minutes. At first I imagined the delay was due to another client who was in the middle of a crisis and could not be interrupted, but a couple of times as I went up to his floor, I passed a cleaning lady coming down the winding stairs carrying a huge bundle of soiled sheets and towels in her arms. When I sat in the car waiting, I looked at the first and second story windows on the rows of townhouses, wondering who lived in them and what they did. There were rarely any passers-by at ten o'clock in the morning, but when a person did walk by the car, I felt a little self-conscious as our eyes met as I sat at the wheel waiting to go in. I imagined that they knew that I was waiting to see a priest on the second floor of the house, a priest who dressed in slacks and a plaid shirt and who had bundles of soiled bedding coming out of his apartment.

After a couple of weeks, Herb agreed to come with me to a session. He talked about his affair but did not show any signs of wanting to discuss our future and Father Bob offered us no direction so we did not develop any significant communication. Eventually the silences drove me to another counselor—a gray-haired psychiatrist with whom I could openly battle for reactions. I exchanged the elegant, slightly down-at-the-heel Marlboro Street townhouse for the long brightly lit white corridors of a modern apartment house in Brookline, a building full of Cambridge-style offices— slightly shabby Danish modern chairs, a bright geometric print on the wall, several hanging green plants, a brownish black tweed wall-to-wall carpet, and a linen-colored couch with more geometric design pillows. I parked in an underground garage in one of the many little slots that were constantly filled and emptied by cars gliding in and out all day.

In June I decided that I needed to get away from all counselors and go on a retreat, so I took an expensive room in a Rockport inn, looking out on the North Shore seacoast, at waves and gray and black rocks and horizons of fog rolling in and smothering the shore, or receding in slow patchy curtains. I arranged a week's working vacation, leaving the children for the first time alone with Herb. I was revising an article for an anthology and I was reading both Erica Jong's *Fear of Flying* and the poetry of Theodore Roethke. I found that Erica Jong seemed to replace male chauvinism with female chauvinism, but I admired her freedom of language and spirit. I was feeling very alone, almost as if I were again in my twenties, trying to make my way. At times, I was despairing and felt rage and a pounding and hurt in the pit of my stomach. When it subsided, I was left feeling calm. I wrote in my journal, "Discipline and habit must take over, push one on." The last sentence seemed to come right out of the code that my father had established for all of us as I was growing up.

I soon found that I hated to leave the fog and surf of my room in the annex to go across the street to the inn where I had my evening meal. The hotel was run by a hearty Scotsman and his wife and was filled with elderly vacationers: matriarchal widows who took several rooms and commanded children and grandchildren to come visit them, wiry eighty-year-old couples with strong Cambridge walking shoes who made the tour around the point three times each day, and other frail gray-haired ladies who spent their seasons alternating between resort spots, enjoying the gourmet meals and participating in the canon of games, slide shows, and recitals offered as evening activities. As the youngest guest, I was placed at different tables each night to add variety to the conversations. I was relieved that Herb and Sarah had brought me to the inn. I had the feeling that otherwise, Mrs. Kenniston or Mrs. Rosenthal or even the Metcalfs, who were terribly gentle and kind, would have found me too difficult to fit into their holiday landscape—a disabled woman alone, who neither participated in their diversions nor seemed willing to accept their offerings of pity.

Coming back one evening after supper when I had felt compelled to rush away from my fellow guests, who suddenly seemed like grotesque puppets bobbing in and out of the tables and chairs and couches of the lounge, I turned on my large color television and the screen expanded into a brilliantly colored close-up of Beverly Sills, a middle-aged opera star, glittering in her purple blouse, reddish blonde hair, and sparkling diamond fingers. Her large confident red mouth laughed constantly, almost raucously. She told the talk show host of her late success, a brilliant career opening up before her with the help of "my Peter" and, of course, her own drive and determination. The skeletal figures of the inn juxtaposed against the image of this bosomy, blossoming self-promoter made me dizzy. I felt a wave of nausea and then a complete emptiness. The curtains were open on the wide picture window, but blackness smothered any view of the sea, so that I looked out into a void. I remembered that the first night after my arrival, I had a dream about my brother, Tom, who had committed suicide twenty-five years before in the summer; when I awoke I particularly noted it in my journal because I had not dreamt of him for a long time. He was the Tom in the photograph, holding his two young nephews, one on each arm beside the maroon car. In the dream I went up to him, trying to tell him about my children, or so I thought afterwards. He kept looking out of the photograph but not at me and a terrible sadness came over me so that I woke up crying and longing to see my children. I almost dressed and went across the street to the inn to use the public telephone to call home, but then I looked at the clock and realized it was only 4 A.M.

Now as my heart pounded and my head ached with the gaudy images, I pressed my face against the picture window, trying to see into the blackness, not daring to turn off the television and leave the room silent. I stared and as my eyes adjusted to the blackness, I began to distinguish the shore, the rocks, subdued waves, and the curls of fog blotting out the stars and moon but still allowing a ghostly light on the coast.

I searched the fog for familiar faces, somehow expecting to see a line of figures, as if out of a Shakespeare play, moving up through the mists of the past to beckon to me and to speak prophetic words: my father and brother, Professor Massignon from France, Mrs. Boas, Miss Baechle from the Wheeler School, and other figures. I stayed by the window for several hours, crouched forward in an armchair, hardly noticing the changing images beside me on the television or the increasing chill of my own body as the night went on and the sea dews fell.

The figures in the mist did not emerge, although I tried to summon them, but one figure kept coming back to me—Elizabeth Winslow, an elderly writer and scholar whom Herb had first met in the Boston Athenaeum and who became a part of our lives. I saw her standing on the lawn in front of her "settler's house" in Sheepscot, Maine, having her picture taken with Herb and then by herself. She was wearing her yellow short-sleeved summer dress—always the same one—and she had a yellow ribbon tied around her graying hair, still brightened with dark streaks and done in a bun in the back. No one knew her age until she died at eighty-nine, but she was in her eighties when we first met, although you would never have known it. She held court at the Boston Athenaeum, where she spent her winters writing her books—biographies of religious figures in American and English literature and history. In March she left for Maine and for her long summer sojourns in Sheepscot, the little town that she had adopted. She supplied the town library with books, attended the historic white church on the hill, and presented the children at Easter with little baskets of chocolate eggs and jellybeans. She fed the squirrels, chipmunks, birds, and other creatures around her house and in her meadows and woods.

The first time I met Miss Winslow—Herb had spoken of her a great deal while he was working at the Athenaeum—she came for dinner wearing a garnet-colored silk dress, a matching hair ribbon of velvet, and one single strand of garnet beads. She said she had given her matching earrings and bracelet and pin to a young woman in Chicago who wanted to marry H. L. Mencken. After she arrived at our house, she gathered the children around her and presented each one of them with a small beautifully made toy animal—a leopard, a bear, and a giraffe. She told me about her years of teaching literature at Goucher College, then at Wellesley College, and of her early years as a graduate student at the University of Chicago, where she had gone at sixteen, having skipped two grades in her California school days.

"I met a young man at Chicago," she said, "a fellow graduate student, and he said to me, 'You know what I'm going to do? I'm going to marry you and take care of you the rest of your life.'" She laughed and her bright black eyes and little birdlike head shook back and forth. "I said to him, 'Oh no you are not, thank you. You will do nothing of the kind.' And he did not."

I felt when she told these stories and many other enthralling tales of her life and of famous people whom she had known that she was talking more to Herb than to me. In fact, her listeners at the Athenaeum were usually male. She held audiences amid the manuscripts and books, talking to them of their work, encouraging their dreams and, above all, their affairs of the heart. She was extremely coquettish and yet completely in control of her scholarship. She continued to publish her books on Jonathan Edwards and John Bunyan and other seventeenth-century figures. She had not started writing them until she was fifty because she had been so absorbed in her teaching. She would walk down each morning to the library from her tiny Mount Vernon Street apartment, rented to her by one of the Boston families who found her someone to cultivate, and return at the closing of the library in late afternoon, sometimes accompanied by one of her courtiers, who would see her to the bottom of Beacon Hill.

Two summers before, when we had begun the painful process of separation, Herb went to see Miss Winslow alone while we were in Maine. He came back and told me that she had said that he was a romantic and would have affairs of the heart. I had felt a shocking betrayal when I heard that. I knew that she was closer to him than to me, but I had exchanged many visits with her and had borrowed books and articles and had shared my own work and writing with her while I was also working at the library. I did not see her again until Christmas time, when Herb suggested that we go to visit her because she had repeatedly asked him to bring me for eggnog to her apartment on Beacon Hill. I made excuses not to go at first but finally agreed and we went on a snowy night to her small, rather chilly rooms filled with books, Indian and Oriental throws and rugs provided by her Beacon Hill patroness—furnishings very unlike the simple early American decor and furniture that she had gathered together in her own house in Maine.

When we went in, Miss Winslow embraced me as usual and I found myself hardly able to speak, a situation that was rare between the elderly scholar and me. We proceeded rather ceremoniously to sit down and I heard myself refusing the eggnog and sherry and all the little Christmas delicacies that she had prepared for holiday visitors. Another woman stopped by while we were there. She embraced Miss Winslow enthusiastically while I watched closely, wondering how she could be so affectionate. After we left, Herb asked me why I had been so uncomfortable. "Because she is not my friend," I said, and I knew for a moment what the Biblical phrase "to harden one's heart" meant. So be it, I felt.

That was not the end of our relationship, however. Sitting in my room in the inn, looking out over the growing light on the horizon, I recalled most vividly our last meeting. I began to shiver with the growing chill in my room but I was too absorbed in the memory to move or to get up and get a sweater. The last time I had seen Miss Winslow was the previous summer in Sheepscott. I had gone to see her because I knew that she had not been well that winter and spring and had almost been brought back to the city and to the hospital for treatment in April. I went alone and when I saw her open the door, smiling with the same winsome and courteous manner as always, I knew that the elderly woman was dying. Her hair hung down in shocking disorder; she was not wearing a ribbon, her yellow summer dress hung on her loosely, and, what was most unusual, she had on no shoes or stockings. There was an odor of old age in the room, not the usual fragrance of lavender mixed with pine and cedar and sweet chocolate. She always served brownies to her guests, made from a box and doctored up, as she said, with secrets of her own.

I sat down a little uncomfortably but my self-consciousness was overwhelmed by compassion as I talked to this frail woman, still razor sharp in her questions and in her responses to our conversation. She got up once or twice—a little unsteadily—and pulled out a book or a magazine or journal for reference. She apologized for not having any brownies but offered a cup of tea. I said I had just finished lunch because I knew that otherwise my refusal would be considered a rejection of hospitality. As we talked and I told her about my current research on two medieval women mystics, I felt that the older woman was getting tired and I wondered when I should break away.

Suddenly Miss Winslow's eyes lit up with particular brightness. "I know what I wanted to give you," she said, as if she had been searching her mind for this piece of information. She went into the next room, her study, also lined with shelves of books, and opened her desk drawer. "A young woman brought me this from England," she said. "It is an essay on one of your women, Julian of Norwich." She handed it to me. "I want you to keep it," she said.

I was very touched. Miss Winslow often lent books and articles but rarely gave them away since she had already decided to give her entire collection to her little library in Sheepscot, hoping to encourage other "seekers," as she called them, to do research in the tiny New England village.

"But I can just borrow it," I had insisted, "and bring it back later this summer when I come up again."

"You must have it," the older woman had said, pressing my hand. "You will make good use of it."

My memories were dulled by an intense fit of shivering. I got up, flipping off the television, and fell into bed exhausted. The next morning was my departure day and I packed my things slowly and had them put into my car by the hotel handyman. I went back into my room several times to check for things I might have forgotten. Each time I returned and found nothing, I was still afraid that I might be missing something that I wanted to take with me.

16

DISCOVERIES

My return from Rockport marked a zero point in Herb's and my relationship, a kind of D day from which we both retreated but which pushed us further apart. Before leaving, I called home, already anxious to get back to see the children. Herb said he was going to have a barbecue. "Margaret is here," he added noncommittally. "I'll ask her to stay. That will be okay, won't it?"

For a moment I was stunned. Then I found myself responding vehemently. "No, it isn't okay."

Margaret was one of the young women from Herb's office whom he had started to include in our weekend family events. She was a pretty blonde Southern student at Boston University who had decided to pursue a career in dance. She was typing for the University Professors Program to make money to take lessons in ballet in a Boston studio. Herb encouraged her dreams, perhaps fantasies.

There was a silence on the other end of the phone when I responded negatively and I realized we were going to have a confrontation when I got home.

When I returned from Rockport, Margaret was gone and the children looked worried. They gave me hugs but soon scattered to their rooms, sensing the tense atmosphere between Herb and me.

We sat down across from each other at the kitchen table. I looked out the big glass window onto our backyard, a wonderful bowl-shaped space with terraced garden beds built on railroad ties going up the hill. I loved digging in the terraces, which were raised as you went up the steps. I still felt waves of anger, but I was losing my resolve for confrontation.

Herb's face was tight and his voice tense with anger but quiet. He rarely raised his tone when angry. "I need to live my own way," he said.

I could not regain the furious strength I had felt when he first left and demanded accommodation to a double life. I should have shouted and demanded, but I could not. I felt drained of my resolve. "There's a limit, you know," I said wearily. I felt at the edge of a tidal wave that threatened to carry my life away.

"I know, I know." Herb was impatient and wanted to conclude the conversation. Our eyes no longer met and we looked in different directions. I looked out into the garden through the glass door. Neither of us could confront the issues, so we reached an uneasy truce that would go on for several years. We tried to keep up a family unity, but our lives were getting further apart. I turned more and more to my own life.

After that confrontation, Margaret came back to the house once or twice when we were having some university people for dinner. She tried to be a friend to Cathleen, who was then a teenager, and she lent her some makeup for her junior prom. Then she disappeared and Herb referred to her rather obliquely, saying that it was hard to know how to handle someone who got too attached. About a year later, Cathleen confided to me that she had seen Margaret walking around the path along the reservoir next to our house almost daily. She had tried to speak to her but Margaret did not raise her head, which was muffled in the hood of her gray sweatshirt.

As I began to be shut out of our marriage and to feel adrift, I became more and more aware of the confinement of my body—a sense I had not had for some time. Once again, I longed for the freedom of movement of the dancer or the athlete or just the ordinary person's daily activities. Looking at the Olympic Games on television at my mother's house in Maine, I was awed by the beautiful images of the diver doing a perfect back flip or the gymnast executing the flawless leap or tumble. It seemed to me that such an articulation of physical form surpassed even a poem or a painting or a piece of music. There was no roughness or pomposity or pride—just the perfect expression.

On another occasion when I was staying for a few days in a peaceful little farmhouse in Maine, writing and reading and meeting a deadline for an article, I had another epiphany and an accompanying longing to be freed of my own body. I was looking out of the window and saw the farmer's wife, a vigorous attractive woman in her late thirties, and a young girl of ten or eleven with long blonde hair—her niece, perhaps—come back to the house in a little red car. They got out and walked off down the road toward the beach, eating apples. Climbing down over the rocks, they disappeared over the hill toward the sea, the image of freedom to me. To take your body where you want it to go and stride in the wind and through the water! It seemed a miracle!

This self-consciousness about my body climaxed in an actual physical event, a catastrophic accident when my brace came unlocked and I fell in the kitchen and suffered a hairline hip fracture. Suddenly I was really confined, first in bed and then in a wheelchair for six weeks.

We set up the dining room as my bedroom study and I had a hospital bed brought in because I had to stay immobile for almost two weeks before I could get into a wheelchair. The doctor decided not to pin the hip because it was a minor fracture and would mend better without intervention. As Dr. Blacklow, our gentle, philosophical family doctor, said of my condition, "At least it is reversible." (His wife was dying of cancer at that time.) I was the chairperson of the English department then and anxious to get back to work. As soon as I was able to use a wheelchair I went into my office, after an exhausting search for a means of transportation. The children were assigned as my nurses during my time in bed, including the bedpans, which they did cheerfully. They always had been willing to do anything that I needed without question, and I never felt that they resented or made an issue of my disability. Sarah claims she thought for years that all mothers were like me until friends in school asked her about my crutches and braces. In any case, all three of them rose to the occasion magnificently after my accident. Mrs. Ames, whom I had hired to cook dinner three days a week and to be with Sarah, who was still in elementary school, was able to take over most of the household matters.

It was clear during this confinement that Herb was not up to the nurturing or caretaking role. He organized things in the beginning and then turned it over to me and the children. It was another revelation about some of the false assumptions on which our marriage was built. The assumption was that I could do everything an able-bodied person could do. I had faked that role fairly well over the years, but now I was in a situation where I had no control.

My hip fracture gave me a fleeting glimpse of mortality. I had never spent much time brooding about age or the inevitable coming of death. I suppose I had actually avoided the subject because it stirred up anxieties about how I would face growing older when I would be less mobile. My accident focused my attention on my physical condition in a very concrete way. First of all, in bed those two weeks I was afraid to move at all, fearful that I would make the fracture worse; then in the wheelchair I had to learn a whole new set of restrictions about using my body. I had always separated myself psychologically from people in wheelchairs. I felt different from them because I could get around without ramps and without elevators.

It was after these episodes of feeling physical entrapment that I actually experienced two moments of reconciliation with my body, experiences that

I reflected upon and which helped to heal my sense of confinement. The first was a recollection of a family trip that we had taken some years before to Moosehead Lake, where we rented a cabin and a motorboat. We started out the next morning to fish and eventually to find a friendly shoreline on which to have a picnic. As we crossed into the middle of the lake, Mount Kineo suddenly loomed out of the water above us. It came as a shock, an unexpected presence. I recalled a passage from Wordsworth's *Prelude* where the poet describes himself as a young boy who has stolen a boat, which he rows away from the shore. All of a sudden he sees a huge peak rear up, blocking his view of sky and stars like a menacing presence. Frightened, he returns the boat to the shore but afterwards he is haunted for days by "huge and mighty forms" which "moved slowly through the mind / By day, and were a trouble to [his] dreams." I felt the same kind of shock and awe as I looked up at the dark form, but it was not menacing to me. It seemed a reality outside of my own physical presence while in some way connected to it. Now in the recollection of that moment I again felt a release from my body's daily limitations and a transcendence beyond my physical self.

The second moment of recollection occurred during a summer when we vacationed as a family at Rangeley Lake in Maine. We had taken a late afternoon ride in a small motorboat that we rented from the lodge where we were staying. As we started back to shore I turned and looked back at the horizon and saw the setting sun and I experienced a momentary flash of revelation about my smallness and insignificance but at the same time my perfect proportion in relation to the vastness of the horizon. This time I did not feel as if I was overcoming my physical body but rather I felt at peace with it because it had its proper place in the universe.

The physical confinement that I experienced from my hip fracture also translated into a new period of creativity for me. It was as if the acceptance of my body and its limitations and the discovery of my relevance to a larger scheme of things gave me a new perspective and renewed energy. I began to turn to my own work and my own interests, realizing I was not going to find strength in my marriage.

I also discovered the work of other women writers—the extraordinary outpouring of poetry, prose, and fiction in the the 1970s, which had been nurtured by the Women's Movement. Although I was aware of the Women's Movement when I was at the Radcliffe Institute among women scholars from 1967 to 1969, I was then still attached to the subjects of my dissertation. Now I found that women were retelling and reshaping their stories and inventing new narratives. I followed the journeys of poets, some of whom, such as Adrienne Rich and Anne Sexton, were my contemporaries, and I read works by African American women writers that expanded my sense of the American experience, giving it an epic quality so often claimed by male writers.

Like many of my women contemporaries, I started to look for the women writers we had lost—the voices we had buried or had not yet discovered. I particularly wanted to know what and how women wrote about themselves, because I had always been intrigued by autobiography and questions of self-identity. In my search for the beginnings of women's autobiographical writing in English, I finally uncovered the voices that I had been trying so hard to hear in France. Women, I discovered, had been writing in Europe since the twelfth century, when many extraordinary women in convents began to record their spiritual autobiographies and other works that started a women's renaissance of learning, art, and scholarship. Famous abbesses such as Hildegarde of Bingen, the playwright, composer, and scientist, created cultural and intellectual centers in their convents. The autobiographical writings of medieval women mystics and saints—some well known, such as Catherine of Siena and Saint Bridget of Sweden in the fourteenth century, and others more obscure—expressed women's particular vision of spirituality and broke the long silence of women.

Looking for English models, I discovered Julian of Norwich, the first known English woman of letters, who was an anchoress in a church in Norwich and known well in her own region for her spiritual counseling. She wrote an autobiographical account of her mystical experience during a serious illness in 1373—a vision of the passion of Christ. This was followed by her miraculous recovery. After twenty years of meditation and study, she revised her first version of her experience and called it *Revelations of Divine Love*. When I read Julian's original autobiographical account of her spiritual experience I found a striking contrast to the well-known model for all autobiographical writing, the *Confessions* of Saint Augustine. Augustine presents himself as the center of a dramatic struggle of opposing forces—the spirit over the flesh—where victory is finally achieved by the spirit, and the sinner is converted and becomes one with God. Julian, on the other hand, although she is describing a dramatic recovery from an illness and a series of revelations, presents an almost clinical account of the experience, and her poetic metaphor for herself and of her role in creation is of a tiny hazelnut in the hand of God. However, despite her lack of self-dramatization and despite her use of the traditional rhetoric of self-effacement—she calls herself "a simple creature"—Julian can adopt an assertive, almost feminist tone in the beginning of her narrative when she protests, "But because I am a woman ought I therefore to believe that I should not tell you of the goodness of God."

Julian spoke to me across the centuries, not only for her unique way of writing about her spiritual experience, but also because despite being a woman in the fourteenth and fifteenth centuries, she was able to meditate, to study and write, and to transform her vision to theological teaching. She could also spiritually and psychologically guide and counsel those who came to her anchorage in Norwich. In short, she was a powerful figure of autonomy who was still uniquely a woman.

I found that a contemporary of Julian's, Margery Kempe, had also written an autobiography, although she, being illiterate, had to dictate hers. Margery's is actually the first known complete autobiography in English. Margery represented the voice of the laypeople and the life of many women in the world who are wives and mothers but who also aspire to another role. In Margery's case, she aspired to a spiritual vocation. Her struggle with these divided responsiblities caused her much suffering. In 1413 she sought advice from Julian and the two remarkable women met in Norwich. Julian reassured her that her vocation was genuine, so Margery pursued her calling, which took her out of her private life as she travelled on pilgrimages around the world and confronted figures of authority in church and state, who often doubted her visions and her vocation. Her spiritual self-narrative is also unlike Augustine's *Confessions*. While he identifies with the divinity, Margery, like Julian, has a relationship with God as the "other." She describes a number of conversations with the deity, who tells her that she must be a "mirror amongst them [mankind]" to reflect her sorrow for Christ's suffering. Her account recreates not only her spiritual pilgrimage and her visions but also the medieval world seen from a woman's point of view. Both Julian and Margery, while part of the medieval world, spoke beyond it and connected to me. Their lives as recorded offered a woman's spiritual way.

The more women's autobiographies I read, the more I became convinced that women wrote differently about themselves than men. Because of the roles and identity constructed for women, even contemporary women's autobiographies, I found, often presented themselves in relation to others—an "identity by alterity," as I described it in an essay on women's autobiographical writing. My research resulted in a collection of women's autobiographical writings, *Journeys,* co-edited with a colleague, Carol Hurd Green, and my theory of women's autobiographical writing became a part of the growing critical discussion of women's writing.

This immersion in the study of the traditions of women's history and women's literature and spirituality was fundamental in giving me a sense of my own relationship to the past. I began to understand my experience of alienation among the postwar Catholic intellectuals in France as part of a gradual awakening on my part to the significance of gender and to an understanding of my own particular journey as a woman. I read Simone de Beauvoir's *The Second Sex* and filled in one of the gaps in my French experience. These revelations also helped me to develop a sense of independence and autonomy, which I would increasingly need in my personal life.

At the same time I was also continuing my journey of reconciliation with my disability. The final turning point came in the summer of 1977 when I spent a week in retreat in Brewster on Cape Cod. It was the beginning of the abandonment of that double in my life—that consciousness or voice that tried to pass as able-bodied—as well as another stage in my acceptance of my disabled body. I did not grasp its real significance then but it later sustained me through more difficult times. I spent a revitalizing week of work, reading, writing, and meditation. I had taught a summer school course that year—the first course in women's studies at the college. One of my students—an adult learner, as we called the older returning students at Emmanuel—asked me to give a course on women's literature and so I created one, a gathering together of many of the discoveries I had made in my reading of women's writing.

The course was exhilarating, but it was an oppressively hot June and Herb had arranged to be away for a month in New Hampshire, where he had found a retreat for himself among other writers and musicians. I had the house and the children's lives to care for as well as my teaching so I was exhausted by the end of the summer session. I had planned my trip away earlier, rejecting a place like the inn at Rockport, which had been too structured and frivolous to inspire work. It also evoked sad memories for me. I had not yet discovered Cummington Community of the Arts in western Massachusetts, which was to become a haven for me to go to in the future. I began to ask around and found my retreat from one of the nuns at the college. She suggested that I ask about renting a room in Brewster where the order of La Sallette had a center. She said they had recently closed the seminary there and sometimes rented out space in the empty building that was still maintained by the local parish priest. I drove to the Cape one Sunday with my friend Charlotte and we stopped off at a beautiful site where the seminary stood, high on a hill looking out to the sea. The priest was in the nearby parish house and was very cordial about the idea of my renting a room for a week. We went over to the seminary and I picked out two small adjacent rooms—one to sleep in and the other for a studio—on the first floor not far from the kitchen. We set the date and the price and drove home.

Now that the summer session was over, I was ready to go to Brewster. As soon as Herb returned, I packed my things and he and Paul followed me to the Cape in another car so they could help me get settled. We arrived in the late afternoon and got the key from the priest. The huge seminary was dark and empty. "Aren't you going to find this creepy being here alone?" Paul asked.

I hadn't thought about that and I was surprised that I had not even considered the possibility that I might be freaked out, knowing my deep-seated fears of darkness and solitariness from the past. However, as I looked around at all the empty spaces, I did not think about how dark and silent it was going to be. "I'll be fine," I said confidently, although internally I quailed a little.

When they left, I unpacked my things, arranging the carefully selected pile of books on a shelf, the typewriter and paper and notebooks on the table, which we had set up, and the chair with the proper cushion. I put my few clothes in the drawers of the bureau or in the closet. The bed was narrow and rather hard but adequate, and I connected my radio on the small night table and placed my clock beside it although it seemed as if I was about to enter a timeless zone. I looked around and relished the lack of clutter and the lack of complexity that the partially filled shelves and the near empty drawers suggested.

We had stopped for lunch on the way down so I was not very hungry but I decided I had better do a little food shopping although I had planned to eat most of my dinners out at one of the local restaurants. Eating alone in a restaurant was going to be a novel experience, one that would test my image of myself as I entered alone and presented myself to strangers. For more than twenty years I had been almost constantly with some part of my familiar world, my husband, my children and family and friends, my students and colleagues. Occasionally I went to conferences alone and took a hotel room by myself. I always enjoyed it, reveling in the anonymity of the hotel decor, trying the television and rising especially early just so I could order breakfast in my room—what a luxury! But in those circumstances I had always felt connected as a professional and I usually had plans with colleagues to eat meals and go to events. Here I would be a complete stranger and perhaps a curiosity. *Oh well,* I thought, *here's a new experience or at least one you have not had for a long time!*

When I came back from the store, there was another car next to mine, and I soon discovered that a middle-aged French Canadian couple, friends of the priest's, had taken a room near mine for a few days of vacation. I was filled with a sense of comfort! Now I was not alone but I was still solitary.

We exchanged greetings, and from time to time, we would see each other for further pleasantries. Mostly I was just aware of their coming and going, preparing food in the kitchen and retiring early at night. They departed before I did, which I regretted, but by that time I was so involved in my work and my thoughts that I did not have time to panic at the emptiness of the place.

A day or so after my arrival, I found my spot behind the seminary where I placed a chair to sit and look at the sea. There was a glorious vista of a gradually sloping hill of grass and wildflowers merging into the shoreline and the ocean. I made a list in my journal of what I wished to accomplish: reading—an eclectic list including Charlotte Perkins Gilman, Ellen Moers's *Literary Women,* more Simone de Beauvoir, a novel by James Agee, and so on; an outline for my collection of women's autobiographical writings; an essay on Julian of Norwich and Margery Kempe for the *New Boston Review;* an article on Anne Bradstreet; a short story; and the list went on. I felt totally engaged in my work but also totally at peace—enjoying the sun, which was not too hot, enjoying the quietness, but with the knowledge that people were not too far away. I felt that social games and human involvements had momentarily receded.

The next few days were a frenzy of activity as I read and wrote and typed as if possessed. I barely slept at night and was frequently awakened by something I had to write down or look up in a book. Occasionally, I felt lonely and spooked out as I listened to the silence of the building with all of its ghosts of earnest seminarians, but then I would turn on the radio and fall asleep to music. It was rather hot and stuffy in the building as the weather warmed up, but I had brought a small fan with me that distracted me from the heat and provided a rhythmic accompaniment to my typing. I ate most of my dinners at the same restaurant and soon became a regular. It was a modest year-round establishment that did not have much of a summer crowd. One day I drove to Orleans and bought a few gifts to take back to the children. The priest stopped by once or twice to see if I needed anything and he sent over his secretary to check on me. I remembered that Herb had talked to her when we had arrived. He must have mentioned my former interest in Huysmans and my translation of Huysmans's life of Saint Lydwine, because she soon revealed that she was a zealot for martyrs and especially ones like Saint Lydwine with gruesome deaths. She urged me to go on with that work and to get it published. "We really need models like that," she said.

I was amused. My interest in such a project was zero and I could not imagine a less needed model for women. I tried to be noncommittal and very preoccupied, which seemed to work. Unless she saw me getting into my car, she left me alone.

My retreat at Brewster was a marked contrast to my experience at Rockport. Here I was solitary—though not isolated—and I did not have to deal with a hotel community completely out of touch with my own mood and purpose. I was at peace with myself, and years of intellectual and creative energy were released. I gave no thought to working out relationships or trying to read anybody's needs or moods. Grief was supplanted by occasional anger but it was a productive anger.

One morning as I sat outside and watched the sun glistening on the water and highlighting the whitecaps, I began to let go all of the images that haunted me. It started with the glittering, self-assured television image of Beverly Sills, and others followed: my father's unrelenting gaze as he told me I had to keep trying to improve; my sisters' unattainable glamour girl image of the 1940s; the sadness of Naomi dancing; Miss Winslow's yellow ribbon; Father Bob's blank eyes in the apartment on Marlboro Street; the angry child holding the Thanksgiving turkey by a string; my silent figure in the study of Louis Massignon; my return to a wheelchair after the fractured hip. Many other images came and slipped by me and lost themselves in the ocean in front of me. I took out my pen and notebook and wrote for several hours, hardly pausing to raise my pen. It was the only time I can remember writing a complete short story in one sitting. I hardly changed a word even for its publication. It was the story of my grandmother's death and of the child who discovered she could not bargain with God, even for love. I had started the story that summer in the writing course with Frank O'Connor although I had not finished it. Now I felt that I was going back to the person who had been a writer that summer, but not the person who had been described "as the perfect wife for a writer." And I resolved my old bargain with God. I could not be cured, but I could face the reality of myself as disabled. I had overcome many barriers and my disability was, in fact, a part of my uniqueness as a person.

I did not realize then how important my week at Brewster was going to be. It was a renewal and it laid the groundwork for future survival. At that moment, when I had finished writing the story, I felt a wonderful calm. Looking at the sea as I sat on that beautiful hillside, I felt that I was seeing it for the first time.

With Herb heading off to Paris, 1957

With Herb in a Paris café, 1960

Posing with Cathleen in her baptism dress, Paris, 1960

With Cathleen, Paul, Herb, and friend Dilip, Boothbay Harbor, Maine, 1964

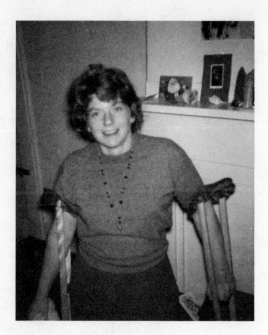

Cambridge, Massachusetts, 1964

Cathleen, Paul, and Sarah, Maine, circa 1973

Preparing dinner for guests, Belmont, Massachusetts, 1970

Visiting New Orleans, Louisiana, for the African literature conference at Loyola University, 1991

The Past is such a Curious creature

—Emily Dickinson, poem 1203

EPILOGUE

1988

When my daughter Sarah and her boyfriend took me out to dinner for my sixtieth birthday in 1988, I had no idea that she had planned a surprise party for me and that her main purpose was to keep me out of the house until all the guests could get there before we returned. I was stunned when I walked in the door to loud shouts of "Surprise!" Familiar faces filled the room—friends and colleagues and family. Both Cathleen and Paul and his wife, Chris, had driven or flown in from their respective jobs or graduate programs. It seemed as if everyone I really cared about was there.

It was a good birthday to celebrate. I had not thought a great deal about turning sixty. Being the youngest in the family, I had never been anxious about aging, even though I married someone almost four years younger than I. In fact, I hardly noticed passing fifty in 1978, after half a century of living. Now I was marking a significant milestone in my life and the celebration made me reflect on the decade that led up to it. Much of the decade, I realized, had been characterized by survival. In the spring and summer of 1979 I experienced some traumatic events: In April Herb walked out peremptorily and permanently. A few weeks later I went to the doctor and was diagnosed with breast cancer. Finally, looking over piles of unopened mail, I discovered we had many unpaid bills I did not know about.

Of course, my first concern had to be the cancer. Although I was numb and in shock, I could not be in denial about the disease. I became completely focused on the diagnosis, the options for treatment, and the doctor I would have. I had no impulse to keep a journal of every moment, but I did want to control my medical experience as much as possible. I interviewed several doctors on the phone and finally went to one who was highly recommended and told him quite frankly what I would demand from him as my doctor. Although he assured me he understood my terms,

I still had a long agonizing wait all summer to get a date for the surgery in August. The weeks of anxiety were interrupted by a trip to Boothbay Harbor to sort out and divide with my sisters the furnishings of the summer house. Mother had decided to sell it, feeling unable to cope with the maintenance and responsibility. Unfortunately, none of us at that point could finance a buy-out. The weekend I spent sorting through china, rugs, and furniture certainly underscored my sense that my world was dissolving.

I avoided the "How to Deal with Your Cancer" books that I was given. Most of them in 1979 blamed the victim and suggested that the patient had brought it on herself. Fortunately, the anger they generated gave me the energy to get through the hospitalization and get home. The operation was a success and the prognosis excellent. My friend Charlotte took over as nurse both in the hospital and at home. Although she almost smothered me with remedies and care, I was eternally grateful to her. Without her, it would have been very difficult. Herb pretty much disappeared after he dropped me off at the hospital. He reappeared at my bedside at home. "I think we should sell the house," he said solemnly. "I'll help find an apartment for Sarah and you."

I couldn't even answer him. I just waved my hand in dismissal. Later I told Cathleen I would not take any calls from him

If the first stage of this experience was trauma, the second stage was recovery, slow and painful because the return to crutches was hard with a healing incision. This time I intensely focused on recovering strength so I could return to work. I needed the income. I felt, however, an incredible weakness as if my body was an unwilling component of my consciousness. I remember sitting on the couch for hours in the family room, which had a picture window looking out at the reservoir, and trying to concentrate my mind on the sloping hillside, as if, by focusing on a point outside myself, I could somehow infuse energy into my body. I hardly noticed people coming and going, although friends and family were there. My sisters came. Cathleen was home and Sarah and Paul returned after camp and work respectively. My mother was no longer able to come and pitch in as she had done for so many years, but others came and went. I was touched when a cousin of Herb's, whom I rarely saw, came by with his wife, and one of Herb's nieces brought a cake. Both visits seemed to be given as gestures of compensation for Herb's lack of support.

I particularly remember the visit of my friend Kate Rushin, a poet whom I had met at Cummington Community of the Arts, who made a special trip to Belmont and brought me some of her favorite healing herbal tea. Kate and I had discovered that we had both been born twenty years or so apart in the not so attractive city of Camden, New Jersey (also the birthplace of Walt Whitman, we noted)—I from a family in a white suburban town and she from the African American community in Camden. She later moved to a town near mine, but our spheres never intersected. Kate was a life-giving person, a wonderful poet and performer, and her special tea, like her gesture of friendship and caring, seemed symbolically to infuse life. Gradually I recovered and could return to teaching a week or two after classes began in September.

The final stage of this traumatic period of my life is best described as the combat stage. I was suddenly a single parent and my battle over the next five years was to keep the house in Belmont open as a haven while Cathleen and Paul put themselves through college and started graduate school. Fortunately, our children could get free tuition at both our colleges so Paul transferred to Boston University from Wesleyan University where he had started. Cathleen, who was already a junior at Wesleyan, stayed there to graduate. They came home for vacations and often for summers while they worked and while Sarah was finishing high school. I kept the house going by the skin of my teeth. I put boarders in every available room and discovered some of the habits and eccentricities of the human race. I rented to a French chemist who would not bathe and to an unemployed teacher who spent her mornings in the bathtub. One year I rented to a reclusive poet who rarely left his third-floor room. He was followed by a Polish astronomer who appeared constantly in the kitchen to talk about what was wrong with America and to wait for me to start mothering him. I also taught full-time in the summer as an adjunct professor of writing at the Kennedy School of Public Policy.

I didn't realize how broke I was until I asked the tight-fisted Belmont tax collectors for a rebate and I got it. Then I knew that I must be poor! My divorce settlement granted me the house but very inadequate child support (Cathleen and Paul were both over eighteen and legally on their own) to supplement my small Emmanuel salary. However, I made it through to Sarah's graduation but then decided it was time to leave Belmont. When we started to sort out and get rid of eighteen years' worth of belongings, we realized the house had seen us through some important times. There were good memories even during the final years. The children always felt they could bring their friends home and we had many parties and cookouts in the backyard, decorating it with candles and piping out music through the windows.

Looking back on those "single" years in Belmont, I realized I had almost gained a sense of invincibility after all the battles. At least I knew I could never passively accept someone else's agenda. My drive for independence, perhaps fostered by my conflict with my father, stayed with me. After I sold the house, I bought a two-family house in the nearby town of Arlington with a friend, a writer whom I also had met at Cummington Community of the Arts, and I moved in.

My birthday party made me realize how much had happened in the last decade. They had been hard years, but I had found new ways to live. I realized that twenty years had slipped by since I had started teaching at Emmanuel College and that I had built a life of my own in a community of scholars and friends. Although Emmanuel was a small liberal arts college, its location in Boston attracted an unusually good faculty and I had found in its academic community a satisfying intellectual home. The interdisciplinary trend in the 1980s drove all of us to interact with each other. I think I either taught or worked on projects with faculty from almost every discipline, whether it was a course in modern art, music, and poetry, or a collaboration with the history or sociology or religious studies departments. I developed a women's studies program and gave conferences and wrote grants and papers.

One of the most successful and satisfying projects was a program in 1982, "Women in Transition," which had grown out of my interest in a large group of women who, divorced or widowed, were forced into the job market after spending most of their adult years as homemakers. My project was funded by a grant and drew together a group of twenty-five women, diverse in age and background, for a program that would give them a context for their own personal experience. Working with a sociologist, a women's historian, and an artist, I put together an eight-week program that explored women's experience in work and family and that celebrated the creativity in women's lives in the past and the present. In weekly three-hour sessions, we discussed readings in women's history and literature, showed films, and invited visiting artists to discuss their work. We also put together a panel of women who told us about their different career experiences. One of the unplanned events—and there were several—was an exhibit of quilts, which members of the group organized from their own homes and communities. Our final project was the creation of a book of memoirs and photos about an important woman in the life of each one of the participants. The book was handsomely designed by our colleague in the art department and it became a treasured memento for every member of the program. Our eight weeks ended with a potluck supper and a reading by Alice Walker, whom I managed to engage. She was an artist in residence at a nearby university and when I asked her if she would come, she accepted, saying she liked the sound of our program. When we picked her up and drove her to the college from Cambridge, she arrived like a star, but she was extremely gracious to everyone and gave a magnificent reading from *The Color Purple*. During all of our events everyone took lots of pictures of each other and the group found it hard to accept the fact that the program was over. They had become so bonded that we had reunions for several years, and I still hear from some members to this day.

My program for women was just one of the many outcomes of my involvement in the late 1970s and 1980s in the Women's Movement generally and with a particular community of women scholars both in my college and in the larger academic community. Many of us were midway through our lives and careers and all of us were profoundly changed by the Women's Movement and by the new approaches and material that we were finding in our fields of study. We met informally in reading groups or formally with the support of grants to exchange ideas and create new ways of teaching and doing research. This helped me to discover my own field of women's autobiographical writing, and also to recreate most of my courses to include the women who had been left out of my Harvard English literature courses, which had concentrated on white male authors. I also developed women's studies courses with colleagues, which we team-taught. It was an exciting intellectual time that transformed my thinking and expanded the walls of my small institution, making me feel part of a larger cultural and political community that had so often been just a male province.

In 1983, I became part of a group of women academics sponsored by a Mellon Foundation grant. We met in a seminar monthly to exchange information and to present our work in women's studies in the humanities. I shared a presentation with a colleague of mine in one of the neighboring colleges in Boston. We had both organized programs in women's studies for adult students and we discovered that we had used many of the same approaches in teaching. Martha and I would drive out to Wellesley every month and return full of ideas to discuss over dinner. We planned to start the Fenway Women's Studies newsletter and perhaps a collaborative women's center.

Unfortunately our plans were interrupted when Martha was struck with cancer. She fought hard to survive but she was not as lucky as I was. When it became clear that she was not going to live, her friends organized a vigil with her at the hospital, taking turns around the clock. Most of us were there when she died, and afterwards, when we sat in the lobby gathering strength to go to someone's house for a meal, the doctor came by and thanked us for our attendance. He said it made Martha's death easier not only for her but also for the entire medical staff, who, he said, often felt inadequate in a patient's last hours. Our coming together for Martha made me feel the power of friendship and community, which I so often experienced with the women I met and worked with at this time.

Our Mellon seminar group provided a graduate student with a doctoral dissertation on the effects of women's studies on our careers. She attended our meetings and interviewed us individually. She asked me to be a reader for her thesis at Harvard's school of education so I became familiar with her conclusions. The study described us "as having transcended our original training and credentials" and as "powerful enough to create new alternative structures, new methodologies, texts, even institutions." It also described the effect our new discipline had on our personal lives as well as our careers. Some of the group acknowledged lesbianism, others decided to divorce, and some made significant adjustments in their marriages or relationships. All of the group, the study noted, described themselves as more "culturally pluralistic," and it concluded that we were "especially attuned to the problems of the underclasses throughout the world." None of the women, the research concluded, felt they had to choose between family or career, although in many cases they were exhausted in maintaining the two parts of their lives. The study seemed to reflect many of my own experiences. I had developed new methods and material in my teaching and scholarship, often relearning things that were gospel in college and graduate school. I had also become more politically aware, particularly of the diversity of the world and of the needs of people without power. Finally, although my personal life had been fractured, I had created a new one that included both career and family.

Of course most of my daily work in the 1980s involved teaching the Emmanuel undergraduates, whom I found appealing for their diversity. The college's mission had originally been to teach poor urban women, but it became a middle-class institution in the 1960s when I first arrived. In the 1970s and 1980s, however, the students reflected again the diversity of the class and race of the college's urban setting and it took in many international students as well. I felt very connected with my students, who made the inevitable frustrations of administrative and institutional life worthwhile. They provided the unexpected, the hopeful, and the creative, making classrooms come alive. I shared their many triumphs: sometimes it was the discovery of a particular author or even just the pleasure of reading; at other times it was the pride in producing an excellent paper or a poem or a challenging idea.

One of my students reminded me of my role at the college when she sent me a copy of her letter supporting the Faculty Excellence Award for teaching. She wrote, "The day I first met Dr. Mason, I had cold hands, a lump in my throat, and SAT scores that weren't high enough to warrant automatic enrollment in her freshman honors English course." I remembered that scene and how she persuaded me to let her in the class. Four years later she graduated with honors and as she noted in her letter, "her confidence in me gave me confidence in myself."

Following the lives of students who kept in touch with me always seemed like a gift and made me feel that I could return some of the mentoring of Mrs. Boas and my Radcliffe sponsors. Foreign students were often among those who continued to share their lives with me. One of them was a lovely and talented Japanese student who had to miss her Emmanuel graduation to return to Japan for her brother's wedding. When she returned, I received a phone call from her. "Dr. Mason, could you give me my diploma?"

"Why, certainly," I said, and then wondered what she meant.

She continued earnestly, "I would like you to hand me the certificate so that I feel that it is real."

I realized she wanted some ceremony to replace the lost graduation event that would have meant so much to her. We arranged to meet and meanwhile I wracked my brain thinking of how I could make the presentation memorable. Fortunately, it was summer so we could meet under the trees on campus. When the day came, the dean of students met us under a flowering tree and handed the diploma to me and then I gave it to Kyoko with a rose attached. Afterwards we recessed to my office for cake and punch—a pale American version of a tea ceremony!

Sometimes I had to share the tragedies of my students. There was Gina, a gifted young woman who had opened up with excitement to new ideas in my classes and had worked with me on a successful honors paper. She had the candor and humor of her hometown of Brooklyn, but she agonized over getting her ideas together on paper and I realized later that she was agonizing over much more serious problems at the time. When she introduced me at graduation to her father and brother and sister (her mother had died when she was a child), she told me how much she appreciated working with me and how much completing her thesis had meant to her. She had decided to go to law school and I wrote many letters of recommendation, but she was turned down repeatedly. Her LSAT scores were not quite high enough although I had no doubt she could be successful in graduate school.

One day I got a call from her. "Dr. Mason," she shouted, "I made it!" She had been accepted at a law school in Chicago and she wanted to know if we could have lunch because she was soon going to move there and share an apartment with another Emmanuel student.

I was thrilled for her. In a few days she arrived at my office for our lunch date, carrying a picture she painted that she wanted to give me. She was a very talented artist and I was touched by her gift. I held up the picture and as I looked at it, I felt a cold shiver go through me. It was a striking group of figures done in pen and ink and pastels, mostly in gray and black tones with daubs of mauve and pink and flesh colors. The figures, dressed in loose jackets and pants, stood together looking out. Their eyes were identical and deep and dark. The picture was titled "Androgynous Misfits." I knew that Gina had recently been struggling with her own sexual identity and the starkness of the picture suggested the pain of her struggle.

We had lunch in the college coffee shop and Gina enthusiastically filled me in about her plans. She seemed energized and optimistic about the year ahead. When she parted, she promised to keep in touch. Three days later, I received a call from the dean's office. Gina had taken her life the previous night. In shock, I attended her wake with several colleagues and spoke to her family. Later at a memorial service for her at the college, I spoke about her a little and read some poetry. The service was crowded with her friends as well as her family, and her father spoke of Gina and of her attachment to the college and to her friends. I thought of the fragility of young people and how they sometimes have such a tenuous grasp on life. The wake and the memorial service were very healing experiences, but I could not help recalling my brother's death. I wished that we could have had such a memorial for him, that we could have shared our grief but also celebrated his life.

In the 1980s I also discovered that the younger generation of professional women had new expectations. While I was a visiting fellow at the Radcliffe Institute in 1983 I met young women who were about the same age I had been when I was first there, and found that they were well advanced in their careers. They had not taken a break to raise children but now some of them were experiencing motherhood later in their lives. I was shocked and amused that our lunch break conversations were often about nursing versus bottle feeding or the latest theory about how to toilet train. One day a fellow was given a baby shower. Unheard of a decade before! Then, we had avoided talking about our children as earnestly as these young women were now discussing parenting and motherhood. We were escaping from our domestic life to try to recapture our professional identity. These women had a clear sense of themselves as successful professionals, but they were anxious about being equally competent as mothers. Mary

Bunting, in her mission as the institute's founder, had succeeded. Women had made their careers a priority. But as always, they had not escaped the conflicts between career and family even though the scenario was playing out differently. They still felt that their role as caretaker and nurturer was an important, perhaps dominant part of their identity Inevitably they found that balancing these roles was difficult.

Now at sixty in 1988, I was buoyed by the sense that I had, belatedly, found my voice. My association with a diversity of women had made me realize I was no longer haunted by feminine stereotypes. I could be myself. In my career, I realized that it was too late to build a power base as younger women were doing by actively networking and publishing; such exposure was necessary to attain a better academic position. However, it was not too late to get satisfaction out of the coherence of my intellectual and my personal life. The seventh decade did not seem like a bad one to begin.

1990

After my sixtieth birthday bash, I announced that we did not need to count birthdays anymore except perhaps backwards, but, of course, my children, who had been brought up on big birthday parties, insisted on giving me a special dinner on my sixty-second birthday. But first, I had an important obligation to keep that afternoon. I was going to my first meeting in the Disability Rights Movement, at the University of Massachusetts campus in downtown Boston. I was invited by a new friend and recent student of mine, who was pursuing a Ph.D. at the Union Institute, where I had been recruited to be on her doctoral committee. Karen was disabled with spinal bifida and was active in the movement. She and I had decided to give a paper together later in June at the New England Women's Studies Association conference on the alliances and differences between generations of disabled women.

I took a taxi from the Emmanuel College campus to the dreary building that housed many important programs of the University of Massachusetts's Boston campus and found my way to the room where the meeting was being held. The sign on the door read "Disabled Peoples Liberation Front," the organization that was holding the meeting. When I went in the room I expected to see many people in wheelchairs, on crutches, and with obvious signs of disability. Actually, it was a small turnout and the group did not seem like a gathering of the disabled but rather just a mixture of people you might encounter on a subway—men and women who were young and old, professional and working class, disabled and able-bodied, from many different parts of society. I picked up one of the flyers on the table alongside the coffee and doughnuts, and it defined the organization as "a progressive group of people with a variety of disabilities . . . street people, blacks, anticapitalists, lesbians and gays, sheltered workshop laborers, parents, recovering drug and alcohol users, militants, unemployed people, students, workers, and demonstrators."

The meeting started with self-introductions accompanied by a signer for the hearing impaired, and then individual members gave reports on their group activities. I had been asked to talk about the current status of and conflicts in the Women's Movement. As I finished my talk, which described the third wave of the Women's Movement that demanded a broader coalition to include all women and particularly women of color, I realized I'd barely mentioned disabled women—only in passing within a list of diversity issues. Typically, I had identified with the causes of other women but I had neglected my own particular issue, the disempowerment of women with disabilities. My talk was followed by a joint report from a young man and woman from Act Up, a gay and lesbian group, who described with colorful wit one of their recent protest demonstrations. Their presentation was followed by a middle-aged woman in a wheelchair who recounted the recent "Crawl-On and Bus Chaining" protest that was carried out to demand total transportation access in Boston. She described how a number of disabled people had actually halted bus service in downtown Boston by hauling themselves out of their wheelchairs and onto the buses or by chaining themselves to the outside of a bus so it could not move. The image created was very vivid and caught my attention. *Now that's what I should be doing,* I thought. And determined to be more active.

After the meeting was over, I bought a tee shirt that said "Disabled People's Liberation" and put it on immediately. Even though it was hidden by my jacket I felt that I was coming out by wearing it. When I went downstairs to get a cab, I ran into a woman in the lobby who recognized me from one of the women's studies conferences we had both attended. She gave me a ride back to the college and we exchanged notes on the different meetings we had attended—hers had been on education and the inner city and the need for solidarity among urban people. I was proud to be able to say that I attended a meeting of the Disabled Peoples Liberation Front.

When I got home I was full of enthusiasm and revolutionary spirit. I took off my jacket and burst into the dining room wearing my red liberation shirt. Cathleen and Sarah were setting the table for dinner. Some friends were going to join us to celebrate my birthday. "I'm going to chain myself to an MBTA bus to demand equal access for the disabled," I announced. Cathleen and Sarah gave me a quizzical look.

"You are going to what?" they queried.

"Yes," I said, but a little less forcefully. "It's the only way to get action, to get the city to make the buses more accessible."

The girls looked at me tolerantly. "Oh, sure, mum, I can just see you chained to a bus."

Slightly deflated, I began to protest their skepticism. Then I thought of myself actually chained to a bus or catapulting myself up high steps onto a bus. Actually, I thought, I had often been put in the position of hauling myself into and onto inaccessible places. Train platforms that were too high. Small commuter airplane ladders that wobbled and allowed no space for crutches. Public buildings whose steps had no railings. Not to mention small removable and narrow steps onto boats and gangways that swayed or developed a ninety-degree angle of ascent from the dock at low tide. I had confronted access barriers all my life without protest. I had succeeded partly because I had denied my disability, but ever since the experience of fracturing my hip and my awareness of my physical vulnerability then and later with cancer and with more and more decreased mobility, I could no longer deny the reality of my body. I had to move from overcoming it or seeing it as unimportant—steps I had achieved in my moments of reflection at Moosehead Lake and at Rangeley Lake—to actually accepting it and claiming it as part of myself.

As for my revolutionary acts, I *would* protest, I insisted, but probably not by chaining myself to a bus. I admired people who did that, but it was not me. I would organize a disability committee at the college and demand more railings and ramps; in fact, I had already consulted with the buildings and grounds people as they began to make the campus more accessible in compliance with new laws. I would give papers, write letters of protest, go to conferences on disability, and ultimately start my own research on disabled women, but I would not go out on the sidewalks.

Was I disappointed in myself? A little, I had to confess. I would like to have been more dramatic, more outrageous, more provocative. But I was not. I had, however, looked steadily at myself as part of a group of diverse disabled people who defied their disempowerment and I had felt one of them.

1996

On August 14, 1996, my mother died at the age of ninety-seven. Five days later, her children and their children and some great-grandchildren gathered to attend her funeral from points all over the country and from Canada. My children and I met in the Philadelphia airport within one half hour of each other and we rented a car and drove to the Medford Leas retirement community in New Jersey to join the rest of the family. It was a gathering of the matriarchal clan and my mother's presence was almost palpable.

For my sisters and me it was a moment to realize that we were the surviving generation now. Furthermore, our relationship would no longer be mediated by my mother, who had taken that role very seriously, keeping us in touch with one another's lives and dividing her treasures and belongings amongst us with equity as she moved from house to town house and then to the retirement community, where another round of inexorable moves began—from apartment to studio to a room with assisted living and finally to the hospital wing where she had been taken after several small strokes. When my sisters and I met in June after she had been moved to the hospital, we had forty-eight hours to clear out her studio. It would then be prepared for another elderly resident, a grim reminder of the cycle of mortality. Before we started on our task of disbursement, we vowed that no disagreement about her possessions would divide us, so we managed to quickly parcel out the remaining chairs, tables, lamps, pictures, jewelry, and personal effects to be distributed among us and the grandchildren. The two needlepoint samplers, the shield back armchair, and the Sheffield candlesticks were reminders to me of the almost sacred significance that my mother had placed in the care of the furnishings of domesticity and the tangible props of the family.

Mother had been fortunate to remain in relatively good health into her nineties, and only in the last years of her life did her memory fail, causing her much anxiety. She grew more and more affectionate and tender as she aged and made a great event out of my visits to her. While still living in her apartment, she would arrange for what she thought would be interesting people for me to meet at dinner, always inviting one of the few surviving gentlemen to join the party. Dinner was served restaurant style in the large attractive dining rooms and often she would have a group of her friends for drinks beforehand. We would attend concerts—there were many events at the community—and sometimes sit together on her patio looking at family photos. When I could not make visits as frequently as I wished, I wrote her detailed letters of the family events she could no longer attend—baptisms and graduations and other occasions. Her letters back were touching. "I have just read your good letter for the 'nth' time," she wrote in an increasingly shaky handwriting. After one visit she wrote, "I am very proud of you as my visitor and daughter. . . . You are very pretty. I love your hairdo." Sentiments that she was once slow to express she now conveyed almost with urgency as if to catch up for lost time. At moments her former bluntness would flash out in a remark, reminding me of a stronger, less accommodating personality. When my son and his wife joined me to take their firstborn child to meet his great-grandmother, my mother, then ninety, gave us one of those moments. Looking closely at Tommy, who was the spitting image of his mother, Chris, my mother pronounced, "Well, he doesn't *look* like anybody." What she meant, of course, was that he didn't look like anybody in *our* family.

The funeral service was held in a small interdenominational church that Mother had attended when she could no longer get to her regular Presbyterian church in Moorestown, the town where she had started her family and later lived until she went into the retirement community. I prepared some recollections about mother's devotion to all the details and events of our lives but also about her independence and curiosity about life, particularly when she visited me in France, characteristics I had only recently recognized as I composed my thoughts about her life and its importance to me. My brother-in-law and a niece also spoke, and my son, Paul, did one of the readings. During the ceremony I felt deeply moved and I was on the edge of tears, but I remained dry-eyed. As I looked around, Cathleen and Sarah and many of my relatives wept openly and I felt almost guilty. I realized I was experiencing a familiar cycle—stoic calmness as I confronted grief, followed much later by a wave of emotion. The release was often unexpected, coming when a person expressed words of sympathy or when a memory of the loss flashed across my mind and brought with it a stab of pain and instant tears. This repression of strong emotions was not only a legacy from my family, but perhaps a pattern that I had developed as a child to handle the anger, frustration, and grief at the loss of my physical freedom. I had changed, however. I no longer experienced the numbness that I remember at my father's and brother's funerals. I was acknowledging my feelings, but I was just delaying their expression. Paul confided in me that he, too, experienced this kind of delayed expression of grief.

My sisters and I led the funeral procession of cars to the Colestown cemetery through the flat southern New Jersey landscape. The black limousine traveled on back roads through a rural setting of orchards, cornfields, and small truck farms, reminding me of the New Jersey of my childhood before the acres of stores, office complexes and highways had developed, which stretched mall to mall toward Camden and Philadelphia.

Our destination was a family plot under a linden tree quite far back in the cemetery grounds. I left the car and walked over to the two rather plain headstones, decorated with the simple raised letters of my father's and brother's names and dates. I did not remember seeing them before. I had not attended my father's burial because his funeral had been in Montreal and my mother had not brought us to New Jersey for his interment. And I couldn't remember coming to the cemetery at my brother's funeral. I had blocked out the memory. Now, as I approached the headstones and my mother's urn (she had requested cremation: "It's more modern, don't you think," she'd said to my sister), I felt a closure, long awaited, to the loss of my father and my brother.

The funeral home had placed two simple bouquets of pink and white summer flowers on the graves and all of us stood without speaking for a few moments. I wanted to linger but my sisters moved toward the car and I realized we were not going to be present for the interment of the urn. I was disappointed as I struggled to give meaning to the ritual of burial. I knew I had not quite grasped its full significance but that it was important for me understand it.

Later as I tried to absorb the reality of my mother's death, so different from my experience with my father's and my brother's deaths, I revisited many times in my memory the visit to the cemetery and the family graves, puzzling over its importance to me. Finally I realized it was the simple fact that I had needed an actual place of commemoration to identify with the deaths of my father and brother. They had been like ghosts to me and the memories that surrounded their images were often ephemeral, even treacherous. I needed a reference point as simple and prosaic as a headstone to literally bring me down to earth in my recollections, out of which I created so much of my past and present identity.

Memory and recollection are both healing and deceiving. In discussing with my sister my renegade act in childhood of cutting off the heads of flowers, she said, "They were tulips." I remember daffodils. If these building blocks of memory, which are so formative of identity, can be called into question, what then is the identity? We can only grasp it temporarily. The story might change. But memory does heal. It has led me to retrace steps I was unaware of and to understand, at least in part, the journey in which old wounds can be closed and healed although much remains a mystery.

My mother's death marked the end of an era and made me stop again for reflection and assessment of another decade of my life. Being a woman alone had its difficulties—from the disappearance of trivial perks such as dinner parties given only for couples or the loss of memberships in clubs and other status symbols, to the serious challenges of managing home and finances and work alone. Above all, I learned the hard lessons of solitude, that crucial state in a life that brings both comfort and pain. But being a woman alone had its compensations. It was satisfying to know that what you had done was all your own, hard won and often without society's traditional rewards but of your own making. I recalled the photograph of the child with the angry expression, holding the string on the Thanksgiving turkey, the child who refused to be the smiling poster child. I kept some of that independence. I had lost it for a while but rediscovered it. I learned that there was much to smile about in the world and I had no regrets about life's experiences—love, marriage, children, work, and career. Now another new phase was beginning for me. I would always connect with the younger generation of students even after I retired from teaching and I would continue to enjoy the pleasures of family and grandchildren, but I would also be ready for the unexpected now that I accepted who I was as a disabled person, a feminist, and a writer. I was hopeful that Julian of Norwich was right when she said, "All shall be well, and all manner of thing shall be well," but I knew my own small voice would still end with a question.

WORKS CITED

Iandoli, Ceci. "Middle-Aged Women's Studies Professors: A Comparative Analysis of Fifteen Educators' Perceptions of Their Personal and Professional Changes." Ph.D. diss., Harvard University, 1984.

Julian of Norwich. *A Shewing of God's Love.* Trans. Anna Maria Reynolds. London: Sheed and Ward, 1974.

Julian of Norwich, *Showings.* Trans. Edmund Colledge and James Walsh. New York: Paulist Press, 1978.

Kempe, Margery. *The Book of Margery Kempe, Fourteen Hundred & Thirty-Six: A Modern Version.* Ed. W. Butler-Bowdon. New York: The Devin-Adair Co., 1944.

Mason, Herbert. *Memoir of a Friend: Louis Massignon 1883–1962.* Notre Dame, Ind.: University of Notre Dame Press, 1988.

Mason, Mary Grimley. "The Other Voice: Autobiographies of Women Writers." In *Autobiography: Essays Theoretical and Critical.* Ed. James Olney. Princeton, N.J.: Princeton University Press, 1980.

Mason, Mary Grimley, and Carol Hurd Green, eds. *Journeys: Autobiographical Writings by Women.* Boston: G. K. Hall, 1979.

Rich, Adrienne. "Diving into the Wreck." In *Diving into the Wreck: Poems 1971–1972.* New York: W. W. Norton, 1973.

Woolf, Virginia. "A Sketch of the Past." In *Moments of Being: Unpublished Autobiographical Writings.* Ed. Jeanne Schulkind. New York: Harcourt Brace Jovanovich, 1976.

Wordsworth, William. *The Prelude; or, Growth of a Poet's Mind.* Ed. Ernest De Selincourt. London: Oxford University Press, 1933.

DISCOVER THE BEST WOMEN WRITING
MEMOIR AND AUTOBIOGRAPHY FROM THE FEMINIST PRESS

Across Boundaries: The Journey of a South African Woman Leader by Mamphela Ramphele. $14.95 paper, $19.95 cloth.

Always from Somewhere Else: A Memoir of My Chilean Jewish Father by Marjorie Agosín. $18.95 cloth.

Among the White Moon Faces: An Asian-American Memoir of Homelands by Shirley Geok-lin Lim. $12.95 paper, $22.95 cloth.

Black and White Sat Down Together: The Reminiscences of an NAACP Founder by Mary White Ovington. $10.95 paper, $19.95 cloth.

Cast Me Out If You Will: Stories and Memoir by Lalithambika Antherjanam. $11.95 paper.

A Cross and a Star: Memoirs of a Jewish Girl in Chile by Marjorie Agosín. $13.95 paper.

A Day at a Time: The Diary Literature of American Women Writers from 1764 to the Present, edited by Margo Culley. $16.95 paper.

Fault Lines by Meena Alexander. $12.95 paper.

Harem Years: The Memoirs of an Egyptian Feminist, 1879–1924 by Huda Shaarawi. $12.95 paper.

Juggling: A Memoir of Work, Family, and Feminism by Jane S. Gould. $17.95 paper.

I Dwell in Possibility by Toni A. H. McNaron. $12.95 paper.

A Lifetime of Labor: The Autobiography of Alice H. Cook by Alice Cook. $22.95 cloth.

Lion Woman's Legacy: An Armenian-American Memoir by Arlene Voski Avakian. $14.95 paper.

The Mamie Papers: Letters from an Ex-Prostitute by Maimie Pinzer. $19.95 paper.

Memories: My Life as an International Leader in Health, Suffrage, and Peace by Aletta H. Jacobs. $18.95 paper.

The Seasons: Death and Transfiguration by Jo Sinclair. $12.95 paper.

Songs My Mother Taught Me: Stories, Plays, and Memoir by Wakako Yamauchi. $14.95 paper.

Streets: A Memoir of the Lower East Side by Bella Spewack. $10.95 paper, $19.95 cloth.

These Modern Women: Autobiographical Essays from the Twenties, edited by Elaine Showalter. $8.95 paper.

To receive a free catalog of The Feminist Press's 180 titles, call or write The Feminist Press at The City University of New York, 365 Fifth Avenue, New York, NY 10016; phone: (212) 817-7920; fax: (212) 987-4008; www.feministpress.org. Feminist Press books are available at bookstores or can be ordered directly. Send check or money order (in U.S. dollars drawn on a U.S. bank) payable to The Feminist Press. Please add $4.00 shipping and handling for the first book and $1.00 for each additional book. VISA, Mastercard, and American Express are accepted for telephone orders. Prices subject to change.